AN AXE AND FOUR BALLOONS

'Of all the factors which make for success in battle, the spirit of the warrior is the most decisive.'

Field Marshal 1st Viscount Montgomery of Alamein

TIM SPICER

AN AXE AND FOUR BALLOONS

The biography of Brian Franks, the man who saved the SAS

BARBRECK

First published in 2026 by Barbreck Publishers

ISBN 978-1-9995891-7-2

A CIP catalogue reference for this book is available from the British Library
 Published in the United Kingdom by Barbreck Publishers, 50 Albemarle Street, London W1S 4BD and distributed by Penguin Random House UK, One Embassy Gardens, 8 Viaduct Gardens, London, SW11 7BW

Typography and typesetting by James Sutton

Printed and bound by CPI, UK

By the same author:
An Unorthodox Soldier, 1999 (Mainstream Publishing)
A Dangerous Enterprise, 2021 (Barbreck)
A Suspicion of Spies, 2024 (Barbreck)

Dedicated to the men and women of Great Britain's Special Forces and Intelligence Services

'Secret operations are essential in war; upon them the army relies to make its every move. An army without secret agents is exactly like a man without eyes or ears.'

Sun Tzu, *The Art of War*

IF

Rudyard Kipling

If you can keep your head when all about you
Are losing theirs and blaming it on you,
If you can trust yourself when all men doubt you,
But make allowance for their doubting too;
If you can wait and not be tired by waiting,
Or being lied about, don't deal in lies,
Or being hated, don't give way to hating,
And yet don't look too good, nor talk too wise:

If you can dream – and not make dreams your master;
If you can think – and not make thoughts your aim;
If you can meet with Triumph and Disaster
And treat those two imposters just the same;
If you can bear to hear the truth you've spoken
Twisted by knaves to make a trap for fools,
Or watch the things you gave your life to, broken,
And stoop and build 'em up with worn-out tools:

If you can make one heap of all your winnings
And risk it on one turn of pitch-and-toss,
And lose, and start again at your beginnings
And never breathe a word about your loss;
If you can force your heart and nerve and sinew
To serve your turn long after they are gone,
And so hold on when there is nothing in you
Except the Will which says to them: 'Hold on!'

If you can talk with crowds and keep your virtue,
Or walk with Kings – nor lose the common touch,
If neither foes nor loving friends can hurt you,
If all men count with you, but none too much;
If you can fill the unforgiving minute
With sixty seconds' worth of distance run,
Yours is the Earth and everything that's in it,
And – which is more – you'll be a Man, my son!

David Stirling

If you can read a map and find your way
And trust your compass and follow where it may
If you can trust yourself when we all doubt you
And make allowance for our doubting too.

If you can walk and not be tired by walking
Or being lost and late don't deal in lies.
Or when silent don't give way to talking
Nor talk too big, nor look too wise.

If you can hump a bergen nor mind the weight
And care for it as tho' it were your life
If you can fight alone yet basha with a mate
And work with him yet never come to strife.

If you can force your heart and nerve and sinew
To serve your turn long after they have gone
And so hold on when there is nothing in you
Except the will which says to them "hold on!"

If you can talk with trogs and keep your virtue
Or walk with "brass" nor lose the common touch
If neither we nor Pen-Y-Fan deter you
If all men count with you but none too much.

If you can fill the unforgiving minute
With sixty seconds worth of distance run
Yours are the wings and everything that's with it
And - which is more - you're SAS my son.

CONTENTS

FOREWORD

There are a great many unsung heroes of war, but Colonel Brian Franks must be right at the top of the list – not only because of his courage, leadership and extraordinary achievement in battle, but because of his determination that the SAS regiment should continue in existence after the war when all other special force units were being disbanded. As David Stirling the founder of the SAS regiment put it, '*Had it not been for Brian Franks, we would have been consigned to oblivion.*'

Brian Franks was one of a small group of people who early in WW2 decided that if they were to fight and die for their country, then they would do so amongst friends, and it was in the bar of White's Club in London that many of them were recruited into the Commandos and the SAS. Their high-level contacts included the Prime Minister Winston Churchill and they ruthlessly used these contacts to bypass officialdom. A *bon viveur* who counted among his closest friends David Niven, Ian Fleming and Evelyn Waugh, he was manager of the Hyde Park Hotel before, and after, the war. Brian Franks had joined the Army as a member of the Territorial Army, and although he remained a civilian at heart, he displayed quite extraordinary military qualities – always judging others by the very high standards he set himself. When his men got into difficulties on Operation LOYTON in 1944, he parachuted into the area himself and managed to extricate most of his men from German encirclement after some vicious fighting.

When 30 of his men, who had been captured, were subsequently murdered by the Germans, he set up an SAS war crimes investigation team that continued in existence long after the SAS regiment itself had been disbanded. He commanded this team secretly from a small room at the top of the Hyde Park Hotel and they succeeded in finally tracking down and arresting the Nazi war criminals responsible, in spite of obstruction and indifference from the British Army of the Rhine.

Seen from an age when political correctness is threatening to undermine the fighting spirit of the British Army, Brian Franks, a superb trainer of men and a shrewd risk taker, was someone who utterly refused to be shackled by the dead hand of the military and civilian bureaucracy. He epitomised the sort of free-thinking soldier who instinctively understood the fundamental difference between conventional soldiering and the use of small uniquely well-trained parties operating behind enemy lines. Known to his men as 'the Colonel', they all knew that he would fight for their interests as fiercely as he would against the Germans.

And so it was, that after the war he successfully campaigned to have the SAS reinstated – pointing out to the military hierarchy that there was an obvious need for stay-behind parties to remain in Europe if the Soviets invaded. In 1947 this was finally agreed by the War Office, and 21 SAS (The Artists Rifles) was duly formed with Brian Franks as the unit's first Commanding Officer. Soon after, the regular component of the SAS regiment was formed in Malaya to help fight the communist insurgency that had erupted there at the end of the war. He later became Colonel Commandant of the SAS when I first met him.

Living in the shadow of the founders of the SAS, many of whom I knew, when I commanded 22 SAS, I made absolutely sure that we operated in the same independent way as our wartime SAS predecessors had done, often using back channels to bypass authority. Shortly before his death Brian Franks visited the SAS in Hereford and spoke after dinner to the Sergeants' Mess. It was an evening that none of us who were present will ever forget. It gave us a privileged insight into what it must have been like to be under his command in war and reminded us of the sacrifices and challenges required. He told us very firmly to keep faith with the guiding principles of the SAS that had been set out by the founders of the regiment in 1941. He was an inspiration to us all.

So, I am particularly delighted that Tim Spicer, who is also something of a risk taker, and with whom I have soldiered in difficult times on operations, has written this long-awaited and well-researched biography of Brian Franks.

General Sir Michael Rose KCB, CBE, DSO, QGM, DL
Former Commanding Officer 22 SAS
and Director Special Forces

ACKNOWLEDGEMENTS

Rather like David Stirling in his address at the opening of Stirling Lines[1] in which he highlighted who, besides him, should be credited with founding the SAS, I can't take sole credit for this book. Over 80 people helped me pull Brian Franks's exciting story together.

In the first instance the Franks clan. The initial idea for me to write the biography came from Susie Lowther-Pinkerton, Brian's granddaughter, picking up on the determination of her late uncle George Franks to achieve proper recognition of his father's achievements, fully supported by 'Le Reseau Franks', Valerie, Brian's daughter and her husband Will, Ingrid, his daughter-in-law, and Brian's other grandchildren, Katie, Georgina and Harry. Also the de Lesseps family Marc, Françoise and Bruno, who first tipped me off about Robert and Operation LOYTON.

Next came approval from the SAS hierarchy Harry Holt, Mark Carlton-Smith, Peter de la Billère and Michael Rose, who kindly wrote the Foreword, and Jamie Lowther-Pinkerton.

I was very lucky to have had considerable help from the friends and family of other dramatis personae in the book: Archie Stirling, Peverel and Eddie Manners, Pip Birtwistle, Ben Laycock, Martha Mlinaric, David Farran, Rupert Johnson, Amy Crossland, Lady Henrietta Dunne, Nicky Dunne, Charlie Maxted, Rooney Massara, Rob Hann and Xan Smiley.

The help and support given to me by the SAS Regimental Association was invaluable: John Allcock, Tracy Hawkins, Grenville Bint and Rebecca Hawtrey and from the Artists Rifles, Patrick Baty and Mike Orr. Other historical archives provided essential detail:

1 See Annex A.

Jane Rosen at the Imperial War Museum, James Kelly at RHQ Scots Guards, King's College, Sherborne School, David Brava at Le Service Historique de la Défence Vincennes, Sally Jennings and her team at Eton, Gil Greenall – the Chairman of White's, and David Anderson the Secretary, Jerome Maubec at Le Fondation de la France Libre in Paris, Bembridge Sailing Club, Bertie Wetherall in Hong Kong, Lugina McConnell, Museum Vliegbasis Deelen in Holland, David Sarsfield of the British Online Archives and Pierre Sauvage at the Varian Fry Institute. All of these archives couldn't have been properly ransacked without the help of my fantastic research team: the Wizard of Kew – Phil Tomaselli, and in France Blodwyn Sheriff and Elizabeth Dorléac.

Historians also played a very significant part. Philippe Get, the world's leading expert on Operation LOYTON whose help was invaluable including guiding me round the LOYTON operational area. Professor Clive Jones the leading authority on the Secret War in Yemen, Richard Head, Alan 'Spike' Hoe, Rupert Allison and Damien Lewis.

Other contributors, friends and supporters: our most eminent historian Andrew Roberts, Jason Philips and the Hambro family at Wiltons, David Walker, Algie Cluff, Gavin Rankin, Bill Duff, James Ellery, 'The Captain', Charlie Anteleme, Don McCullin, Caspar Hobbs, Nicholas Soames, Danny Katz, Chris Dodkin and Lynn Amos.

On the production side, of course my gallant publisher David Campbell who has now trusted me with three books, his sidekick the intrepid Nell Richmond, and Christina Usher and her team at Penguin. My very long-suffering PA Lauren Smith who must have typed 50 iterations of the manuscript – third time around she has also become a skilled editor and researcher. James Sutton for graphic design, Rachel Glen once again for her excellent maps. Editorial rigour was provided by 'Tom the Book', Tom Bromley who kept me on the straight and narrow, Henry and Francis Jones-Davis who looked at an early version, Chris Parker for copy editing, Paul Potgeiter at Focus Media for photography and Alex Hippisley-Cox for PR.

Finally Pauline and Sam, and 'Walsingham' for your meticulous espionage and diplomacy.

Tim Spicer, Devon 2026

INTRODUCTION

Every biographer's nightmare is the nagging worry that they have missed something important, or that as soon as the button is pressed for printing, something new would turn up. Sure enough, after the publication of *A Suspicion of Spies* my publishers received an email. It was from Marc de Lesseps saying that he had very much enjoyed the book, and noted that his father Robert was mentioned – a '*Frenchman working for Biffy Dunderdale in London in 1940, cover name GOODFELLOW*'. He also said he had personally taken several of the photos in the book, and that Biffy was his godfather!

I got in touch with Marc and our conversation led to a meeting at his house in Burgundy. There I found a treasure trove of photos and anecdotes about Biffy and Robert which of course would have been helpful to have had six months earlier. Over a very serious Burgundian lunch, Marc's son Bruno asked me about his grandfather's involvement in a wartime SAS operation, codename LOYTON. When I looked rather blank, he explained that GOODFELLOW had taken part in this operation with 2 SAS.

This made me very curious. It wasn't the norm for an SIS officer working in London, with access to the many secrets in Biffy's office, to be deployed behind enemy lines with the SAS (although I discovered much later that 'GOODFELLOW' had already been on operations in France for Biffy).

The operation Bruno referred to, Operation LOYTON, was the final operation of 2 SAS in the Vosges mountains in eastern France during the autumn of 1944. It was a complicated operation which ran into considerable difficulties, and was unusual in that the Commanding Officer of 2 SAS had parachuted in to take command when things got sticky.

That Commanding Officer was Lieutenant Colonel Brian Franks.

By a remarkable coincidence, on my return from France, I got a phone call from a very old friend, Jamie Lowther-Pinkerton, who had enjoyed a distinguished military career in the Irish Guards and SAS. Jamie reminded me that his wife Susie was the granddaughter of Brian Franks. He had been an enthusiastic supporter of the Biffy project and his question for me, at Susie's suggestion, was that on the back of the Biffy book, would I consider writing Brian Franks's biography?

Even with the little research I had done about Operation LOYTON I knew that Brian was another of these tough, capable, charismatic and charming individuals who had contributed significantly to this country's clandestine war fighting and intelligence work in World War II, and beyond. He, like Biffy Dunderdale and David Birkin, was another *'famous man you've never heard of'* outside of the intelligence and special operations world. It was a great honour to be asked and I immediately accepted, with two provisos – that the Franks family needed to be fully behind the project, and that the Special Air Service hierarchy was also happy. One always has to tread carefully in this arena. Luckily both agreed.

The British public has a seemingly insatiable appetite for books about the SAS, spies, adventurers, special operations and intelligence. This fascination seems to be deep in our national DNA, stretching back to Queen Elizabeth I's adventurers, Drake, Raleigh, Hawkins and her spymasters Walsingham and Cecil. There are more than a thousand books in print just about the SAS, and plenty of biographies of David Stirling, Paddy Mayne and Roy Farran, but there is no biography of Brian Franks, in spite of his being named by David Stirling as one of the five co-founders of the SAS.

On the 30th of June 1984 David Stirling was invited to open the newly refurbished SAS barracks, Bradbury Lines, which had been renamed Stirling Lines in his honour:

> *At this point I want to emphasise that I have always felt uneasy in being known as the founder of the regiment. To ease my conscience I would like it to be recognised that I have five co-founders: Jock Lewes and Paddy Mayne of the original L*

Detachment; George Bergé who started the French SAS; Brian Franks who re-raised the SAS flag after the war and John Woodhouse who created the modern SAS during the Malayan Campaign by restoring to the regiment its original philosophy.[2]

Brian was born in 1910 into a very comfortable, well-connected family. His father was a professional soldier who had served in the Boer War and throughout the First World War. The family, like many of their class, would spend the summer at Bembridge on the Isle of Wight, where Brian became friendly with a young scallywag called David Niven. They would share many adventures and become life-long friends.

After prep school at Wixenford,[3] and Eton, family circumstances prevented Brian from going to Oxford. He took a job in the hotel business. Starting in the kitchens of the Dorchester, he made a strong impression and rose quickly into management. He was soon head-hunted by the Bennett family, owners of the Hyde Park Hotel, who had heard of Brian's reputation in the business and hired him.

As war had become more likely in the late 1930s, Brian joined the Territorial Army. In 1939 his regiment was mobilised and sent to Palestine. After a frustrating and dull period, Brian extricated himself to join the Commandos which were then commanded by his friend Robert Laycock. Early in 1944 he was posted to 2 SAS as Second-in-Command, taking over from Bill Stirling in June, and successfully commanding the regiment in France, Germany and Norway.

In 1945, the decision was taken to disband the SAS, a decision that Brian and many others thought very short-sighted. He left the Army with two driving ambitions. First to track down and bring to justice the war criminals who had murdered his soldiers, and their Resistance helpers, during Operation LOYTON. Secondly, to have the SAS restored to the Order of Battle of the British Army. Brian contrived to set up an 'off the books' SAS war crimes investigation team that operated for the next three years, successfully bringing to justice the war criminals who had murdered SAS soldiers in France.

2 For the full text of this address, see Annex A.
3 Wixenford was absorbed into Ludgrove Prep School in 1937.

Ostensibly fully returned to civilian life, Brian also worked for SIS, as part of their clandestine war planning team, using his wartime experience to help plan the future of special operations, and making preparations for the possibility that the Cold War would soon turn hot. He went on to force through the resurrection of the SAS, and helped with the development of the regiment into what it is today.

In his private life, Brian Franks was a dashing *bon viveur*, a gastronome, and a terrific sportsman. As a soldier, one of his officers described him as '*an excellent commander, full of initiative and brave ... with a clear and decisive mind*'. He was always the adventurer but never sought the profile of many of his contemporaries, although his war record was well known, and spoke for itself.

Under Brian's leadership, the Hyde Park Hotel went from strength to strength. It continued to be a favourite of the Royal Family, and the hub of London Society in the 1950s and 1960s. Brian made many friends across the whole social spectrum, from Royalty to the young soldiers of the SAS and the villagers of Moussey. His story boasts an extraordinary cast of characters, including David Niven, Winston Churchill, the Stirling brothers, Paddy Mayne, Roy Farran, Robert Laycock and Ian Fleming. Evelyn Waugh, in particular, features throughout. The chronicler of the 'Bright Young Things' of the so-called Jazz Age, Waugh set his early fiction in grand country houses, townhouses, clubs and hotels both upmarket and seedy. It was in this environment that Brian first met Waugh in the 1930s.

From a biographer's perspective, researching and pulling together the various strands of Brian's life – hotelier, soldier, sportsman, *bon viveur* and family man – was both fascinating and challenging. Private papers, archives, in particular the SAS historical archive, and personal interviews, all played a part. Luckily there are a good few people still alive who knew Brian well.

What was also unusual during my research were the many personal connections that emerged, between Brian's and my own life. First there was a very strong link with Bembridge, where I lived between 1960 and 1973. Logan Scott-Bowden, 'Scotty', was a close family friend. During this time I was at Sherborne School and was taught by both Sam Hey and Doughey Randolph. I served briefly in

21 SAS before joining the regular Army. Later I was entrusted by the Director Special Forces with rewriting SAS doctrine after the first Gulf War. Based in the Special Forces Headquarters, I could most definitely feel the ghosts of the Stirling brothers, Paddy Mayne and Brian Franks peering critically over my shoulder. Later I worked directly for both General Peter de la Billière and Michael Rose. Finally I wrote this book in the house that used to belong to Cyril Maude, an alumnus of Brian's prep school. The grounds of the house were used by John Durnford-Slater and 3 Commando for training for Operation AMBASSADOR, an early commando raid on the island of Guernsey.

The title of the book comes from a letter Brian wrote to his parents from his prep school Wixenford in 1918. It was the classic '*Dear Mummy and Daddy, I hope you are well ...*' letter written on lined, dusty pink paper. '*Please send me an axe and four balloons ...*'. In a time before the scourge of 'health and safety', the axe and four balloons were duly sent. There was never any explanation forthcoming from Brian about their intended or actual use.

This biography is not yet another history of the SAS. It is about Brian Franks and will navigate the adventure, fun and laughter of his life, overt and covert, civilian and military. Inevitably his time in command of 2 SAS will feature prominently, as will the re-formation of the regiment, and it will put him in his rightful place in the pantheon of the SAS.

Leadership has been described as:

> *pre-eminently the art of the man who dares to take the risk; of the man who thinks deeply and clearly; of the man who, when accident intervenes, is not thereby cast down, but changes his plans and dispositions with the readiness of a resolute and reflective mind, which so far as is possible has foreseen and provided against difficulties.*

Brian Franks showed all these qualities, both in peace and in war. This is his story.

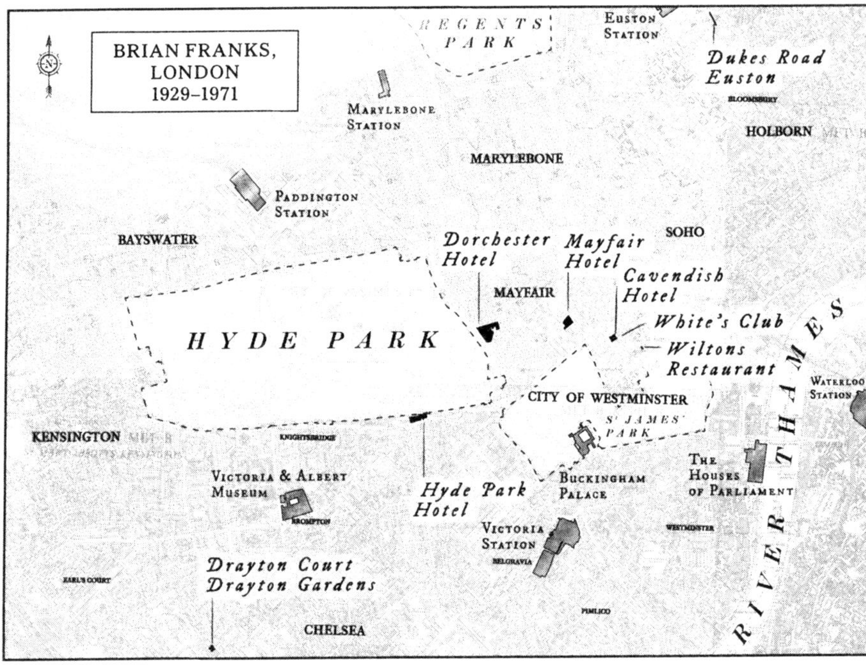
BRIAN FRANKS, LONDON 1929–1971
REGENTS PARK
EUSTON STATION
Dukes Road Euston
MARYLEBONE STATION
HOLBORN
MARYLEBONE
PADDINGTON STATION
BAYSWATER
Dorchester Hotel
Mayfair Hotel
SOHO
MAYFAIR
Cavendish Hotel
White's Club
Wiltons Restaurant
HYDE PARK
RIVER THAMES
WATERLOO STATION
CITY OF WESTMINSTER
ST JAMES' PARK
KENSINGTON
KNIGHTSBRIDGE
THE HOUSES OF PARLIAMENT
VICTORIA & ALBERT MUSEUM
Hyde Park Hotel
BUCKINGHAM PALACE
BROMPTON
VICTORIA STATION
WESTMINSTER
BELGRAVIA
Drayton Court Drayton Gardens
EARL'S COURT
PIMLICO
CHELSEA

TIMELINE

1910 12th September: Brian Franks born

1918 Wixenford prep school
8th October: Father killed in action

1923 Eton

1929 Leaves Eton and takes a job at the Dorchester Hotel

1930 Joins the Mayfair Hotel on promotion

1938 The Hyde Park Hotel General Manager

1939 12th January: Marries Zoe Quilter
10th June: Franks commissioned in Middlesex Yeomanry (TA)
3rd September: War declared on Germany
28th December: Embarks for Palestine. Remains in Palestine until February 1941

1941 20th February: Posted to Egypt
18th March: Appointed signals officer for LAYFORCE at Kabrit
19th/20th April: Bardia raid, then admitted to hospital
27th June: Joins Phantom GHQ Signals Regiment. 'H' Middle East Squadron
August: In hospital, returns to UK September
15th November: Disembarks in UK. Attends Special Training Centre
1st December until 14th April 1942: Phantom E Squadron

1942 14th April: Posted from Phantom to Special Service Brigade as Staff Captain
15th August: Brigade Major Special Service Brigade

1943 July: Operations HUSKY, LUSTY, BLACKCOCK, BAYTOWN
3rd–7th October: Operation DEVON, Termoli. Awarded MC
17th November: Returns UK to Headquarters Combined Operations. Liaison with Combined Operations Pilotage Parties

1944	21st February: Brian appointed 21C 2 SAS Parachute Course 15th March: 2 SAS returns to UK 4th June: Takes over command 2 SAS on resignation of Bill Stirling 6th June: D-DAY 26th July–17th September: Operation HARDY / WALLACE 13th August–12th October: Operation LOYTON 31st August: Franks parachutes to join LOYTON, subsequently awarded DSO November: Preliminary investigation into missing soldiers
1945	25th March–10th May: Operation ARCHWAY, commands FRANKFORCE 12th May–25th August: Operation APOSTLE, Norway 10th June: Establishes War Crimes team October: Disbandment of the SAS. Forms SAS Association
1946	Returns to the Hyde Park Hotel until 1971 Works part-time for SIS War Planning Group Successfully lobbies for reinstatement of SAS into the Order of Battle
1947	1st May: Appointed CO newly formed 21 SAS (Artists) TA
1948	SAS War Crimes Unit closes investigation
1951	Honorary Colonel 21 SAS
1952	22 SAS formed
1959	23 SAS (V) formed
1962	Secret war in Yemen
1968	The Hyde Park Hotel bought by Forte Group
1971	1st December: Brian Franks resigns from the Trust House Forte board
1976–1980	Colonel Commandant SAS
1980	30th April–2nd May: Iranian Embassy siege
1982	2nd April: Argentina invades Falklands 6th May: Brian Franks dies

CHAPTER 1 – AN AXE AND FOUR BALLOONS

> 'From the whole decade before 1914 there seems to breathe forth an atmosphere, as it were, of eating everlasting strawberry ices on green lawns to the tune of the Eton Boating Song.'
>
> George Orwell's autobiographical essay, '*Such, Such, Were the Joys*'

Brian Morton Forster Franks was born on the 12th of September 1910. His father, Lieutenant Colonel George Franks, was a professional soldier, in the 19th (Queen Alexandra's Own) Royal Hussars. George Franks had fought in the Second Boer War, where he took part in actions in Natal, at Rietfontein, and Lombard's Kop. He was involved in the defence of Ladysmith and further actions in the Transvaal and Orange River where he was Mentioned-in-Dispatches.

Brian's mother May was the daughter of Gerald Morton, and cousin of Desmond Morton.[4] They lived in London at 3 Halkin Place and also had a country house, Hale House at Farnham in Surrey. The family was a typical upper-class Edwardian family with private means to supplement George's army salary. Holidays were taken every summer at Bembridge on the Isle of Wight, where initially George rented a house called the 'Moorings' and then took a lease on a more substantial property, 'The Mill House'.

On the back of the high-profile international yacht racing at Cowes run by the Royal Yacht Squadron, and the Royal residence at Osborne House nearby, the Isle of Wight had become a very fashionable summer holiday destination for the upper classes. Bembridge was at its centre. At the start of the century it had been a small village but very quickly expanded when wealthy families would come down from London for July and August. They would take the train from Waterloo to Portsmouth and catch the ferry to Ryde Pier and then

4 Desmond Morton, SIS officer, Churchill's close adviser and Brian's lifelong friend.

Bembridge Sailing Club

travel on by train to Bembridge Harbour Station. More exclusively, some would catch the paddle steamer *Island Queen*, which would take them direct to Bembridge, mooring alongside the Sailing Club, the social epicentre of the village during the summer.

King Edward VII was a regular visitor to Bembridge, as was Queen Mary, who would shop for antiques at William Couldrey's shop on the High Street. Alfonso XIII, King of Spain, would rent a house, as would the Countess of Limerick, James Ismay (Chairman of the White Star Line), the Oppenheimers and the Earl of Ducie. Others lived there permanently: the Thornycrofts at Steyne House, the Belvilles at the White House and the Moretons, who owned the whole of Ducie Avenue.

King Edward had come to the throne in 1901 after the death of his mother Queen Victoria. He ushered in a more vibrant era of pleasure, sandwiched between the great achievements of the Victorian age and the looming catastrophes that would follow in 1914. The Edwardian era is fondly remembered as an idyllic and leisurely time, a golden age of long summer days, endless garden parties, '*a time when women wore picture hats and did not vote, when the rich were not ashamed to live conspicuously and the sun never set on the British flag*'.

The King set the tone for the nation. While still Prince of Wales, Edward had already earned himself something of a reputation as a playboy and a *bon viveur*. Even though he had married in 1863, he continued to live the bachelor lifestyle, and his numerous mistresses were common knowledge among the upper classes. Edward led the 'fast set' in the grand lifestyle that typified the era.

The Royal timetable seemed almost completely dominated by the social calendar: in August the King would be yachting in Cowes and Bembridge; in September he would be abroad in the fashionable resorts of Germany or Austria; in October stalking in Scotland; winters were spent at Sandringham. If not hosting shooting parties, he would be attending them. A month on the French Riviera in the spring would be followed by three months in London for the summer season.

Weekend house parties were the norm for the upper classes. Country pursuits were de rigueur: hunting, shooting and racing. When not in the country and back at their houses in London, nightclubs, cabarets, the theatre and the embryonic cinema were very much in vogue, all assiduously documented by *Tatler* magazine's social barometer 'Bystander'.

In France (Britain's newest ally, after the Entente Cordiale, signed in 1904), this period was known as 'La Belle Époque', but also, rather ominously, as the 'Fin de Siècle'. It was a time of contrasts, decadence and high living on the one hand, optimism and change on the other. Society was no longer confined to the aristocracy, the arts were thriving, travel was easy. The motor car, air travel, luxury liners, champagne and ragtime coexisted with the beginnings of socialism, women's emancipation and workers' rights, and the ever-present 'Irish problem'. In Britain 'class' was still a major factor but the classes generally held each other in mutual respect.

In spite of the embarrassing wake-up call of the Boer War, Britain was still the most powerful nation on earth. In 1922 Britain ruled one quarter of the world's land mass and 24 per cent of the world's population. Germany had become Britain's *bête noire*, and a rush to reform the Army and increase the power of the Royal Navy had begun. The Entente Cordiale was reinforced with a treaty signed with Russia in 1907, creating the Triple Alliance, which pushed Germany, already flexing its military muscles, into a state of paranoia, fearing encirclement by its perceived enemies.

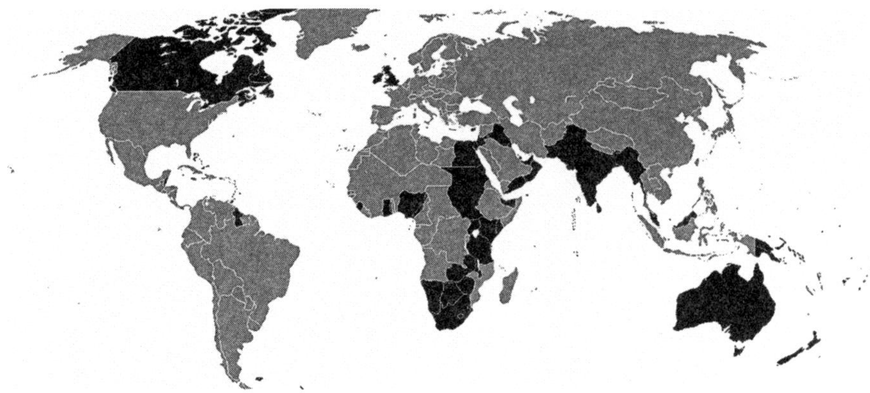

The British Empire 1914

In Bembridge the locals liked their summer visitors:

Bembridge came next to Cowes for aristocracy. They come with their maids and valets and butlers, and take one of the big houses. They'll take another one for the children and nannies. The real aristocracy treated you more or less like friends. They'd talk to you and call you by your Christian name ...

The Franks family were very much part of this happy scene – long days on the beaches of Ducie or Lane End and evenings at friends' dinner parties or at the Sailing Club.

In 1914 war changed everything. Brian's father deployed with his regiment to France as part of the BEF. The regiment took part in the Battles of Le Cateau, Mons and Aisne in 1914, the second Battle of Ypres in 1915, the Somme 1916, Cambrai 1917 and Amiens 1918. He was appointed Commanding Officer of the regiment in time for the pursuit of the retreating Germans in the autumn of 1918.

George came through all the fighting on the Western Front unscathed. He would come home on leave regularly, always accompanied by his orderly and Trumpeter Sergeant, Edward Levingston. Levingston would deliver George home, settle him in and then make his way to his own family in Southampton.[5] Brian would see his father

5 Edward Levington was commissioned into the Army Service Corp in 1918 and missed the final action at Brancourt.

George with Brian on leave

during his leave and they would spend as much time together as possible. At home on leave in 1917 George learned he had been awarded the DSO. He had also been elected to White's.[6] Sadly he would be unable to enjoy the White's conviviality and network for long.

*

At 1600hrs on the 6th of October 1918 the Commanding Officers of the 9th Cavalry Brigade were summoned to an Orders Group at Brigade Headquarters for the next phase of the cavalry pursuit of the retreating Germans. The 19th Hussars were to be the advance guard of the brigade. On the morning of the 8th of October George, together with his squadron leaders, watched the infantry advancing and attacking pockets of enemy resistance in Poncheaux and Genève. At 0855hrs George gave the order to patrol forward towards Vaux le Prêtre. The patrols under Lieutenant Fullerton reported the area to their front clear of enemy. The regiment then moved forward in tactical bounds from dead ground to dead ground. By 1045hrs Lieutenant Scott-Coburn with his troop from A Squadron had pushed forward and came under fire from an enemy machine-gun post which they attacked and captured. The remainder of A Squadron were told to follow up and exploit Scott-Coburn's success.

6 White's. The oldest gentleman's club in St James's. See Chapter 15.

Although the regiment was making good progress, it was not moving fast enough for the rather agitated Brigade Commander, who sent George a peevish message: '*Get a move on.*'

George paused the advance to give out some quick battle orders: '*B Squadron left, A Squadron right, C Squadron in reserve. Advance.*'

The regiment was moving forward in column, at the trot, when it came under sustained fire from a fortified farmhouse. George immediately took control of A Squadron, ordering them to follow him and attack the machine guns and artillery on the right flank. '*Draw swords, form line ... Trot ... Canter ... Trumpeter sound the charge.*'

One of the officers of A Squadron remembers: '*I think that was the last time such a trumpet call has been sounded in action, but to hear the chaps yelling their heads off behind me and the rush of galloping horses following mine to goodness knows where is a thrill that will stay with me forever.*'

George led the charge, getting about twenty yards in front of the main body. He and his horse were killed as they broke into the enemy position, leaping the first barricades on the edge of the farm. His men captured the position and gave the enemy '*a taste of the sword*', but it was not without considerable cost. Three officers and 18 other ranks killed, and eight officers and 36 other ranks wounded, 113 horses were killed. In the words of the war diary '*this gallant charge enabled the infantry to get forward and had a very demoralising effect on the enemy who were very rattled and jumpy*'.

One of the officers killed by machine-gun fire alongside George Franks was Lieutenant Norman Birtwistle MC; 26 years later his nephew would join 2 SAS under Brian Franks's command in 1944. After the war George was posthumously awarded a CMG '*for valuable service*' and a second Mention in Despatches.

In September 1918 Brian, aged eight, had started at his prep school, Wixenford near Wokingham. Brian had been put down for Eton at birth and Wixenford was one of its main feeder prep schools.[7]

7 Wixenford closed in 1934 and the buildings were taken over by Ludgrove, which continues to be the main feeder prep school for Eton. Old Wixenfordians include George Curzon, Viceroy of India and Foreign Secretary; George Trevelyan, historian; Duff Cooper, diplomat; Kenneth Clark, art historian; Cyril Maude, theatre impresario and William Whitelaw, Home Secretary.

George Franks in full dress uniform

He had been there barely a month when he was summoned to the headmaster's study to find his mother, who broke the terrible news about the death of his father. Brian took it stoically and elected to stay at school rather than go home. He was not the first boy at school to be in this situation, but his was all the more poignant given the war would be over in barely five weeks.

*

Gradually the pain of this tragedy subsided. The war was over and normality began to creep back. Holidays in Bembridge were resumed and Brian met and became friendly with a young fellow his exact same age whose father had been killed at Gallipoli in 1915. David Niven lived at Rose Cottage with his mother, brother and sisters, their London house having been sold after the death of his father. Rose Cottage was in the centre of Bembridge, about half a mile from Mill House where Brian would continue to go with his mother for school holidays. Niven was wild, and he and Brian soon formed a strong friendship which would last all their lives.

In 1920 Brian contracted pneumonia at Wixenford. Confined to the school sanatorium under the strict control of the school matron, he received a parcel from David Niven at the nearby school of Heatherdown where he was also on track for a place at Eton. The

Brian's mother, far right

parcel consisted of a chocolate box with a smaller box inside, then a smaller box etc. leading to a final matchbox. Matron decided to open the parcel for Brian as he was very weak. When she got to the matchbox, she opened it with a flourish and considerable force. Out flew a reasonably fresh dog turd, which flew into an open medicine cabinet before being extracted with a pair of forceps. Brian thought it was hysterical and immediately began to feel a lot better. Matron, however, was not amused. For this and many other misdemeanours Niven was expelled from Heatherdown aged ten and a half and lost his chance of a place at Eton.

Back in Bembridge Brian and David continued their friendship. Niven's mother was very tolerant of her boys and their friends and as they became teenagers she had an extension built at the back of Rose Cottage so that she would not be woken up when they came home from carousing with their friends. It was known as the 'Sin Wing', and the scene of much teenage debauchery. Brian's mother, May, complained to Niven's mother that at age ten David had told Brian the facts of life. Unfortunately Brian then asked his mother for detailed corroboration!

Both boys developed a keen interest in sailing. David's mother had bought him and his sister Grizel a 14-year-old sailing dinghy called *Merlin*. In 1925 Brian and David set up the Bembridge Dinghy Sailing Club for children between 12 and 18. Niven was the first secretary and Brian the first sailing captain. At the end of its first year the

Hugh Elles

Hugh Elles with King George V

club was in profit to the tune of £2 12s 6d, with which they promptly brought some brandy. The next morning they woke up face down in a nettle patch feeling very sorry for themselves!

In 1923 Brian's mother remarried an old family friend, Lieutenant Colonel Sir Hugh Elles,[8] the first Commander of the Tank Corps during World War I. Hugh Elles, like George Franks, was a career soldier. He served in the latter stages of the second Boer War, where he first met Brian's father. He went to France with the BEF in 1914, was wounded in the second Battle of Ypres. Once recovered, he was one of three officers selected by General Sir William Robertson, soon to be Chief of the Imperial General Staff, to liaise in person with frontline units and pass the information directly to GHQ. This ad hoc arrangement was the antecedent of the GHQ Liaison Regiment or 'Phantom' in which Brian was to serve during the next war and which was to prove vital to SAS operations.

In the summer of 1916, Elles was tasked to report back from the Somme, where tanks were first used. Promoted to the temporary rank of colonel, Elles was appointed to Head of the Heavy Branch (the first tank units) in France on the 29th of September 1916. Having seen the tanks achieve little success during the Battle of Passchendaele because of the exceptionally wet ground conditions of the autumn of 1917, he pressed Haig to use massed tanks on the drier, open ground at Cambrai. On the 20th of November 1917 he personally led 378

8 Later Lieutenant General Sir Hugh Elles KCB, KCMG, KCVO, DSO.

tanks and 98 support vehicles into battle at Cambrai in a Mark IV tank called 'Hilda', named after a favourite aunt. Promoted to brevet colonel in June 1918, Elles continued to command the Tank Corps until Germany's surrender in November 1918. He later became ADC to King George V and Master-General of the Ordnance.

He would prove to be an excellent step-father.

*

On the morning of the 24th of September 1923, the first day of the Michaelmas Half,[9] Brian was delivered to Eton by his mother and step-father.

Eton College, on the banks of the River Thames, under the shadow of Windsor Castle, was founded by King Henry VI in 1440 as a charity school to provide free education to 70 poor boys who would then go on to King's College, Cambridge, also founded by Henry in 1441. He used Winchester College, which had been founded in 1382, as a model, appointing Winchester's headmaster as the first Provost[10] and transferred some of Winchester's scholars as a quorum to start the school. Eton was to grow into the most famous and prestigious private school in the world.

To a new boy Eton is mystifying. It has a strange language of its own, unusual dress code and even more unusual institutions and traditions. Brian was to spend his first Half in the holding house before moving to Headlam's house in the Lent Half of 1924. Headlam's was run by Geoffrey Headlam, known to all as 'Tuppy'. Tuppy had himself been educated at Eton and Balliol, and became a 'Beak' in 1905. He fought in the First World War with the Coldstream Guards until his discharge on medical grounds. Returning to Eton, where he was to remain until 1935, he was considered to be an excellent housemaster by his charges. They liked his relaxed but authoritative style. Brian got on extremely well with him.

9 At Eton, 'Half' is a term. There are three Halfs in an academic year: Lent Half, Summer Half and Michaelmas Half. 'Beak' is Eton speak for Master.

10 Chairman of the governing body of Eton. Chosen by the Crown, he oversees the governance of the school above the headmaster.

Anna May Wong

One of Tuppy's supervisory duties was to check letters arriving at the house for the boys:

> *Eton housemasters are really supposed to glance over all the letters that reach boys in their houses. The main idea is to guard against letters being written to them by bookmakers. On occasion I have had to question boys on more trivial matters such as the arrival of photographs of naked ladies.*

Brian would later recall one incident when Tuppy asked him to open an envelope which Brian knew for certain contained risqué photos '*of a certain actress*'. Brian couldn't quite remember which actress it was, hoping it wasn't Anna May Wong with whom 'Tuppy' was '*especially friendly*'. Luckily it was a photo of another lady.

All the boys knew about Anna May: 'Tuppy' taught history in a classroom in the house. Brian Johnston[11] a contemporary of Brian's who became a lifelong friend, takes up the story:

> *Tuppy would often receive phone calls and we took it in turns to be on telephone duty and answer them for him. One day, just*

11 Brian Johnston was two years behind Brian at Eton. They were both in Headlam's and both cricket fanatics. They became great friends. Johnston went on to win an MC in the war with the Grenadier Guards, eventually becoming one of the most famous cricket commentators for BBC Television.

after Anna May had been down to see him, the telephone rang and Martin Gilliat (who later became the Queen Mother's Private Secretary) was on duty. There was much speculation among us ... There was quite a lot of excitement and a hush as Gilliat returned. 'Who was it?' asked Tuppy. 'Sorry sir,' said Gilliat, completely straight-faced, 'Wong number.'

Academically Brian was above average, among other things learning to speak fluent French, which would stand him in good stead both in his business career and in the SAS. His French report from the Lent Half 1926 describes Brian as '*intelligent and keen but sometimes rather tiresome. He is one of the youngest in the Division*[12] *but one of the very best.*'

As he rose through the school his interest in politics and international affairs was developing. He joined the Eton Political Society and became a competent debater. Brian also joined the Officers Training Corps in which he showed a natural aptitude for matters military, rising to the rank of Cadet Sergeant. Tuppy Headlam noted in the house book: '*Franks was unlucky, I believe, not to be a Cadet Officer.*'

There is a strong military tradition and connection at Eton, particularly with the Brigade of Guards. Of Brian's father's generation during the First World War, Etonians won 13 VCs, 548 DSOs and 784

12 Another Eton codeword for 'class'.

MCs. When Anthony Eden, himself an Old Etonian and winner of one of the 784 MCs, visited Hitler at Berchtesgaden in 1935, all that Hitler wanted to talk about was his conviction that Germany's defeat in the First War was entirely due to the military ethos of Eton.[13] In the Second World War the tally was five VCs, three GCs, three GMs, 254 DSOs and 355 MCs.[14] One extraordinary small record: six successive occupants of a room at Headlam's between them won two VCs and four MCs. The rooms either side were also occupied by MC winners. Brian was one of them.[15]

However it was on the sporting field that Brian really excelled, and made his mark. He represented his house at fives in the Lent Half, football in the Michaelmas Half and in the summer his favourite, cricket, at which he also made the School XI. He subsequently played for the Eton Ramblers up until the outbreak of war and again afterwards. Extracts from the house record book include: '*Franks scored 100, and bowled 40 overs magnificently in the second innings and got 7 wickets for 23.*'

He was also to become a fanatical fisherman, a keen shot and stalker.

13 During this meeting Eden did discover that he and Hitler had faced each other across the frontline in March 1918 during the German spring offensive.
14 During World War I, 5,650 Etonians served in the Armed Forces. 1 in 5 were killed, the equivalent of a whole year at Eton and the equivalent of another year wounded. This tally of decorations does not include the Royal Navy.
15 Commemorated by a plaque in the Hopgarden.

Other than cricket, Brian's greatest joy was food! Together with three friends, Hugh Vivian-Smith, Peter Tiarks and Raymond Lambert, he founded 'The Thursday Club', a breakfast dining club.

These breakfasts were elaborate affairs. The menu for their leaving breakfast on the 25th of July 1929 is a case in point:

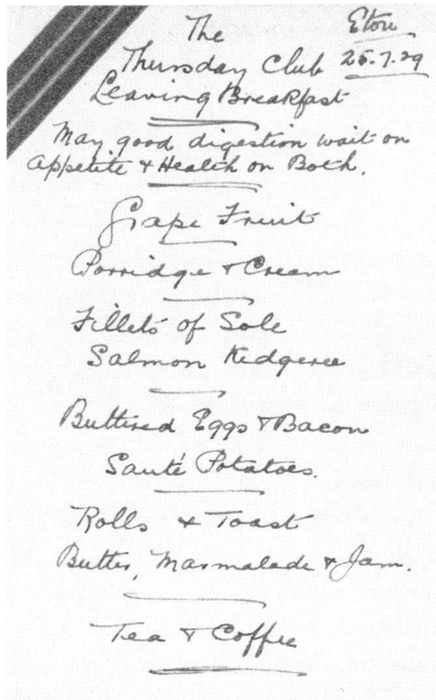

The Thursday Club
Eton 25.7.29
Leaving Breakfast

May good digestion wait on appetite & Health on Both.

Grape Fruit

Porridge & Cream

Fillets of Sole
Salmon Kedgeree

Buttered Eggs & Bacon
Sauté Potatoes.

Rolls & Toast
Butter, Marmalade & Jam.

Tea & Coffee

His love of food would stay with him for ever. The Christmas lunches, known as 'Franks' Feasts', at the Hyde Park Hotel, would become legendary.[16]

It was probably his sporting achievements and his gastronomic eccentricity that got him elected to the Eton Society at his first showing on the 16th of December 1928. 'Pop' is the nickname for the society which comprises the most effective, well regarded and confident senior boys in the school, who are in their last year. The members of 'Pop' take on the role of school prefects. 'Pop' has 16

16 See Chapter 14.

The Thursday Club

members; new members are elected by the existing members. It is very exclusive, and like anything exclusive, is hugely sought after. Not everyone makes the cut. To be elected first time round, as Brian was, was quite an achievement. There is no application process and potential members have to be outstanding to join this privileged elite. Elections were bitterly contested and often protracted. Members of 'Pop' wear their own stylish variant of the school uniform – a braided tailcoat, a buttonhole, white and black houndstooth check trousers, a white bow-tie and, most distinguishingly, a flamboyant silk waistcoat of the individual's own design.

Tuppy's end-of-Half report described Brian as '*of wild appearance with long hair and his tie out of place, with plenty of spirit and enjoys life*', and '*a very interesting and charming boy, cheerful, friendly, trustworthy. He looks like an imp but is one of those who make life pleasurable.*'

Brian's step-father, Hugh Elles, had supported Brian throughout his time at Eton, notably by paying his fees and continuing their family trips to Bembridge in the holidays. But the family money was running low and for the latter part of his time at Eton, his fees were waived by the school. As a result he was unable to join many of his friends at Oxford, although he continued to visit them and have lots of fun. '*I had lots of friends at Oxford, especially at Trinity. When I could escape the kitchen I went there – played golf, got plastered and all that.*'

'Pop' 1929

Curiously, Brian had another frequent family visitor while at school, Desmond Morton,[17] who was Brian's mother's cousin. Morton was in the Secret Intelligence Service. Brian later recalled that '*he was always delightful and always amusing – full of anecdotes and fun. Never once did he give me any inkling of his job*.'

One of the great advantages of having been to Eton was the friendships formed and the ability to tap into the Old Etonian network. Eton may not be the oldest school in the country but it is certainly the grandest. Etonians emerge with a relaxed nonchalance, very confident and with standards of old-fashioned excellence, all masking a strong sense of duty and a steely determination to succeed, without '*an extravagant declaration of principles*'. George Orwell again: '*It has one great value. It is a tolerant and civilised atmosphere which gives each boy the chance of developing his own individuality,*' and Wilfred Thesiger,[18] who served in the wartime SAS, remembered: '*Eton was one of the most formative influences of my life. It gave me responsibility, the decencies of life and standards of civilised*

17 Before 1929 Morton had been a frequent house guest of Winston Churchill, but in 1929 Churchill began to prepare for war. Winston would constantly question him about classified matters, which put Morton in a difficult position given that he was in SIS. Morton went to see Ramsay MacDonald, the Prime Minister, explained his position and asked for some advice. 'Tell him whatever he wants to know. Keep him informed.' 'Will you put it in writing, Prime Minister?' Desmond replied. MacDonald wrote the necessary authority on a sheet of 10 Downing Street notepaper.

18 Wilfred Thesiger (1910–2003). Born in Addis Ababa, attended Eton and Oxford. Boxing Blue and Chairman of the Exploration Society. Sudan Political Service 1935–40. World War II: Sudan Defence Force (DSO), SOE and SAS. Post-war: explorer and author.

behaviour.' Brian Johnston would describe it as '*a wonderful club, some people call it the best Trades Union in the world*'.

The Eton 'old boy' network is indeed very powerful, particularly when combined with other 'networks' such as the Guards, Oxford and Cambridge, White's and the SAS. It is well summarised in the 'Eton Boating Song':

But we'll row for ever,
Steady from stroke to bow,
And nothing in life shall sever,
The chain that is round us now.

It is often assumed that Etonians are successful because of their connections alone, but this is not really true. The school instils responsibility, self-reliance and resourcefulness from an early age. The boys are treated more like undergraduates with a 'sink or swim' philosophy. The restriction of school rules, and isolation during term time, meant that there was always an undercurrent of 'escape and evasion' and outwitting the 'beaks', which would have made James Bond proud and stood Brian in good stead later in the Vosges mountains. Julian Amery would describe Eton '*as the perfect preparation for a splendid series of adventures*'.

Brian made many friends at Eton, including Hilary Bray, Brian Johnston, Ian Fleming and Robert Laycock, with whom he would work closely in the coming war, still some ten years off. Brian left at the end of the Summer Half in July 1929 and started looking for a job, settling on the hotel business. Later, when asked why hotels: '*he gave a nonchalant Eton smile and said I don't know why really, I often wondered. I wanted a job and there it was …*'. It was an inspired choice, and he would become very good at it.

CHAPTER 2 – MARBLED HALLS

'I dreamt I lived in Marbled Halls...'

Alfred Bunn, *The Bohemian Girl* (1843)

Behind Brian's nonchalant approach was a real need to find a job. There was to be no private income support available from family funds for three years at Oxford or to assist him with an Army career, where a private income was pretty essential; it was a case of 'get a job'.

His search was not helped by the economic climate in Britain. The Wall Street Crash of 1929 and its knock-on effect on the British economy coincided with Brian leaving Eton. It was Britain's most profound economic depression of the twentieth century, and hit the country hard when it was still a long way from recovering from the effects of the First World War. Britain's world trade fell by half between 1929 and 1933. By the summer of 1932 unemployment had reached three and a half million and many more could find only part-time work. Particularly badly hit were the industrial and mining areas in the north of England, Scotland, Northern Ireland and Wales, with unemployment reaching 70 per cent in some areas.

Ten years before Brian left school it would have been unheard of for an Etonian to take a job in a hotel, but Brian and another Etonian, David Rhys (son of Lord Dynevor), took the plunge.[19] Brian was put in touch with Hugh Wonter[20] of the Hotel and Restaurant Trades Association, who arranged for him to meet Sir Francis Towle, the Managing Director of Gordon Hotels. During the First World War Towle had been Assistant Inspector of the Quartermaster General's Service, and Controller of the Navy and Army Canteen Board. He was knighted in 1919. Towle interviewed Brian, and liked what he saw. But he warned him that he would have to start at the very bottom, offering him a job in the kitchens of the newly built Dorchester Hotel, which was just about to open.

19 David Rhys, like Brian, advanced quickly to become a manager at the Savoy.
20 Sir Hugh Wonter, later Managing Director of the Savoy Group and Lord Mayor of London.

Towle was a key player in the development of the Dorchester, in which he had a personal holding of 10 per cent. He had tried to persuade his own company, Gordon Hotels, to develop the project but they were unwilling to take the project on directly. Instead Towle formed a syndicate together with Sir Robert McAlpine, and Gordon Hotels. The Dorchester House Syndicate Ltd was incorporated in August 1929, and the hotel opened its doors on the 18th of April 1931. On the 28th of March Towle had given Queen Mary a personal tour. This was to set the scene for the hotel's long association with Royalty, the aristocracy, artists, writers, musicians and actors. Cecil Day Lewis, Somerset Maugham and Alfred Munnings were among the early patrons.

As Towle had promised, Brian started work at the Dorchester before it opened, learning what was going to be expected of him. He started right at the bottom, working as a 'pan diver', fish cleaner, potato peeler and the chef's general dogsbody. He also had a spell as a waiter. Brian quickly came to the attention of the management, as an enthusiastic and capable young man whose hard-working ethos and affable manner soon marked him out as management material. Having an Old Etonian tie around the hotel would not go amiss either.

David Niven saw him at Bembridge and commented: '*He was working his way up through the kitchens of the Dorchester but was filled with enthusiasm and painted a glowing picture of his prospects.*' Within two years Brian had made his way from menial jobs in the kitchen to Banqueting Manager, one of the most responsible positions in the hotel. His hard work and reliability were recognised in a personal letter from Francis Towle, dated the 9th of April 1934:

Brian Franks, Esq.
Dorchester Hotel W1

Dear Mr Franks,
I have pleasure in enclosing herewith a cheque for £100[21] *as a bonus for the special services you have rendered since you have been at the Dorchester.*

21 Worth £9,146 today. To put this in perspective the average house price in London at the time was £750.

I should like to take this opportunity of congratulating you upon the hard and successful work you have put in since your appointment at the Dorchester and I am quite sure that we can rely on your continued efforts at a time when the banqueting business wants more careful watching than ever.

Yours faithfully,
Francis Towle

*

As well as working hard, Brian also found time to play hard, continuing his love of sport. Brian spent time on the golf course, and took part in the British Amateur Squash Championship at the Bath Club in 1934 and 1935. He also indulged his love of cricket, often playing at Lord's for the Eton Ramblers.

He was much in demand socially, a regular feature in the gossip columns of the *Express*, *Sketch*, *Evening News*, *Queen* and most often in *Tatler*'s *Bystander*, where he was often referred to as '*smiling, suave and sophisticated*' or as a '*notable guest*'. He attended many weddings of his friends as an usher and was best man for D'Arcy Lambton when he married the Hon. Monica Brand, Lord Hampden's daughter, at St Martin-in-the-Fields on the 10th of October 1933, with a reception held at the Duke and Duchess of Buccleuch's London house in Grosvenor Place.

In June 1932 *Bystander* published an article called 'The Dance List':

The Dance List. Have you seen it? For years I used to think it was a myth, a phantasm. 'Is he on the Dance List?' It began long years before the war. It has been added to, subtracted from, increased, erased, altered out of all recognition from its original self. It is handed round discreetly. It is spoken of reverently. Mothers of debutantes up from the Cotswolds or Scotland or Missouri, or wherever debutantes come from, would be lost without it. They say to their friends, 'My dear, how can I get hold of the dance list? Can you help, my dear? Of course, I know it's all very humiliating

Hard day on the cricket pitch

Late night at Ciro's

to ask you a thing like this.' Then the fun begins. It is all so very awkward. They unwisely ask Mrs Snodgrass who also had a debutante daughter last Season. She opens her saucer-blue eyes and says, 'A dance list? My dear, how funny you are. Is there such a thing? Really? Well, of course, we've never needed it. We know far too many young men as it is.' The liar. She paid through the nose for a glimpse of one in 1931. Not that it did her ugly daughter much good.

Well, who is on the dance list? Automatically, unmarried officers in the Cavalry and the Brigade of Guards are on it, and so are unmarried peers, baronets, and sons of peers up to the age of thirty-five or so. If a young man arrives at a dance early in the Season with Lady Pansy Peabody or that rich Miss Wallop, he is likely to find himself on the list in no time. Within a week his mantelpiece will bristle with invitations to dances from strangers of whom he has never heard ...

And now for the list. Are you on it? Here you are, then: Lord Mornington, Lord O'Neill, Lord Kelburn, the Duke of Norfolk, Lord Mulgrave, Sir Hugh Smiley, Lord Buckingham, Mr Max Aitken, Lord Walpole.

The list continues and of course always included '*Mr Brian Franks*'.

As well as enjoying himself in smart restaurants or on the dance-floor, Brian also spent time at Bembridge with his mother and step-father who were great 'Bembridgites', being spotted there in April, May, August and September 1932. He kept up with his chum David Niven and they continued to race dinghies at the Bembridge Sailing Club. He would continue to visit regularly until the war intervened, seven years later.

*

On the 14th of April 1936, Francis Towle wrote to Brian confirming that he would like him to take over the management of the Mayfair Hotel in Stratton Street, '*at a salary of £600 a year, plus a commission amounting to 3% on any increased profits of the hotel in each year, above the average trading profits for the years 1933, 1934 and 1935, such commission to be based on the accounts as shown in the company's books*'. The post would start immediately and be subject to six months' notice on either side. Brian continued to shine. By July his salary had increased to £650.

As well as his new responsibilities, Brian continued with both his social and sporting lives. He spent as much time as he could in Scotland with his friend Hilary Bray. They would stay with the Lyles in Perthshire to shoot grouse, and fish on various lochs, and on the Tay. This would be followed by a visit to Hilary's uncle Arthur Anderson, who owned Glen Etive for some great days' stalking:

> *No stalker, no pony, just a rope to drag a beast down to the lochside. H. divided the hill, dominated by Beinn Treacle (my name), into Lower Club, Middle Club, Upper Club. Lower C. a fairly easy drag, Middle C. hard work, Upper C. impossible. I remember missing a stag on purpose in late afternoon on U.C. The drag would have been awful and home at midnight at best. I never knew whether he realised what I had done. I suspect he did. On getting a beast to the lochside, one of us had to fetch a boat and row it to Barrs to be skinned and butchered. At the end of a bottle of whisky it was done with some loss of temper and some very odd joints. We did not improve with practice.*

Stalking with Hilary Bray

It was fishing for salmon on the Awe that really began Brian's love affair with fishing. One evening the fishing party was assembled for drinks in the drawing room at Inverawe. The telephone rang and the hostess Francis Campbell-Preston went to answer it. A few minutes later she returned looking somewhat puzzled. '*The strangest thing ... That was our neighbour who has the fishing opposite us. He was complaining that one of his guests was fishing this afternoon, when someone started pelting him with rocks from our side of the river. I told him that couldn't possibly be the case.*' '*On the contrary,*' *said Brian,* '*it was me. He was a horrible little shit at school and still is. He deserved it.*'

Brian also kept in touch with David Niven, who had gone to Sandhurst and been commissioned into the Highland Light Infantry. Niven was stationed in Malta but sneaked off to London whenever possible. Brian had him put up for Boodles and arranged riotous dinners at the Mayfair Hotel. One of the more notable took place before the Caledonian Ball. Niven takes up the story:

> *A most colourful spectacle awaited us. Scots from all over the world were present in full regalia and the pièce de résistance was always the set reels. The girls we were to partner wore the sashes of their clans and had been carefully selected by the Ball Committee for their territorial connections with the regiment and not, we noticed, with some alarm, for their good looks. However,*

Lady Elles with William

we had just arrived from a riotous dinner in a private room at The Mayfair Hotel which Brian Franks had arranged, so we were not too unnerved when introduced to our horse-faced partners from far-away glens.

The Pipe Major had been polishing up our dancing for days before the big night and we were quietly confident of holding up the good name of the regiment in front of hundreds of pairs of critical eyes. The unknown girls were expert dancers and it was the dawning look of horror on their faces as they realised we were not.

One event marred Brian's successful progression through the luxury hotel business. On the 7th of December 1937 Brian's mother collapsed and died on a train coming back from Birmingham, where Hugh Elles had been giving a speech. Her death was sudden and unexpected. But while very upset, Brian met it with the same stoicism with which he had dealt with the death of his father.

*

Brian made such a success of running the Mayfair that he soon came to the attention of Leonard Bennett, the owner of the Hyde Park Hotel, one of London's grandest and one with which Brian was to be hugely involved for the next thirty-five years.

The Hyde Park Hotel was built in 1889 as an exclusive apartment block with 138 bachelor flats. It was originally known as Hyde Park Court, and was situated between the park and Knightsbridge, with the original entrance on the park side. The entrance halls, corridors and main rooms were lined with marble, the building having been '*designed to meet the requirements of a large section of the upper class*'. In 1904, however, it was badly damaged by fire, after which the building was sold off relatively cheaply to the Bennetts, a family of property dealers who refurbished it and reopened it as an opulent hotel in 1908. Period fireplaces were installed, and the furniture was English and French eighteenth-century in style.

Queen Victoria had insisted that no advertising signs should appear anywhere in Hyde Park. The original main entrance, facing the park, was closed. The rear entrance, on the Knightsbridge side, became the main entrance instead. The hotel was unique in that it retained the atmosphere of an exclusive apartment block as well as having a restaurant, bar, seven banqueting suites and a ballroom. In all, there were 205 bedrooms and 19 suites, frequented both by London and international society and by nobility and Royalty, either still reigning or in exile.

The Royal Family were regulars at the hotel, and used the original entrance in Hyde Park, which was opened only for their use. Because of its well-known connections to the Royal Family, many grand debutante parties and balls were held there. Many of the suites were occupied by long-term residents, and there was an enormous staff, including dozens of valets, who catered for every need of their pampered clients. The atmosphere at the Hyde Park was like a highly exclusive gentleman's club. No guest was accepted without first having their references checked and considered; it was preferable to have a title. Politicians were an exception to this elitist ruling, and figures such as Beaverbrook and Churchill were favoured clients because they were important, influential and gave the Hyde Park an edgy 'style'. The hotel thus became the destination of choice for the aristocracy, visiting Royalty, diplomats, celebrities and socialites. Brian was often in the bar and grill room, and came to know many of the regulars.

The 1920s swept into the Hyde Park Hotel with a bang. Most of

The following was written by a member of The Times Advertising Staff after an independent investigation.

BACHELORS' SUITES.

WHAT are the ideal quarters for a man living in town? The question is answered at the Hyde Park Hotel. Take a "Bachelor's Suite" there and you will have, firstly, just that comfortable sort of retreat that a man can call his "den"; secondly, exceptional hotel advantages; thirdly, the most agreeable and convenient situation in London. You will have bed-room, sitting room, and private bathroom, all compactly enclosed within the walls of your own suite. Can any-thing be more comfortable? For your meals you have at your disposal the finest dining room in London, overlooking Hyde Park, as well as the well-known Grill Room. The reasonable charge for the apartments includes service; you may, therefore, dispense with a valet. Do you enjoy music? A first-rate string orchestra plays each evening in the handsome smoke lounge. The situation of the Hotel is unrivalled in London for agreeableness and con-venience. It stands on the edge of Hyde Park, on high ground; for club-men and theatre-goers it is the central point of their world; while May-fair and Belgravia are quite close to hand. Are not such quarters rightly described as IDEAL?

Plan of a Bachelor's Suite at the Hyde Park Hotel.

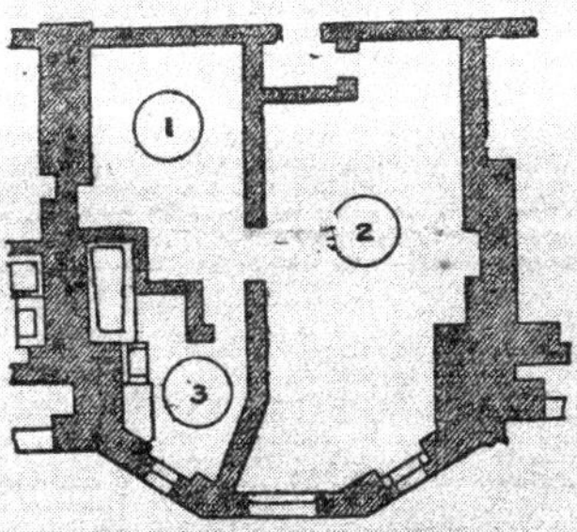

No. 1.—*Bed room.* No. 2.—*Sitting room.* No. 3.—*Bath room.*

The Hyde Park Hotel,

Albert Gate, LONDON.

Most charming and healthful position in London, overlooking Hyde Park, and the hub of the world of fashion and pleasure.

Family and Bachelor Suites of various sizes, with bath and lavatory, complete within themselves; single rooms.

The finest Dining Room in London with open Terrace directly overlooking Hyde Park.

GRILL RESTAURANT. LOUIS XVI. LOUNGE.
AMERICAN BAR. ELECTRIC LIGHT.

For Tariff, terms of Hiring the Banqueting and Ball Rooms, and other particulars, address: The Manager.

For Balls, Weddings, Receptions, Banquets, a magnificent suite of rooms is available, possessing a separate and private entrance. These rooms derive from the contiguity of Hyde Park the charm and beauty that belong to a great mansion set in its own garden.

The American Bar

The Grill Room

the hotel's upper floors were still occupied by the very rich permanent residents, as well as by various exotic Sultans and Maharajas from all corners of the British Empire. In 1929 the Sultan of Zanzibar arrived with 12 goats, who roamed the upper floors, causing chaos and making more than a little mess.

Rudolph Valentino had also moved in for an extended stay. The ground-floor suites and banqueting rooms were dominated by the Royal Family, in particular the Prince of Wales, who would regularly arrive with his close friend Dudley 'Fruity' Metcalfe, for a 'sharpener' or two before heading off to the Café de Paris, Ciro's, the Gargoyle, or the Kit Kat Club. They would often return for a nightcap on their way home.

The 'Bright Young Things' or 'Flappers' of the 1920s and early 1930s found the Hyde Park too grand and stuffy. They wanted something a bit more exciting and preferred the nightclubs or the naughtiness of Rosa Lewis's newly opened Cavendish Hotel on the junction of Jermyn Street and Duke Street. Rosa Lewis had started out as a cook for Lady Randolph Churchill, and is famous for chasing the young ten-year-old red-haired Winston out of her kitchen shouting '*hop it copper knob*'. She had a dalliance with Edward VII and it is rumoured that he bought her the Cavendish. She had also been hired as the cook at White's, but she lasted a very short time there, sacked when a member complained that she had called him '*a damned old woodcock in tights*'.

The Sultan of Zanzibar

Rosa Lewis

Evelyn Waugh, who was introduced to the Hyde Park by Brian, became a regular. He loved its grandeur, but also loved the loucheness of the Cavendish and he would flit between the two. The distinction was similar to the difference between White's and the Colony Room[22] in Soho, both utterly perfect but for the right occasion. Rosa Lewis would have a love/hate relationship with the Bennetts and the Hyde Park which would last all her life – but it was where she took refuge when the Cavendish was bombed in the Blitz. Eventually things would turn full circle. Rosa died in 1952, and in 1964 the derelict site of the Cavendish was acquired by the Hyde Park Hotel.

The Coronation of George VI in 1937 was a particular high spot for the Hyde Park. The hotel was packed with Royalty and the aristocracy: King Gustav of Sweden, King Christian of Denmark, the Duke of Norfolk, the Marquis of Salisbury, the Duke of Abercorn, and the Marquis of Londonderry were all guests. As the threat of war started to cast its shadow over London, the Bennetts decided it was time to modernise the Hyde Park and started looking around to see who might fit the bill to oversee the work. They knew of Brian's reputation at the Dorchester and the Mayfair, his ability, excellent managerial skills and his strong social connections. So they set out to headhunt him.

22 Colony Room: a private members' club in Soho, one of the premier drinking dens, with a very louche atmosphere. It was presided over by the owner, Muriel Belcher, 'an imperious lesbian and benevolent witch with a fondness for insulting banter'. Francis Bacon, Lucien Freud, George Melly and Jeffrey Bernard were members. Visitors regularly included Royalty and rock stars. It had an 'atmosphere of delectable depravity'.

Basil Bennett took on the job, as he knew Brian well. The recruitment took place during the spring of 1937. Throughout March, April and May they discussed salary and future prospects, in letters between the two parties. On the 17th of April Basil wrote, '*I offer you this post on purely commercial grounds. Rightly or wrongly I consider you could be very useful to this company in developing our business* ...' In May they had further discussions:

> *... then there is every prospect of your becoming General Manager in future years – with cash and lodging it is worth £2,000 p.a. I want you to consider very carefully whether or not you would be influenced in accepting my offer by the fact that your own job at the moment is not very salubrious. Another point is this. You will probably be sufficiently rash and injudicious one day to embark on a course of matrimony. You would of course have a decent flat here to live in; but it might not be a particularly pleasant prospect either for you or 'The Unknown Wife'. In other words I don't want to seduce you from a job where you are doing well and will no doubt do better unless you think very hard about it. You are of course under no obligation to accept anything that I may offer. I shall be only too glad for you to consult with anyone you like about this matter. Thank you so much for lunch the other day.*
> *Yours,*
> *Basil Bennett*

In June 1937 Brian accepted the job, gave his notice and parted amicably with Francis Towle, taking up his new post in January 1938. He had of course been '*sufficiently rash and injudicious*' as Basil Bennett predicted; on the 29th of November 1938 he became engaged:

> *The engagement is announced and the marriage will shortly take place between Brian Morton Forster Franks, only son of the late Lieut.-Colonel G. D. Franks, CMG, DSO, 19th Hussars, and of the late Lady Elles, of Foulis Terrace, London, SW7, and Zoe Gwynedd, second daughter of Sir Cuthbert and the Hon. Lady Quilter, of Methersgate Hall, Woodbridge, Suffolk. Miss Quilter*

Zoe Quilter

is 26 and through her mother is a cousin of Lord Penrhyn and of Viscountess Portman. Her father, the second holder of the baronetcy, succeeded to the title in 1911.

Basil Bennett had been quite right in assuming Brian's thoughts would sooner or later turn to marriage. He had had ten years since leaving Eton to play both the London and country fields with the ladies, as the suave, charming debonair man about town. With an impending war he felt that it was about time to settle his domestic arrangements. His attention homed in on Zoe, whom he had got to know at the Mayfair, where she was in charge of all the floral decorations.

Brian and Zoe were married on the 11th of January 1939. The inevitable *Bystander* announcement followed:

Mr Brian Morton Forster Franks and Miss Zoe Gwynedd Quilter were married at St Clement Danes, Strand. He is the only son of the late Lieut. Col. George D. Franks, 19th Hussars, and the late Lady Elles. She is the second daughter of Sir Cuthbert and the Hon. Lady Quilter, of Methersgate Hall, Woodbridge, and 28, South Street W1. Her younger sister, Sonia, is marrying Patrick Pole-Carew, Coldstream Guards, next week at the Royal Military Academy Sandhurst. The Rev. W. Pennington-Bickford and the Rev. F. Wilkinson officiated. Given away by her father, the bride wore a gown of ivory-tinted velvet. The bride was attended by

Sonia Quilter (sister of the bride) Gillian Elles (step-sister of the bridegroom), Hermione Peel, and Renée Alston. Mr Ian Lyle was the best man. The reception was held at 21 Belgrave Square. Later the bride and bridegroom left for the honeymoon in the South of France.

One of the Quilter family members present was Zoe's brother, Raymond, who was to have an unusual connection with Brian later in the war. Raymond Quilter was a parachute pioneer. He developed parachutes – not only for parachutists but for parachuting Jeeps and equipment containers for the SAS and SOE. Brian and his men would use them on Operation LOYTON.[23]

On the 1st of February Brian received a very welcome wedding present, being elected to the board of directors of the Hyde Park Hotel Management Company. As the threat of hostilities intensified a feeling of malaise permeated the Hyde Park. The Bennetts were already

23 See Chapter 9.

trying to reorganise the hotel's catering, which was the primary reason Brian was brought in. At the Mayfair, Brian had employed a restaurant manager called Ronald Massara. Both Brian and Massara would play a hugely important role in reversing the fortunes of the hotel after the war. Massara had previously worked at the Savoy, the Paris Ritz and the Berkeley. Brian also brought in Tommy Kinsman and his orchestra, one of the top dance bands in London.

The permanent residents of the Hyde Park – mainly crusty bachelor types – decided that they would ignore the atmosphere of malaise. They were an extraordinary breed, long-term residents who took a highly idiosyncratic approach to their day-to-day lives in the hotel. They all had their own solitary tables in the grill room and they would be furious if a casual guest dared to stray into their territory. Their clothes were valeted daily, their shoes were highly polished to Brigade of Guards standards; taxis waited at the door for them; and they were treated like Royalty. The very thought of having to leave the protective comfort zone of the Hyde Park was anathema to them.

Later in the year, with preparation for war at the back of his mind, Brian joined the TA. He, like many others, felt that the country had been living on borrowed time since the Munich Crisis of 1938.

The last function held at the Hyde Park before the outbreak of war was the annual dinner of the Chelsea Arts Club. By Hyde Park standards, the menu was fairly basic: only eight courses, including soup, lobster mousse, roast turkey, cold veal, pudding, savoury, cheese and coffee. Among the guests were Sir Edwin Lutyens and J. B. Priestley. Brian, as ever watching proceedings closely, sensed that there was a false gaiety masking a feeling of impending doom.

On the 3rd of September 1939 Brian and the staff gathered around a wireless, set up in the ballroom to hear Neville Chamberlain announce that Great Britain was at war with Germany. Eight minutes after the end of the broadcast air-raid sirens sounded, marking the start of the 'Phoney War'. Life would not return to normal at the Hyde Park for six years.

CHAPTER 3 – WAR

> 'Four elements make up the climate of war: danger, exertion, uncertainty, and chance.'
>
> Carl von Clausewitz, *On War* (1832)

Brian reported for duty with the Middlesex Yeomanry at the Duke of York's Headquarters on the King's Road, Chelsea.[24] He would keep in touch with the hotel throughout the war, even finding Basil Bennett a place in the Commando Brigade Headquarters in 1943 and later in the SAS. In 1944 Brian would use the hotel as his London office while commanding 2 SAS.

The Middlesex Yeomanry was considered a 'gentlemen-only' TA cavalry regiment, which had distinguished itself in both the Boer War and the First World War. During the 1920s there was an extensive round of defence cuts and many of the TA Yeomanry cavalry regiments were disbanded, amalgamated or rerolled. In order to survive, the Middlesex Yeomanry elected to join the Royal Corps of Signals. Brian had chosen this regiment because it was full of people with whom he had been at school: George Grant, Dick Schuster, John Smiley and Geoffrey Heyward. The Commanding Officer Leonard Messel and the Second-in-Command were also Old Etonians.

The regiment remained in London between the outbreak of war and its move north to York in November, to join the 15th Cavalry Division as the Divisional Signals Regiment. Their time in London was spent in basic training, the issue of kit such as steel helmets and respirators; of neither was there enough to go round. Key point defence and air-raid drills took up a lot of their time. By November boredom and frustration were setting in. On the 24th of November they received a warning order to move north to York to join their divisional headquarters and to move with them to Palestine. The War Diary for the period of the 24th to 27th of November makes interesting reading.

24 Later the Duke of York's barracks became the headquarters of 21 SAS and the secret location of the Directorate of Special Forces.

Brian in Yeomanry uniform

Anyone who has been a soldier will recognise the atmosphere of 'order, counter-order and disorder!'

24.11.39 *Mobilisation conference. To proceed to Palestine. Division in a somewhat chaotic state.*
25.11.39 *Drawing of stores in London District cancelled and indents forwarded to York. This results in a great deal of extra work and seems to be utterly pointless.*
26.11.39 *State of chaos begins. Most men on leave or flat on their backs owing to inoculations. No orders received from anywhere and it becomes difficult to organise anything.*
27.11.39 *Chaos increases by leaps and bounds; absence of any written orders increases muddle; fog of war descends in an impenetrable blanket.*
28.11.39 *Further small parties move north and things begin to get out of control entirely. Still no orders.*
29.11.39 *Fog clears a little and preparation for move go forward. Generally a less depressing day.*
30.11.39 *The road party left five minutes ahead of schedule, probably for the first time in the regiment's history.*

Eventually orders were received and the regiment moved north by road and rail. Brian commanded 'L Troop', B Squadron allocated as the brigade signal troop for the 6th Cavalry Brigade, which consisted of three cavalry regiments: the Warwickshire, Staffordshire and Cheshire Yeomanry. The brigade was commanded by Brigadier John Chrystall CBE MC.

No sooner had the Middlesex arrived in York than the division was ordered south to Southampton and embarked for Cherbourg on the 26th of December 1939. From Cherbourg a rather uncomfortable 36-hour rail move across France followed, with the division embarking on the *Devonshire* in Marseille. Arriving on the *Devonshire* was a relief: '*... Comfortable and ship's company very helpful. Considered a first-class hotel after 36 hours on train.*'

On the 3rd of January 1940 the convoy, consisting of two troop ships, four horse ships and two destroyers from the Australian Navy, set sail for Haifa. During the journey, Brian became sick with a throat infection and retired to bed with a temperature of 103°. Arriving in Haifa on the 9th of January the regiment moved to Netanya, where they were expecting to have a period of training but were told to '*train on the job*'.

The 1st Cavalry Division's role was internal security. Palestine, which had been under British mandate since the end of World War I, was in a state of unrest. The Arabs were bitterly anti-British following the Balfour Declaration[25] and had been in open revolt since 1936, when the Higher Arab Committee led by Hajj Amin al-Husseini, the Grand Mufti of Jerusalem, ordered a general strike. This was accompanied by significant terrorist activity, armed attacks on British troops, roads blocked and trains derailed. The Germans were of course keen to encourage and exploit this.

Before Brian could get to grips with his role at 6 Brigade he was detached on temporary duty to Jerusalem to 'mother' the evacuated married families from Egypt, but he was back within a week to resume command of 'L Troop' at 6 Brigade headquarters, first at

25 The Balfour Declaration was a public statement issued by the British Government in 1917 expressing support for the establishment of a 'national home for Jewish people' in Palestine. It was a letter from Arthur Balfour, the British Foreign Secretary, to Lord Walter Rothschild, a leader of the British Jewish community. It was published in the press on the 9th of November 1917. The declaration is a key document in the history of the Israeli–Palestinian conflict. It is seen as a cornerstone of the establishment of the State of Israel. However, it is also a source of controversy and resentment among Palestinians, who view it as a betrayal of their rights.

Brian in Palestine

Nazareth, then Nablus. He took his duties seriously. On the 23rd of December 1940 the Brigade Commander wrote to him:

Headquarters,
6th Cavalry Brigade,
Nablus
23rd December 1940

My Dear Brian,
The training season for 1940 has closed. I thank you personally again for the manful way you have supported me all through. No one could have been better served and the measure of success obtained during manoeuvres has been largely due to your efforts. The brigade is now ready for war and before long will be called upon to play its part.

I feel so appreciative of your efforts that today I wrote the attached 'Special Order of the Day', and I would be grateful if you would let all ranks know its contents. As I said once before, I have asked a great deal of you. I can truly add that I have received much more than I asked.

Good luck to you and yours, and a Happy Christmas and Prosperous New Year.

Yours ever,
John Chrystall

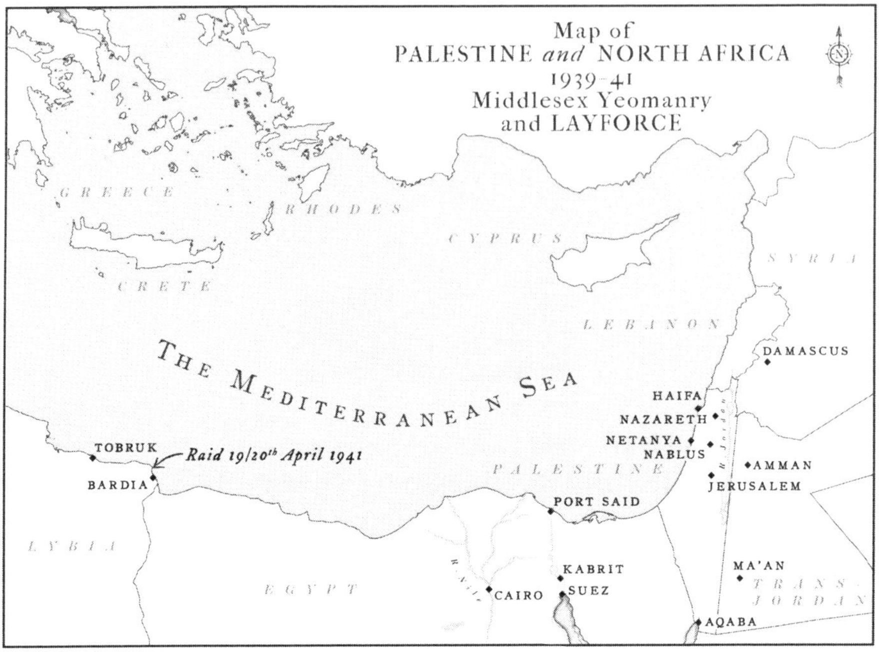

A second handwritten letter followed, congratulating Brian on '*really first class efficiency combined with good cheer*'.

One of the key achievements that Brian had overseen was the mechanisation of the brigade headquarters – the move from horses to vehicles: from 'Oats to Oil'.

*

Brian's next move was to North Africa. He was posted to the 2nd Armoured Division Signals Squadron on the 20th of February 1941. This was an armoured division in name only, having been reduced in strength to three armoured regiments and was further weakened by some of its units being taken for an expeditionary force to Greece. In March it would be destroyed by a German–Italian counter-attack which led to the British being ejected from Cyrenaica.

During this rather slack period Brian began to look around for something more exciting to do. Cairo, behind the scenes, was rapidly

Shepheard's Hotel

becoming a hotbed of guilty pleasures. Besides the unofficial 'headquarters' of the British Army, Shepheard's Hotel, and the Mohammed Ali Club, Madame Bardia's nightclub and casino with its anti-Nazi cabaret and raunchy dancers, the Auberge des Pyramides and the Kit Kat Club, all provided intriguing entertainment and were also fertile ground for German intelligence. The famous belly dancer Hekmet Fahmy was well known as an Abwehr informant.

They were a magnet for a '*gathering of the clans*', which would form the genesis of British Special Forces, the SAS, Long Range Desert Group, Popski's Private Army and SOE: the Stirling brothers, Neil 'Billy' McLean, Paddy Leigh Fermor, Vladimir Peniakoff and Stanley 'Billy' Moss were all regulars in Cairo, and very soon Brian would bump into them. Many of them lived at Shepheard's Hotel.

As fate would have it, Robert Laycock, whom Brian knew from Eton, had just arrived in Cairo with his force of the newly raised Commandos. Due to a directive designed to confuse the Germans (and everyone else), the unit designation of 'Commando' was changed to the more conventional 'battalions' and the formations commanded by Laycock renamed, from 7, 8 and 11 Commando, to LAYFORCE.[26] Bob heard that Brian was in Cairo and looking for action so immediately arranged for him to be posted as the LAYFORCE signals officer on the 18th of March 1941. This was the start of Brian's lifetime

26 This administrative 'ruse de guerre' has led to confusion with Brian being reported as having joined 8 Commando. In fact he never served in 8 Commando.

Robert Laycock

association with the world of special operations, and he found this type of soldiering '*very much to his liking*'.

Robert 'Lucky' Laycock was three years older than Brian and came from a similar background. Their friendship at Eton developed largely through their shared love of cricket. Laycock was also a friend of David Niven and they were eventually to be related by marriage, when Niven married his niece Prim Rollo. Niven slightly disingenuously claimed that he had recommended Bob, who was in the Household Cavalry at the time, for the Commandos. In fact Niven had only helped the administration process of entry. Having joined, Laycock raised No. 8 Commando – otherwise known as 'The White's Commando' – from Guards regiments in London District. The term '*recruited in the bar of White's*' stems from this period, and there is some truth in it, as we will see. 8 Commando's headquarters was at 32 Cadogan Square. David and Bill Stirling, George Jellicoe, Randolph Churchill, Shimi Lovat and Evelyn Waugh, all members of White's, were early recruits. Bob Laycock was firmly of the view that '*if you have to go to war, you might as well do it among friends*'.

One of his other early recruits was Eric 'Bill' Barkworth, a fluent German speaker who was later to become Brian's intelligence officer in 2 SAS. When tested on his German, the German lady recruited for the purpose reported that she thought he was a German '*as no Englishman could speak German like that*'. 8 Commando spent its early days in Arran and Largs in Scotland. Evelyn Waugh described it

8 Commando at Largs. Philip Dunne (centre) and Evelyn Waugh (left)

as '*boisterous, xenophobe, extravagant and witty*'. From here it was ordered to Egypt, where it arrived on the 8th of March 1941.

One evening Brian and Bob Laycock went round to see David Stirling at Shepheard's. His room was on the top floor, which looked out on to a centre well. In the passage outside his room there was a long shelf on which were a number of room service trays each with teapot, cup, saucer and sugar bowl, in readiness for the next morning. It was late and only a few of the night staff remained on duty. David asked them if they would like a whisky and soda. When they accepted he went out into the passage, picked up one of the trays, returned to the room and dropped the tray and its contents out of the window. It fell with a resounding crash at the bottom of the well many floors below. Shortly afterwards the night porter arrived with three whisky and sodas. When they had finished their drinks they thought they had better have some more so David fetched a second tray and repeated the performance. Almost immediately three more whisky and sodas arrived. He explained that the first night he had been at Shepheard's he couldn't get anyone to answer the bell after midnight until in exasperation he had thrown a tray down the well. This had worked so well that he had never adopted any other procedure. It confirmed Brian's view that the Stirling family were often unorthodox in their methods.

Brian's trajectory was now set for the rest of the war, taking him from LAYFORCE, a short spell with the GHQ Liaison Regiment, or

'Phantom', to the Special Service Brigade and eventually to command of 2 SAS. In the words of Fraser McLuskey, padre of 1 SAS, *'he would spend the rest of the war looking for trouble and finding it'*.

*

Brian joined LAYFORCE at Kabrit on the 18th of March 1941. Kabrit was a large and strategically important RAF base 75 miles east of Cairo on the west bank of the Suez Canal. LAYFORCE was now a force roughly the same size as a normal infantry brigade (2–3,000 men) consisting of 7, 8 and 11 Commandos, now joined by 50 and 52 Commandos.[27] The new arrivals contained a number of Jews, Arabs and Spanish Republicans who had fought in the Spanish Civil War. With this increase in establishment, Bob Laycock should have been promoted to brigadier but his youth and lack of seniority upset the stuffed shirts in the Military Secretary's Department. A compromise was reached and he was promoted full colonel. However he was allowed to increase the size of his headquarters staff, to include a brigadier major and staff captain, with Brian as the signals officer and Evelyn Waugh as intelligence officer.

Evelyn Waugh had been desperate to join the forces on the outbreak of war. Initially no one would take him. He lobbied hard and eventually Brendan Bracken, Winston Churchill's Parliamentary Secretary and close friend, arranged for him to join the Royal Marines. He took part in the ill-fated Dakar expedition in August 1940. By September he was back in Britain and in touch with his friend from White's, Robert Laycock, who agreed to have him in 8 Commando, eventually taking him on as the intelligence officer for LAYFORCE which is where he met Brian when Brian became the force signals officer. They became great friends although Brian was firmly of the view that while Evelyn was engaging, brave, highly intelligent and very amusing, he should at all costs be kept as far away as possible from soldiers. He was curt, condescending and abusive. Soldiers had no respect for him.

27 As part of a rather useless deception plan, 7, 8 and 11 Commandos were redesignated A, B and C Battalions. 50 and 52 Commandos were amalgamated into D Battalion. This nonsense didn't last long before the 'Commandos' designation was reinstituted.

Evelyn Waugh with unpromising moustache

Laycock tolerated him because he was good for morale. Somewhat the court jester, always scruffy, sometimes sporting a very unpromising moustache, and wearing an absurd solar topee and over-size shorts. In educating Waugh into the role of intelligence officer and brigade liaison officer, Laycock told him to act as his shadow, always available without being summoned, and otherwise never to disturb him.

David Stirling floated the idea for his brainchild, the SAS, with Bob Laycock, who encouraged him to lobby GHQ in Cairo. He was eventually successful and the SAS was formed at Kabrit in July 1941.

As soon as he arrived, Brian was thrown into the planning of Operation CORDITE, the invasion of Rhodes, which was scheduled for the first week of April. On the 6th of April CORDITE was postponed, then cancelled. On the 31st of March General Erwin Rommel, Commander of the Afrika Korps, had launched an offensive which shattered the British defences and caused a rapid retreat, during which three British generals were captured.

The situation was dire. Both Cairo and the Suez Canal were threatened. Urgent defensive action to stabilise the situation was put in place, including an attempt to employ LAYFORCE as ordinary infantry. Laycock knew that morale would suffer after the cancellation of CORDITE and the potential misuse of his Commandos. He lobbied hard that offensive action by LAYFORCE would make a much more significant contribution to the defence plan than holding ground as conventional infantry. His perseverance was rewarded. He was

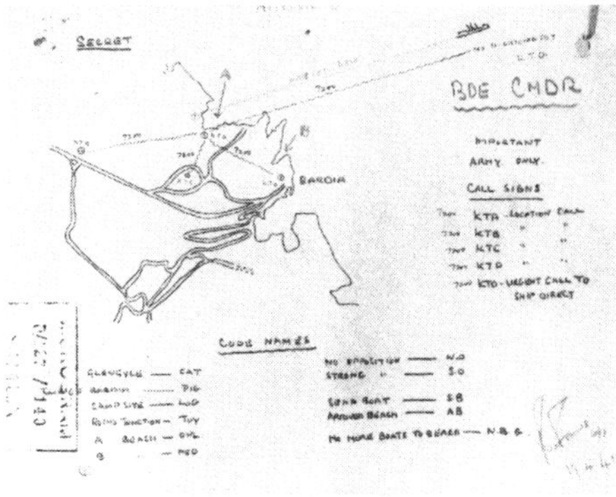

LAYFORCE Signals plan for Bardia raid
signed by Brian

called to a conference chaired by the Commander-in-Chief Admiral Sir Andrew Cunningham on board his flagship HMS *Warspite*. The purpose of the conference was to discuss the immediate use of LAYFORCE in two coastal raids that were to take place the next day on Bomba and Bardia.

The raid on Bomba was to interdict the road west of Tobruk between Derna and Gazala, and destroy logistics convoys. Bardia was a much bigger operation, to attack the port, do as much damage as possible, capture prisoners and put Rommel on notice that his rear areas were not safe.

Brian's job as the force signals officer was to produce the signals plan for the operation for both ground units and ship-to-shore communications. The lot of a signals officer is not a happy one. Communications on operations are critical. If they work well the signals officer is a hero. If they fail, he is the villain of the piece. Happily in this case the communications worked well, but unfortunately not so the other parts of the plan.

The operation was postponed due to bad weather on the 16th of April, and the Bomba raid was cancelled altogether. Better weather was forecast and a reduced operation involving only A Battalion was planned. They would raid Bardia with the objective of disrupting enemy lines of communication and inflicting as much damage as possible to installations and equipment. The force embarked on a converted merchant ship, the *Glengyle*. The plan was to land

Walter Cowan

simultaneously on four beaches, using *Glengyle*'s assault landing craft (LCAs) with the battalion being split into eight detachments.

Bob took a small tactical headquarters with him, Brian, Evelyn Waugh, Robin Campbell[28] and the 70-year-old Admiral Sir Walter Cowan who had appointed himself 'naval liaison officer to LAYFORCE'.[29] The headquarters had been ordered not to go ashore, an order Laycock chose to ignore, a decision with which Brian wholeheartedly agreed.

The landing was unopposed, the only enemy being some motorcycle combinations which immediately fled to raise the alarm. No. 1 detachment deployed to secure and protect the beachhead. No. 2 detachment set up a roadblock on the coast road, but no vehicles came through. No. 3 detachment reached the camp it was intended to attack, only to find it empty. They set fire to the camp and a stores dump. No. 4 detachment found Bardia unoccupied but had to return

28 Later to be awarded the DSO for extreme gallantry on Operation FLIPPER, a raid to kill or capture Rommel. The raid was led by Geoffrey Keyes, who was killed. Campbell was badly wounded and ordered his men to leave him. Keyes was posthumously awarded the VC. There was a strong view that Campbell should also have been awarded a VC.

29 Admiral Sir Walter Cowan, Bart., KCB, DSO, had commanded a river gunboat on the Nile during the Sudan campaign in the 1890s. He joined Kitchener's staff in South Africa. In 1902 he had taken over a destroyer flotilla. In 1941 he was 74. He had been attached at his own request to the Indian Cavalry (Mechanised) Regiment with the 8th Army. He had been captured and taken to Italy. He was repatriated as being 'of no further use' to the British war effort. Infuriated by this slight, he got himself posted to the Commandos as a naval liaison officer. He was to go on to win a bar to his DSO in Italy in 1943. The first DSO had been awarded in 1892.

to the pick-up point due to the tight schedule, before it could complete a detailed search. No. 5 detachment, having landed at the wrong beach, was unable to reach Bardia from the other direction. No. 6 Detachment split into two parties; one party went to the water pumping station, had difficulty finding it, and again due to the strict timetable was forced to return to the beach before it was able to blow it up. The second party tasked with road and bridge demolition was also unable to do much damage. No. 7 detachment found no trace of the mobile artillery that it was tasked to destroy but did locate four old Italian naval guns used for coastal defence, which they blew up.

Bob and his headquarters landed with the first detachment and started to make for some high ground overlooking Bardia, from where they could watch the action and direct operations. En route they were unpleasantly surprised to come across a wadi full of stagnant water and contaminated by the putrefying remains of dead Italians. Returning later across the wadi Brian and Robin Campbell leant over the edge to pull up one of the other members of the headquarters group, who was having difficulty clambering up over the rim of the wadi. Thinking it was Waugh, they decided to bounce him along the side of the wadi on his fat belly for a few yards before heaving him over the top. To their dismay, they discovered that they had roughly manhandled Walter Cowan, who was extremely cross!

All the LCAs except two returned safely to the *Glengyle*. One had broached-to in the surf and could not be refloated, so was destroyed. Another lost its way but managed to sail along the coast to Tobruk; its problem appeared to be a faulty compass. During his return trip, Bob realised that the coxswain of his own LCA, attempting to hold the prescribed bearing, was steering west towards Tobruk rather than north and out to sea. It emerged that the compasses in all the landing craft had been affected by the surrounding metal casing and were giving wholly inaccurate bearings. The recovery therefore took much longer than planned, but the *Glengyle* and her escorts eventually weighed anchor before dawn and reached Alexandria that night.

In spite of the lack of tactical success, many lessons were learnt for future amphibious operations. The raid did have one operational benefit. A German brigade was diverted from the frontline to secure the Africa Korp lines of communication. Casualties were very light but understandably, morale following the raid could have been better. It wasn't helped by a continuing stream of changed or cancelled plans and orders. Bob Laycock wrote a strongly worded letter to the theatre headquarters:

> *Since our arrival here, however, we have pursued the same heart-breaking course of working the men up to concert pitch for projects which have eventually been cancelled.*
>
> *For the last nine months the troops have borne well with the conditions which they cannot be blamed for considering to be examples of 'Order counter order disorder' but, as I have already stated, I judge that they are now definitely beginning to feel that we have recruited then under false pretences and that they belong to a formation which is unlikely to contribute to our war effort.*
>
> *We have prepared for so many expeditions; and yet again last Saturday we got as far as loading our stores on to a train only to be told at the eleventh hour to offload for reasons not stated.*
>
> *I admit that one of the battalions recently carried out an unopposed raid behind the enemy's lines and that it was not very skilfully executed. We did however learn many valuable lessons and I am convinced that there is tremendous scope for our activities against the enemy's L of C where, if we are lucky, we might create considerable havoc. I am sure that all ranks share this view and I most certainly entreat that employment may be found for us soon, if only in the form of small but frequent raids carried out by say from 50 to 100 men.*
>
> *Continuous unemployment must lead to deterioration in the type of man we enlisted and I cannot but believe that even the best troops in the world would suffer from being brought continually to concert pitch to no end.*

When A Battalion finally escaped the *Glengyle* at the beginning of May, the following inscription was found written on a partition on one of the mess decks: '*Never in the whole history of human endeavour have so few been buggered about by so many.*' Laycock had to agree: '*Frivolous as this may seem, I cannot but sympathise with the sentiments expressed*'... particularly as things were about to get even worse for LAYFORCE.

*

On return from the Bardia raid, Brian developed a raging fever and reported sick. He, like everyone else in North Africa, had been suffering from 'desert sores'. 'Desert sores' sound like something malingerers develop to avoid duty, but in fact they can be very serious and unpleasant. They are a general form of skin ulcer that easily developed in the desert environment. The poor hygiene of field conditions, harsh climate, with sand penetrating everywhere and flies carrying bacteria all contributed to the development of these sores, which were extremely painful. Limited access to clean water and medical treatment only exacerbated the condition. Constant treatment with antiseptic sulphanilamide and clean dressings were essential. Some sores could lead to the development of cutaneous diphtheria, a virulent bacterial infection which can be very contagious.

When Brian reported sick, he was told that, much to his disappointment, he would be hospitalised for at least a week in order for the sores to clear up and to monitor him for diphtheria. His sores may well have become seriously infected during the Bardia raid crossing and recrossing the wadi full of dead Italians. He would not be going to Crete.

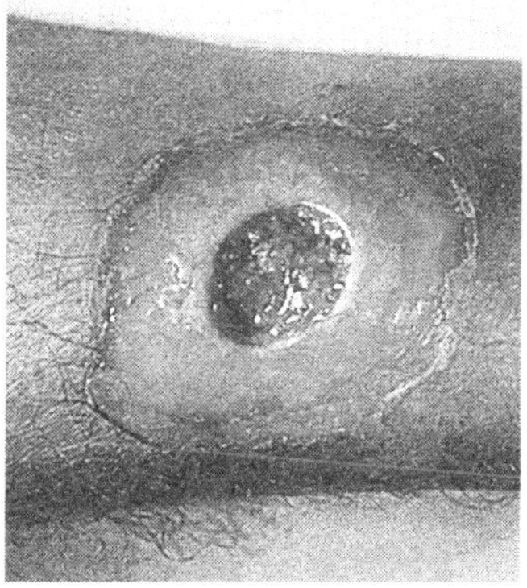

Desert sore

On the evening of the 20th of May 1941, the Germans began the invasion of Crete. After six days of preliminary bombing, General Students XII Airborne Corps began an airborne assault on key targets, aimed at capturing the strategically important island, which was part of the chain of islands keeping open British lines of communication to support the war in North Africa, Gibraltar, Malta and Crete.

Despite the vulnerability and inherent risk of an air assault, the Germans got lucky early on by capturing the airfield at Maleme. Whoever held Maleme held the key to the battle and therefore control of the island. The Germans were able to reinforce quickly and by the 26th of May General Freyberg,[30] the commander of the defence forces, signalled to the Commander-in-Chief North Africa General Archibald Wavell that the loss of the island was only a matter of time.

On the 23rd of May Bob received orders to embark A and D Battalions of LAYFORCE on four destroyers as a matter of urgency, and head for Crete, as they were the only available reinforcements.

LAYFORCE arrived into what was a chaotic and disintegrating situation. Bob and the ever-faithful Waugh commandeered a truck and made their way to Freyberg's headquarters, where they were told the battle was lost and that all that remained was to conduct a fighting withdrawal in order to extricate as many troops as possible by naval evacuation. LAYFORCE's role would be to cover the withdrawal. Bob suggested that his men might be more use if landed behind the enemy to break up the momentum of their advance, as they were trained and equipped as Commandos rather than regular infantry. He was told in no uncertain terms to do what he was told.

Bob deployed his forces and conducted the most difficult of tactical operations, a fighting withdrawal. LAYFORCE fought well, with many acts of extreme gallantry. A and B Battalions fought hard although the Commanding Officer of A Battalion, Lieutenant Colonel

30 Lieutenant-General Bernard Cyril Freyberg, 1st Baron Freyberg VC, GCMG, KCB, KBE, DSO and three bars, KStj (1889–1963), was born in Richmond, Surrey but raised in New Zealand. He served with distinction in the First World War both in the Gallipoli Campaign and on the Western Front, where he was awarded the Victoria Cross. He was one of the most highly decorated soldiers of WW1. In WWII he commanded the 2nd New Zealand Division in Greece, Crete, North Africa and Italy. After the war he served as Governor-General of New Zealand from 1946–52.

Colvin, did not cover himself in glory. Evelyn Waugh was decidedly unimpressed to find him reluctant to emerge from his hiding place under a table until German bombers had left the area. Waugh conducted himself very bravely throughout and rather surprisingly did not receive a Military Cross. He later used his experience with LAYFORCE as a significant part of his masterpiece, the *Sword of Honour* trilogy. The Commanding Officer of A Battalion is thought to be the model for Major Hound.

Eventually Bob and his small staff withdrew. Some of LAYFORCE were captured and there has been some controversy as to whether Bob should have remained and been captured with them. This extract from the LAYFORCE War Diary sums up the situation:

> *On finding that entire staff of CREFORCE had withdrawn, Col. LAYCOCK, accompanied by B.M. & I.O. proceeded to SPHAKION to obtain authority for withdrawal. On finding that entire staff of CREFORCE had embarked, in view of fact that all fighting forces were now in position for embarkation and that there was no enemy contact, Col. LAYCOCK, on own authority, issued orders to Lt. Col. YOUNG to lead troops to SPHAKION by route avoiding the crowded main approach to town and to use his own personality to obtain priority laid down in Div. orders. LAYFORCE reached SPHAKION outskirts in good time for boats but were unable to penetrate rabble; flanks dets. were able to reach beach but main body remained ashore. Col. LAYCOCK, accompanied BY B.M. and I.O. embarked HMS KIMBERLY. Total numbers of LAYFORCE evacuated 23 Officers, 186 O.Rs.*

On balance, he did the right thing. He carried out his orders, enabling much of the force to escape, and for such an effective commander to surrender and spend the rest of the war as a prisoner would have been a great loss.

Like all soldiers, Brian was disappointed to be left behind when all his comrades were on operations, but he accepted his lot. Getting fit again was the priority, and other operations would soon come his way.

Bob reported to GHQ in Cairo, and to add insult to injury was told that there was no possibility of reconstituting LAYFORCE, indeed it was to be disbanded.

When Brian was released from hospital he briefly rejoined LAYFORCE headquarters, just in time for its disbandment, leaving them on the 27th of June 1941. LAYFORCE was disbanded on the 1st of July. By now Brian had built a solid reputation as a really capable signals expert, combined with bravery, and a taste for daring operations. With this in mind he started to look round for something that would suit both his style and temperament. He most certainly did not want a conventional signals or staff job.

*

The GHQ Liaison Regiment, or 'Phantom' as it became known, was designed as a Special Reconnaissance Regiment but that description does not accurately define its role, which was to '*transmit vital information from the battle front, ignoring the usual channels, to the Commander*' to enable him to make quick decisions in a fast-moving battle – '*the eyes and ears of the Commander-in-Chief*', allowing him to build up an accurate battle picture as to what his own units and flanking formations were doing, in addition to what the enemy were up to. Its speed and accuracy of delivery enabled the operations and intelligence staff at headquarters to read the battle and provide solid assessments and advice to the commander. Phantom would prove to be a success and this was in part due to the organisation being totally self-contained. Every link was Phantom-owned and -operated. Phantom, like all successful World War II innovations, or 'private armies' as they were jealously and disparagingly referred to by the more slow-witted staff, was conceived by a very eccentric TA colonel, George 'Hoppy' Hopkinson MC.[31]

'Hoppy' was highly intelligent, eccentric and wild, small, stocky, with a crew cut, twinkling eyes and a beguiling grin. After distinguished service in the First World War, he went up to Cambridge to

31 Later Major General Commanding 1st Airborne Division. Killed in action in Italy in September 1943 supervising an assault by 10th Battalion the Parachute Regiment.

'Hoppy'

read engineering. There, he thoroughly enjoyed himself playing hard as well as working hard. He rode in point-to-points, raced motor-cycles, sailed, preferably in rough weather, and flew *'long distances in insecure aircraft'*. But his first love was soldiering.

He had developed his ideas for what would become Phantom during the BEF operation in Belgium and France in 1940 when working with an RAF ground/air liaison unit commanded by Wing Commander J. M. Fairweather DFC. The Phantom concept was so successful that a permanent unit was formed after Dunkirk, and 'Hoppy' was given command. As a commanding officer he was completely unorthodox, a showman, single-minded, tough on everyone but with a twinkle in his eye, always insisting on the highest professional standards from officers and men alike. He was much loved, and collected around him an eclectic mix of men. Officers were recruited for their character, style, dash and initiative. They included David Niven, Jakie[32] and Michael[33] Astor, Viscount Maurice Macmillan,[34] Carol Mather,[35]

32 Major Sir John Jacob 'Jakie' Astor VII, MBE, ERD (1918–2000). British Army officer, Conservative MP, and agriculturalist. The youngest son of Nancy Astor, prominent racehorse breeder and steward of the Jockey Club.

33 The Hon. Michael Langhorne Astor (1916–1980). Educated at Eton, became an MP in 1945.

34 Maurice Harold Macmillan, Viscount Macmillan of Ovenden (1921–1984). Educated at Eton and Balliol College, Oxford. Son of former Prime Minister Harold Macmillan. Active service in north-west Europe after the Normandy landings. Conservative politician and MP 1945–74.

35 Carol Mather (1917–2001). Educated at Harrow and Trinity College, Cambridge. Officer in British Special Forces during WWII, including operational service with the Commando and with the SAS in north-west Europe. Became an MP after the war.

Eric Barkworth at Kabrit 1941

Peregrine Worsthorne,[36] Sir Robert Mark,[37] John Hislop[38] and young cavalry officers '*whose persistence combined with personal pleasantness, made up for their deficiencies in rank*'. John Hislop described Hoppy as '*having much about him of the soldier of fortune, with no ties or permanent home, at his best in war*'.

David Niven described his Phantom Squadron as including journalists, a Frenchman, a weightlifter, the assistant bursar at Eton, a concert pianist, an amateur steeplechase jockey, a gay interior designer, garage mechanics, bookmakers, stockbrokers and burglars, or as someone else described them '*bounders and bankers*', all of them under the eye of a steely sergeant major from the Scots Guards.

Phantom filled a capability gap which, at the time, the Corps of Royal Signals could not provide. By the time LAYFORCE was disbanded, Phantom was deployed around Britain training hard for their role in future operations. A detachment had been sent to Greece and after the withdrawal from there ended up in North Africa, where it was brought up to squadron strength by a draft from England. By May 1941 it was designated H Squadron and looking for a new commander. Phantom was viewed in Cairo as a cross between a commando

36 Sir Peregrine Worsthorne (1923–2020). Phantom during the Italian campaign. After the war a prominent journalist and editor.

37 Sir Robert Mark (1917–2010). After the war he joined the police, Commissioner of the Metropolitan Police (1972–77).

38 John Hislop commanded the Phantom detachment on Operation LOYTON. See Chapter 9.

and signals unit, so Brian, as the first squadron commander, fitted the bill perfectly. Sadly he was to command it for only two months from June to August 1941 when he was again hospitalised, this time for more serious investigation of the recurrent desert sore complications. Brian handed over to Dermot Daly, a Scots Guards officer with whom he had served in LAYFORCE. After a month in hospital in Cairo, Brian's condition was considered serious enough for him to be evacuated by sea to Britain. He was successfully treated on board ship and arrived in Glasgow in November 1942.

CHAPTER 4 – SERVICE OF A HAZARDOUS NATURE

'The good soldier brews tea on the battlefield, finds extra food in the desert and laughs all the time.'

Roy Farran

Special Service Brigade insignia

Brigadier Dudley Clarke,[39] who was instrumental in the founding of the Commandos and Special Air Service, described the type of person ideally suited to these special units as having the independence of spirit and resourcefulness of an Elizabethan pirate, the ruthlessness and cunning of a gangster, and the resilience, adaptability and survival instincts of a frontier tribesman. Men who were not afraid to take risks, who were utterly fearless and self-reliant, who '*treated darkness as an old friend*', and who would be willing to press on to their objective regardless. Brian was perfect commando material.

Brian had been nominated to command E Squadron of Phantom, which was training in Scotland for the invasion of North Africa, Operation TORCH. He took over the Squadron on the 22nd of December 1942. Before taking command, he attended a week-long course at STC-1 (Special Training Centre) at Inverailort Castle. Set up in late autumn 1940 by Bill Stirling and Brian Mayfield of the Scots Guards, it specialised in teaching the techniques of irregular warfare: sabotage, demolitions, silent killing, instinctive shooting, camouflage and concealment, navigation, fitness and the more esoteric tradecraft for working behind enemy lines.[40]

39 Brigadier Dudley Clarke CB, CBE, pioneer of military deception. Saw active service in the First World War, the Iraqi Revolt (1920), Palestine, and the Second World War, Egypt, Lisbon and London.

40 ST-1 had a very eclectic group of instructors including William Fairburn and Eric Sykes (silent killing), Gavin Maxwell (shooting) and Johnny Ravensky (lock picking and safe cracking) who was suspected 'of not having fully retired'. Discipline was maintained by John Royle, a former officer dismissed for punching two senior officers and was now an RSM in the Scots Guards.

Inverailort

Brian commanded E Squadron until February 1943, by which time Robert Laycock had re-established the Special Service Brigade at Castle Douglas, also in Scotland. Laycock conspired to get Brian, whom he '*highly regarded and much liked*', posted to his brigade. On the 26th of March he wrote to his wife Angie from the King's Arms Hotel, Castle Douglas, '*I am very pleased about getting Brian Franks back, and wonder whether you will like him as much as I do.*' On the 11th of June 1942 Brian took over the post of Staff Captain 'A'[41] in the Special Service Brigade HQ.

Arriving in Ardrossan, Brian set about his duties with his customary professionalism. He was pleased to find Evelyn Waugh already back in the fold. Bob Laycock, who still found Evelyn amusing, had pulled strings to get him out of the Royal Marines, have him transferred to the Blues, and back on board as a supernumerary intelligence officer whose primary role was liaison with Combined Operations Headquarters in London. Bill Barkworth had also returned from the Middle East and was sharpening his skills on the intelligence staff.

Brian subscribed to Bob Laycock's view that if you have to go to war you should do so among friends, and as his duties included postings and promotions, he was easily able to arrange for Basil Bennett and Hilary Bray to join the brigade headquarters, with Basil as Camp

41 Staff Captain 'A': the officer of captain rank who on the brigade staff is responsible for 'A' matters – personnel, discipline and administration, including postings and promotions.

Basil Benett

Philip Dunne

Commandant and Hilary as a 'liaison officer'. Basil Bennett was very popular with everyone, particularly as he managed to use his hotel contacts to make significant improvements to the food in the mess and with the wine cellar. He was regarded as something of a father figure in the officers' mess, which was established in the Kilmany Hotel. Other familiar old faces and friends had gravitated to Bob's headquarters including Philip Dunne[42] and Bill Stirling. Philip Dunne was described by Evelyn Waugh as *'the sort of man Hitler hadn't reckoned with'*.

The disastrous Dieppe Raid, Operation JUBILEE,[43] had taken place on the 19th of August, the only really successful part of which was the action of Shimi Lovat's 4 Commando and John Durnford-Slater's 3 Commando. Bob and his team were frustrated that they were kept out of the operation by Combined Operation Headquarters, fortuitously as it turned out. In spite of his frustration Bob was biding his time for the moment when his headquarters would be deployed on operations as a force headquarters. This would happen soon enough. In the interim, staff work and planning would continue. Brian was impressed how Evelyn Waugh could condense complex and long-winded material into a concise, accurate and readable document.

42 Philip Dunne. One of the original members of 8 'White's' Commando recruited from The Blues, served as Brigade Liaison Officer between Brigade Headquarters and the Commando units. He won the MC at Salerno.
43 6,086 men were landed of whom 3,623 were killed or wounded or captured.

The Commando units which made up the Special Service Brigade were dispersed all over Britain. This necessitated much travelling and wasted time. As is normal in wartime, there were many rumours about future operations including a move back to North Africa, pending involvement in the invasion of Sicily and Italy. Eventually the Commando units were moved to the south of England, the Marine Commandos to the Isle of Wight, 3 Commando to Weymouth and 4 Commando to Winchester. In October 1942 Bob followed and moved his headquarters south to 'Station 62',[44] Sherborne in Dorset. Evelyn Waugh and Basil Bennett were sent ahead as an advance party to arrange administrative matters. Offices were set up in Sherborne Castle. The Plume of Feathers pub was taken over, as well as other accommodation in and around Sherborne. Evelyn and Basil Bennett found lodgings with Mrs Lucy Maxwell at Westbridge House at the western edge of the town overlooking the school playing fields. This was not a happy arrangement. Evelyn and Basil regularly crossed swords with Lucy Maxwell over everything from the quality of the food to the use of the telephone. Eventually peace broke out but more in the form of an armed truce. Brian wisely kept out of it.

At the end of September 1942 Alan Smallman, the brigade major, left to go to the Army Staff College. Brian was promoted major and took over from him. This was a serious step up. The post of brigade major is very prestigious within the British Army. The brigade major is the brigadier's right-hand man. He directs and oversees all staff branches within the headquarters ensuring that their work is entirely focused on the intentions of the brigade commander, and the brigade major speaks with his authority. Although a rank below that of the unit commanders, who are lieutenant colonels, it is a foolish Commanding Officer who does not listen to, or get on with the brigade major. Equally a good brigade major will walk the line between his brigade commander and the Commanding Officers with skill, competence and diplomacy. Brian had all the necessary qualities, which earned him the respect of everyone in the headquarters, and the Commanding Officers of the Commandos.

44 All military locations in Britain were given a codename and number, in an attempt to maintain security.

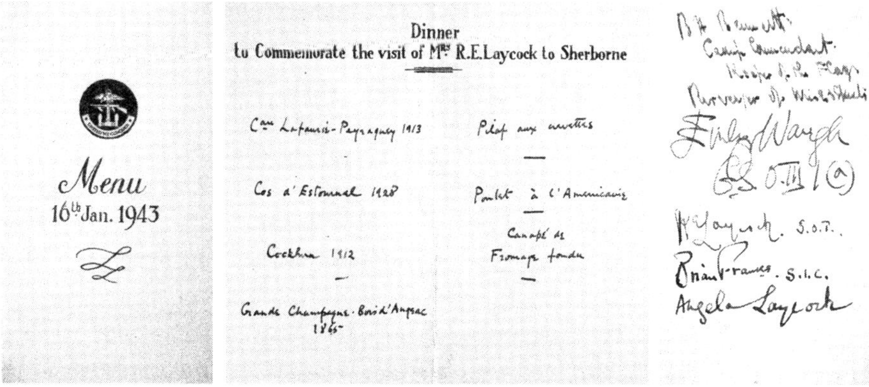

The autumn of 1942 and the beginning of 1943 were exceptionally busy for the brigade and for the brigade major in particular. Much time was spent travelling between units, planning and conducting training and test exercises, liaising with Combined Operations Headquarters, where Brian had inserted Hilary Bray as his eyes and ears, and in highly secret planning for future operations. During visits to London he would use the Hyde Park Hotel as an unofficial 'office', snatch some time with Zoe and then race back to Sherborne. Occasionally Zoe and Angie Laycock would come down to Sherborne for a few nights when the schedule was not too manic. One of these visits took place on the 16th of January 1943, marked by a dinner at which Basil Bennett excelled himself as the self-appointed '*purveyor of wines and spirits*' to the brigade, by producing a 1913 Château Lafaurier-Peyraguey, 1928 Cos d'Estournel and a 1912 Cockburn Port.

*

Meanwhile back at the Hyde Park Hotel, the privations of war were beginning to bite. Brian had kept in touch as best he could but had spent almost all of the first three years of the war overseas. Gradually many of the male staff were conscripted. Basil Bennett volunteered to join his old regiment the Rifle Brigade, in which he had served in the First World War, and from where Brian was soon to get him posted to the Commandos. Basil had handed over the running of the hotel to his brother. The hotel slowly emptied of guests and the restaurant, like the banqueting rooms and ballrooms, closed, leaving only the grill room open. The once glamorous hotel fell silent, reduced to a shadow of its former glory.

The Blitz had begun in earnest on Saturday the 7th of September 1940 on a beautiful early autumn afternoon without a cloud in the sky. It was to last for the next eight months until the 11th of May 1941. Zoe Franks had remained in London, living in their flat in Drayton Gardens while Brian was in North Africa. She had volunteered for the London Fire Brigade, and became the driver for the Chief Fire Officer Frederick Delve.[45] She drove him nightly throughout the Blitz to the scenes of the worst bombings.

The Hyde Park seemed to have a charmed life, but it was not without its share of drama. After a particularly heavy raid, Mary Shiffer[46] emerged from a local air-raid shelter and walked back to the hotel. There was a large hole in the middle of Knightsbridge just in front of the hotel, by the grill room entrance. Lying on a pile of debris was a metal ring. Mary picked it up, deciding to keep it as a war souvenir. The fire brigade and bomb disposal teams felt there was a bomb somewhere in the area, but couldn't find it. The incident was closed for the night, the area cordoned off, and the hotel staff sent home. Back in Wandsworth, Mary showed the ring to a friend, who was an ARP[47] warden. He didn't know what it was, but the next morning he was going along to a Royal Engineers lecture about telltale objects an ARP warden should look out for when identifying where unexploded bombs might be, so asked her why didn't she come as well? As Mary had the next morning off, she agreed. They went to the lecture and, during questions, her friend held the ring up for the lecturer to see.

45 Sir Frederick Delve. Joined the Navy at 16 and saw active service during the Russian Civil War. In 1922 he left the Navy and joined the Brighton Fire Brigade. In 1934 he moved to the London Fire Brigade and in 1936 was involved in the Crystal Palace fire. He was part of a group of far-sighted fire officers who were pressing the government to train and equip the service for war and to create a National Fire Service. He was appointed to command No. 5 Region London from 1940 and remained in post until 1962. He was appointed CBE in 1942 and knighted in 1962.

46 Mary Shiffer, long-time employee of the Hyde Park Hotel between 1916 and 1977.

47 ARP: Air Raid Precautions warden.

'Where did you find that?'
'A friend picked it up – in the street.'
'Recently?'
'A day or so ago to be precise. Why – is it important?'
'It's a Kops ring. It's part of a high-explosive bomb – and if you find a Kops ring lying about, then you can guarantee there's a 2,000lb bomb close by.'

Mary was already moving fast to find a telephone. She rang the hotel and told the duty manager Louis Burdet,[48] who evacuated the hotel. The Royal Engineers dug around the hole for the next week. Eventually, deep under the hotel, they found an unexploded 2,000lb bomb. It was brought up, defused and given to the hotel, who put it on display in the foyer and used it as a collecting box for the dependants of bomb disposal and rescue workers killed in the Blitz.[49]

The second dangerous event of the Blitz was the arrival of Rosa Lewis from the Cavendish, who still maintained her love/hate relationship with the Hyde Park, grudgingly using its deep air-raid shelter when things got too hot in Jermyn Street. The Hyde Park with its elitist atmosphere and regal dignity was a far cry from the champagne- and cigar-sodden atmosphere of the promiscuous Cavendish where Rosa played decadent hostess at what Mary Shiffer described as her *'tarts' paradise'*. On a particular heavy night of bombing in October 1940, a large stick of bombs fell on Jermyn Street. King Street and the St James's church, which sits between Jermyn Street and Piccadilly, were badly hit.

The Cavendish was also hit. Rosa was unhurt and with difficulty she was persuaded to leave and go to the Hyde Park. Rosa's greatest concern was to take with her a hamper of champagne that was loaded on to the taxi. As they were driving off, she stuck her head out of the window and shouted to her faithful manager Charles, *'Jerry's been very naughty tonight. Very naughty indeed. I want all that mess*

48 Louis Burdet, a Frenchman, left soon after this incident to join the Free French. He was trained as an agent and parachuted into France to work with the Resistance.
49 In 1948 Brian and the Bennetts gave a grand party for the local air-raid wardens and bomb disposal teams who had saved the hotel.

St James's church

Burlington Arcade

cleaned up and everything put back straight by Monday.' She stayed away for two days and no sooner was she back, than the Cavendish was hit again. The nearby Savoy Turkish Baths at 92 Jermyn Street were destroyed by a bomb at the same time. This wonderful exotic establishment had become essential to Rosa's male clientele, who depended on it as a recovery centre for the excesses of the hotel.

On the same night Olaf Hambro,[50] who like many was beginning to become blasé about the nightly bombardment, was eating oysters alone at the bar of Wiltons[51] in King Street when a bomb landed on St James's church, Piccadilly, shaking not only the restaurant and its fittings, but also the owner, Bessie Leal. She had had enough. Unpinning her apron, she said to Hambro that she could no longer take the war and was going to close Wiltons and go home to Cornwall. On the spot he offered her £1,200 for the business, which she accepted. '*Put it on the bill ...*' said Hambro. Waking up the next morning Hambro couldn't believe what he'd done. He rang his friend Bruce Offley, who agreed to cover 30 per cent of the purchase price, and Wiltons reopened the following week.

50 Olaf Hambro (1865–1961) Chairman of Hambros bank 1932–61. Educated at Eton and served with the Coldstream Guards in World War I. His nephew Charles was head of SOE for part of the war.

51 Wiltons was and still is one of the best restaurants in London and still very much part of the White's/Wilton axis. In 1964 it moved to Bury Street, and then to its present site in Jermyn Street, number 55, which had been the site of the old 'Knights 55', a brothel, rather appropriately about 100 yards from the Cavendish Hotel.

Olaf Hambro - the morning after

Rosa Lewis was a nightmare at the Hyde Park. She was uncontrollable in the grill room. When she spotted a regular from the Cavendish, she would accost them with a volley of ribald abuse: '*Hallo mutton chops,*' to one ageing Marquis, '*Still fancy a nice clean whore?*' Or to a Duke, '*How's the old water works? Still as unreliable as ever?*' She nearly finished off a senior Guards officer by asking if he still got the '*lover's droop*'. The staid Hyde Park found it all too much. The manager tried, ineffectually, to remove her from the public rooms, but unlike the 2,000lb bomb, she refused to budge.

*

Not long after Brian had taken over as brigade major, Sherborne School[52] asked if the headquarters could help with the training of the CCF. Brian agreed that they would write a training exercise for the CCF Field Day on the 24th of October 1942. Brian, Evelyn, Basil Bennett, Tom Churchill and Johnny Atkinson would act as umpires.

All military exercise instructions start with a 'scene setter' – the general narrative, which was as follows:

52 Sherborne School, one of the oldest schools in England, founded in 705, has a long list of distinguished old Shirburnians including military officers, diplomats, politicians and writers. Two heads of SIS, Alan Turing and Evelyn Waugh's older brother Alec, Henry Druce, the hero of Operation LOYTON (see Chapter 9) were also Shirburnians.

> *The German army, having effected a successful landing on the Dorset Coast, has moved northwards, and is in contact with British troops in the neighbourhoods of CASTLE CARY and WINCANTON. There are still isolated bodies of British troops in the field south of this line, and one such force of about two companies of infantry with attached troops is in the general area of SHERBORNE PARK. A German force of two companies of infantry has been given the task of mopping up this area and on the morning of October 24th this force is situated in the wooded country near CRACKMORE LODGE. During the morning movement has been observed by the Germans in the OLD DEER PARK and patrols have been sent out to investigate. When the exercise opens at 1500hrs, these patrols have returned, having been intercepted, they have had some casualties and have lost some prisoners; they have brought two prisoners back with them. From the information received from the patrols and from the interrogation of prisoners, the force commander believes that the British force consists of about two companies of infantry with some artillery, variously estimated as 1 battery and 1 troop; it is also thought that the British have an ammunition and supply dump in the neighbourhood of what appears to be a keeper's cottage in the Park. The force commander decides to attack, with a view to destroying both the dump and the British force. At 1700hrs the attack is launched.*

The timetable for the day instructed that two companies of boys from School House, the Green and Lyon House under the command of Captain Sam Hey were to assemble wearing battle dress at Crackmore Lodge at 1500hrs. Between 1515hrs and 1630hrs the patrols were to reconnoitre the river crossing, with the attack commencing from 1700hrs. The night attack was to begin at the instigation of the force commander, with ceasefire at 2130hrs.

An amusing account written by 'Commando'[53] subsequently appeared in the school magazine, *The Shirburnian*:

> *Dear Sirs, On field day I was deeply impressed with the whole-hearted vigour and, I might say, realism, with which the exercise*

53 There is much speculation that the author was Evelyn Waugh.

was carried out. The first attack was doomed to be a failure (per plan). The force commander was heard to say that in practice, of course, he would not have attacked until night. The smoke from a smoke-bomb was scattered by the wind, but the umpire was informed that it must be imagined as a dense cloud. The final touch was when a whole company crossed the river by a bridge, the umpire being forced to believe that they had waded over at many points, because 'their housemaster said that they must not get wet', as the Second-in-Command put it. I only hope that, if I ever meet any Germans, they know the rules, too.

John 'Doughey' Randolph,[54] a housemaster at Sherborne and Commanding Officer of the CCF, had invited the umpires to his house, Abbeylands, for beer and sandwiches. Brian could not attend but Waugh and Bennett accepted. Unfortunately they drank a bottle of 1920 Dows Port before dinner and another afterwards. At some point they remembered their invitation and turned up very late, somewhat drunk and embarrassed to find 'Doughey' sitting behind a mountain of sandwiches. He was not amused; neither was Brian, who gave them an almighty dressing down the next day.

Another much more significant event would also take place on the 24th of October 1942: authority was given for all members of the Special Service Brigade to wear green berets.

*

Rather like Dieppe, the Special Service Brigade did not take part in Operation TORCH. 1 and 6 Commandos were involved and yet again were not properly utilised, being placed under command of conventional military formations. The key lesson learned – again – and

54 Sam Hey taught the author Latin and 'Doughey' Randolph mathematics, which he had taught Alan Turing. John Hervey Randolph (1898–1975), known by everyone as 'Doughey', was one of Sherborne's 'characters', a force of nature, described as being a 'rather small, and for much of his life, rather stout man, stalked, and sometimes strutted upon, the Sherborne stage for nearly half a century, choleric, and at times infuriating, gay and companionable at others, quick-witted and full of humour, temperamentally nervous and unpredictable, enthusiastic and excitable, imperious and diffident in turn, deeply affectionate but embarrassed to admit it, exceptionally clever and gifted'.

one that Bob and his team rammed home at Combined Operations – was that Commandos must be commanded by a capable and forceful headquarters that understood the role of Commandos with a proper staff to manage the operation, and used only for what it had been specifically trained to do.

The time in Scotland and Sherborne, together with the lessons from JUBILEE (Dieppe) and TORCH (North Africa) enabled Bob to brainstorm the future of the Special Service Brigade, notably with Brian, Bill Stirling and Philip Dunne. Brian was tasked to write a paper which set out ideas for the future entitled '*Role of the Special Service Brigade and the Desirability of Reorganisation*'. The main thrust of the paper was a fundamental restructuring whereby the brigade would be split into three groups of three Commandos, each commanded by a full colonel and a small staff of a brigade major, staff captain and intelligence officer. The groups could act collectively within the brigade or be detached to work independently or with other formations as required. The three proposed commanders were Shimi Lovat, Tom Trevor and John Durnford-Slater. With a few amendments the paper was accepted as a blueprint for future operations.

At the Casablanca Conference in January 1943, it was decided that the next strategic phase of the war would be the invasion of Sicily and subsequently Italy. The codename for Sicily was to be HUSKY and the target date would be July 1943. Bob fought and won the battle for his headquarters to take part as the headquarters for all Commando operations in the invasion. He would have under command 3, 40 and 41 Commando.

On the 12th of April Bob split his headquarters, taking Brian, Tom Churchill and Philip Dunne and associated administrative staff to set up an advanced headquarters back up in Scotland at Troon. The rest of the staff, the rear headquarters, initially stayed at Sherborne, then moved to Cowdray Park near Midhurst. Evelyn Waugh was no longer at either headquarters but was sent back to London as liaison officer at Combined Operations. Hilary Bray took his place at Cowdray Park. Admiral Walter Cowan had also reappeared on the scene and Bob was happy to have him back.

Evelyn had had a growing feeling that he was becoming unpopular and that Bob Laycock and Brian were losing confidence in him. He was right. He had been passed over for promotion on several occasions, and while his staff work was exceptional, it was his disdain and dislike of some of his fellow officers, but principally the NCOs and men that was to fix him. Jakie Astor had brought his squadron of Phantom to Sherborne to work with the brigade and he noticed it. '*He never hesitated to take advantage of the fact that while he was a highly educated man, most of them were barely literate. He bullied them in a way they were unused to. He bewildered them, purposely. I found it embarrassing*.' Bob had wished to take Evelyn with him for HUSKY but many of Evelyn's fellow officers felt with good reason that this was unwise. Their objections were conveyed to Bob by Brian, an ironical circumstance, as it turned out. '*You will regret it, Brigadier,*' he said. '*Evelyn's appointment will only introduce discord and weaken the brigade as a coherent fighting force. None of us can see that you will get anything from it at all. And apart from everything else, Evelyn will probably get shot.*' '*That's a chance we all have to take.*' Brian gave a wry smile: '*Oh I don't mean by the enemy.*' As a result he was left behind, only to come back to haunt Brian barely a year later.

In preparation for HUSKY Brian was tasked with finding beaches in Scotland that resembled as closely as possible the beaches in Sicily, and writing realistic training exercises. A full-scale rehearsal, Exercise STYMIE, was carried out on the 18th of June between Troon and Irvine. The day before the exercise, Brian had received an IMMEDIATE signal telling him that Zoe had given birth to their daughter Valerie. On the 23rd of June Bob and Brian went to London for a final briefing, and Brian was able to snatch a quick visit to see his new daughter.

The headquarters embarked on a recently converted landing ship, the *Derbyshire*. They sailed from the Clyde on the 28th of June. The *Derbyshire* was quite luxurious, with excellent food and drink, and plenty of cabin space. On the 1st of July operation orders for the invasion were issued and on the 3rd of July Bob gave out his own orders.

The *Derbyshire*

Brian would have helped plan the operation, and at the orders group Bob would have set out his concept of operations, and Brian would have delivered the detail. Bob started the 'O' group: '*It is my great pleasure to inform you that at dawn on July 10th you will land on the south-eastern tip of Sicily where you will join battle with the enemy in this first dagger thrust into Fortress Europe.*'

Delivery of orders was complicated by the fact that only Lieutenant Colonel 'Pop' Manners commanding 40 Commando was on board the *Derbyshire*. Lieutenant Colonel Lumsden and 41 Commando were sailing on HMT *Durban Castle*. He would have been transferred aboard with his command team for the orders group. Much more complicated was the fact that 3 Commando after the Dieppe Raid had been stationed at Weymouth under command of John Durnford-Slater, brought up to strength, with a draft of 120 former policemen who had volunteered for the Commandos. In January 1943 they were sent to Gibraltar and in April 1943 to North Africa in preparation for HUSKY. Their role in the operation was to be separate from the operations of 40 and 41 Commando and the brigade headquarters, with them coming under command of General Dempsey's 13 Corps with the specific task of going ashore ahead of the main landing to destroy a gun battery, just behind the town of Cassibile. This battery was sited to fire directly on to the main landing beach for the British 5th Division and would make the landing very uncomfortable. The operation was a complete success and 3 Commando went on to conduct

On board *Derbyshire*. Front row L To R: 'Pop' Manners, Bob Laycock, Brian

other independent operations, returning to the fold only at the end of the Sicilian campaign.

The rest of the brigade in the *Derbyshire* and *Durban Castle* arrived off the island of Gozo on the 9th of July. At 0110hrs the next morning the LCAs carrying 40 Commando and brigade headquarters were lowered into the water and took up a holding position to the right of a naval motor launch marking the centre line for the run into the beach. 41 Commando took up position on the left. So far they were undetected. The naval landing commander gave the order to start the run in. At 0230hrs the navigation launch stopped to check its position; however it was too late to stop the momentum of the assault, and both Commandos pushed on to the beach, landing at 0300hrs. 40 Commando and brigade headquarters landed near Punta Castellazzo 400 yards to the west of their intended landing site. Both Commandos headed inland with brigade headquarters between and slightly behind the advancing troops. Opposition was light but some casualties were sustained from heavy machine-gun fire covering the landing beaches. All the brigade's targets were knocked out or captured by 0600hrs.

Brian quickly established the brigade headquarters in a strongly-built house inland from the beach. In exploring the cellars Philip Dunne found it very well stocked with wine, and insisted they took a photograph posing in front of three hogsheads of Marsala, which they would later present to Evelyn Waugh, who was particularly fond

Commandos ashore in Sicily

of this particular wine, as a rather cruel way of rubbing salt into his wound.

On the 11th of July there was a half-hearted counter-attack which was seen off by 40 Commando supported by some heavy-duty artillery and mortar fire co-ordinated by Brian, with the Canadian Division, which had landed to their east. Later that day the brigade was withdrawn into reserve. The Special Raiding Squadron (SRS) commanded by Paddy Mayne, like 3 Commando normally part of the brigade, but in fact working direct to corps headquarters, had also captured their objective at Cape Murro di Porco and the port of Augusta which was critical for the build-up of logistics.

On the 14th of July Bob and Brian attended a planning conference at General Dempsey's headquarters in Syracuse to discuss future operations. It was here they caught up with 3 Commando and the SRS exploits and heard that John Durnford-Slater had won a bar to his DSO for his action at the Malati Bridge.[55]

The British advance across the island was slowing in the face of tough resistance. Operation CHOPPER was planned to release

55 The Malati Bridge was a very important bridge across which ran the main road to Catania, some seven miles ahead of the advance. 3 Commando was inserted behind enemy lines to seize and hold the bridge, which it did, removing all demolition charges. German paratroops counter-attacked. In the face of rising casualties, Durnford-Slater ordered his men to break up into small groups and exfiltrate to the British lines. The operation to hold the bridge was a failure but the removal of the demolitions enabled the bridge to be captured intact the next day before the Germans had a chance to replace the charges.

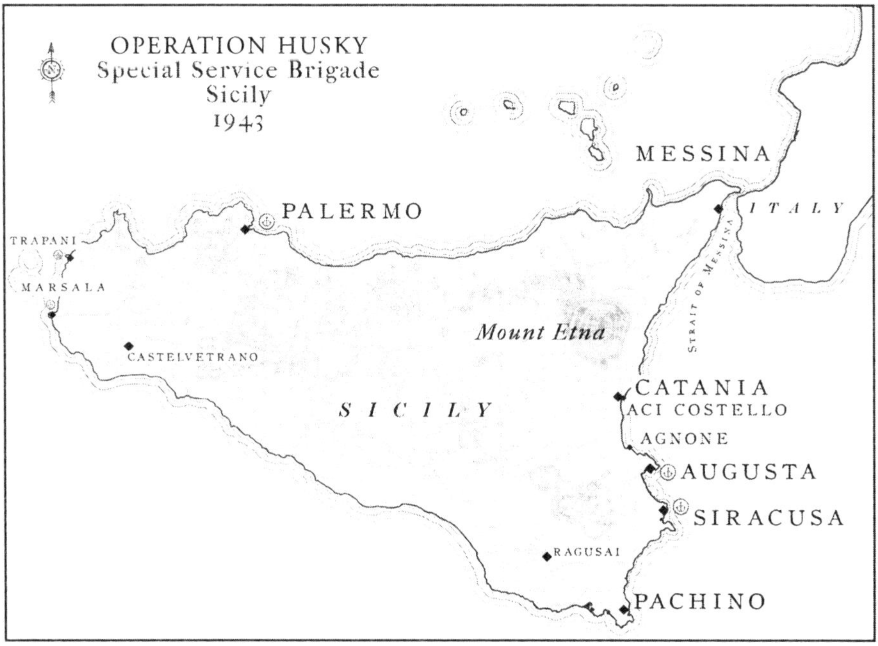

pressure on the advance. 40 and 41 Commando and the SRS under Bob's command would land behind the enemy and seize the port of Catania. The brigade headquarters and all units embarked on their landing craft only to have the operation cancelled due to intelligence reports of large enemy reinforcements in Catania. For the next few days the brigade was stood down and moved to a beach near Brucoli where the troops could relax and swim. Brian and the brigade headquarters, now augmented by Randolph Churchill, spent their time swimming and playing beach cricket.

During this lull in the battle, a deception operation, Operation LUSTY was mounted on three consecutive nights between the 25th and the 30th of July. The operation consisted of a force of destroyers and landing craft carrying out dummy landings to keep the enemy guessing. The operation was accompanied by Brian on the first night, Tom Churchill on the second and Bob Laycock on the third. There was little or no response from the enemy.

On the 1st of August Bob Laycock was summoned to Algiers for a planning conference to discuss the brigade's involvement in the next phase of operations in Italy. John Durnford-Slater was appointed brigade commander in his absence, with Brian remaining brigade major. This change of structure would remain in place until the end of the year with the brigade split into two: Bob would command 2 and 41 Commando on Operation BUTTRESS, and John Durnford-Slater with Brian as brigade major commanding 3 and 40 Commando and Paddy Mayne's SRS for Operation BAYTOWN. Both BUTTRESS and BAYTOWN involved landing in Calabria on the coast of mainland Italy on the opposite shore of the Straits of Messina.

While in Algiers Bob had written a letter to Angie on the 25th of August, '*Please ring Zoe and Peggy* (Dunne) *and say I have nothing but praise for the soldier-like qualities of their respective husbands. They are both superb*.'

The Commando brigade headquarters was established at Aci Costello, a Norman castle just north of Catania. A number of other operations were planned but subsequently cancelled due either to rapid changes in the tactical situation, weather, or availability of ships.

Brian attended various BAYTOWN planning conferences at corps headquarters, but before BAYTOWN was launched, there would be one final amphibious landing further up the coast of Sicily – Operation BLACKCOCK, to insert a mixed force of 3 Commando and supporting tanks and artillery at Capo Ali. The force would then move inland and block the enemy's escape route across the Straits of Messina. The operation would be commanded by the Commander 4 Armoured Brigade, Brigadier Currie DSO, MC. Brian attended a final planning conference for BLACKCOCK then embarked with a very small headquarters and sailed on the 15th of August. It could easily have been a fiasco. The force landed three miles north of their correct landing beaches. However, some fast planning on the ground included Brian himself organising an 'ad hoc' resupply[56] and Tom Churchill, commanding 3 Commando, developing an aggressive advance to link up with the Americans in Messina. 2 Commando and Brian's

56 The landing force had taken no 'Q' (logistics) staff with them.

organisation of resupply from the beach to 2 Commando turned what could have been a disaster into a blinding success. *The Times* war correspondent who accompanied the operation wrote an article titled '*BRITISH MARCH TO MESSINA – Commandos' bold venture*'.[57]

> *MESSINA, Aug. 17th*
> *A handful of British tanks, commandos, sappers, and gunners astonished everyone else and mildly astonished themselves by entering Messina from the south at 10 this morning. They found that they were not the first allied forces there, for American troops greeted them in the streets, but they had had the satisfaction of pulling off successfully an enterprise in the true buccaneering tradition of the commandos and that famous tank formation, the 4th Armoured Brigade, which, as part of the 7th Armoured Division, saw years of service in the desert. The force was a small part of the 4th Armoured Brigade and commanded by its brigadier.*

Brian had the article copied and distributed to all those who had taken part in the operation.

Brigadier Currie, the brigade commander, issued a Special Order of the Day:

> *I wish to express to you and all ranks under your command my gratitude and admiration for the manner in which our recent expedition to MESSINA was carried out. We were a scratch force, drawn from all quarters of the Army, and yet everyone worked together as if we had been training together for some time. The dash and determination shown by all ranks, the way in which officers and men alike worked tirelessly and willingly day and night to achieve the object, was beyond praise.*
>
> *I have received a letter from Lieut-General Sir Oliver Lease Commander of 30 Corps, in which he says:*
>
> *'I realised that you were landed on the wrong beach and I congratulate you on the way in which you retrieved a difficult*

57 Brian had the full text copied for distribution throughout the Brigade.

Commandos waiting for the off

situation. I know how difficult your task was made by the constant enemy demolition and the shelling from the mainland, and I congratulate you on forcing your way into MESSINA so quickly. I shall be grateful if you would congratulate and thank all ranks under your command.'

Will you please pass on these words together with my own thanks to all ranks who took part in the expedition.

21 August '43.

On the 18th of August Brian was back at headquarters after Operation BLACKCOCK. On the 24th of August he attended a final planning conference for Operation BAYTOWN. BAYTOWN took place on the 3rd of September and had little or no strategic significance except as a diversion for the allied main effort, Operation AVALANCHE, the landings at Salerno, which took place a week later. The Germans didn't buy the deception and largely ignored it, maintaining their concentration of force to counter the landings at Salerno. The Commando Brigade involvement was swift and successful, capturing all their objectives in very short order. On the 17th of September Brian drove to Salerno to establish contact with the other half of the brigade, which had taken heavy casualties. Two days later on the 19th of September he received a warning order that 13 Corps would move to Bari on the east coast of Italy and that the Special Service Brigade would move with them.

On the 21st of September Bob Laycock left Italy for Britain on promotion to major general and to take over as Chief of Combined Operations, leaving John Durnford-Slater to command the Special Service Brigade with Brian providing continuity as brigade major.

CHAPTER 5 – TERMOLI

> 'Without courage all other virtues lose their meaning.'
>
> Winston Churchill

By September 1943 Brian had been at war for nearly four years. He was experienced in combat operations and had seen the friction of war and the foibles, weakness, incompetence and jealousy of military bureaucracy, what David Stirling referred to as the '*fossilised layers of shit*'. On the other hand he had served with some exceptional soldiers and commanders. The very effective partnership with Bob Laycock had just come to an end, with his promotion to major general. Their friendship continued and by the end of the year they would be working together again.

Brian would have just as an effective relationship with his new brigade commander John Durnford-Slater, another hard-charging, unconventional and competent commando officer, who believed very much in leading from the front. Together he and Brian would set the tone for the brigade headquarters on future operations. Both of them believed that a Commando brigade headquarters needed to be stripped down to essentials. Small, agile and devoid of unnecessary admin. The headquarters should be close up to the fighting units and concentrate on the essential tasks for short-duration raiding operations: command, communications, fire support and resupply. Anything else was superfluous. Brian's dislike of unnecessary admin was shared by Durnford-Slater, who was delighted that Brian kept the paperwork to a minimum. '*Paperwork was nil; Brian used to pull a few bits of paper out of his pocket occasionally and write something down. This was our filing system.*'

In spite of this sleek organisation both men believed in the old military adage that '*any fool can be uncomfortable*' and so Brian had little problem getting Basil Bennett brought in as 'Camp Commandant'.[58]

58 Camp commandant in this context meant dealing with the admin and creature comforts of the headquarters, not combat logistics.

Termoli

Paddy Mayne at Termoli

Basil also disliked paperwork: '*When Basil was asked to hand over the mess accounts to his successor, he startled this rather solemn young man by telling him that there were none.*' John Durnford-Slater noted:

> *We lived very well indeed and every now and then Basil asked us for a small contribution of lire. These two men now control the destinies of the Hyde Park Hotel and the same atmosphere of efficiency is to be felt there. Alas, the paperwork in the hotel is now no longer confined to Brian's pocket, and Basil's minions seem to want quite a lot of lire every time I leave the place.*

Allan Peile completed the headquarters team as intelligence officer.

So the brigade headquarters heading to eastern Italy with General Miles Dempsey's 13 Corps was no ordinary headquarters, but one which suited the type of operations they would carry out. It also suited the units under their command, 3 and 40 Commando and Paddy Mayne's Special Raiding Squadron.

*

The campaign in Sicily had been dogged by the terrain. Main roads essential for the advance tended to be squeezed between the coast on one side and mountainous or other difficult terrain in the other.

The road passed across numerous bridges or through tunnels and all the withdrawing Germans needed to do was man small delaying positions in front of a bridge or tunnel, delay the advance for a short period, withdraw across the bridge and blow it up.

In a planning conference for the move to Italy General Dempsey explained that his concept of operations would be to maintain the momentum of advance by continuous commando landings on the coast several miles ahead of the advance to seize key features such as ports, bridges and other key terrain. The first of these successful operations were carried out first at Bagnara on the 5th of September by Paddy Mayne's SRS and the second on the 9th of September at Vibo Valentia by the Commando Brigade. After the breakout at Salerno, 13 Corps and the Commando Brigade were told to move to Bari to join the Eighth Army advance. It looked as though the Germans were planning a defence line on the River Biferno which, if established, would be a tough nut to crack, involving an assault river crossing, one of the most difficult operations of war and one which Montgomery wanted to avoid at all costs. He decided to outflank them before they could get established, by inserting the Commando Brigade at Termoli on the coast, two miles north of the river. Termoli was a small port, the capture of which would not only unbalance the Germans and force them to withdraw, but would be useful for logistic resupply.

The brigade was moved in landing craft to Bari where the brigade headquarters set itself up in the Albergo Imperiale. Basil Bennett had identified it as the best hotel in town. There they began the detailed planning for Termoli – Operation DEVON. Termoli was garrisoned by a battalion of German paratroops, 3 Commando's old adversaries from the Malati bridge operation. Brian correctly predicted that they were about to have '*one hell of a battle*'. They would be about twenty miles ahead of the advance, and a speedy linkup would be critical.

Durnford-Slater's plan was simple: 3 Commando and brigade headquarters would secure a beachhead about half a mile west of Termoli. 40 Commando and the SRS would then land, and pass through the beachhead. 40 Commando would seize the town and port, and the SRS a road junction a mile and a half south east of the

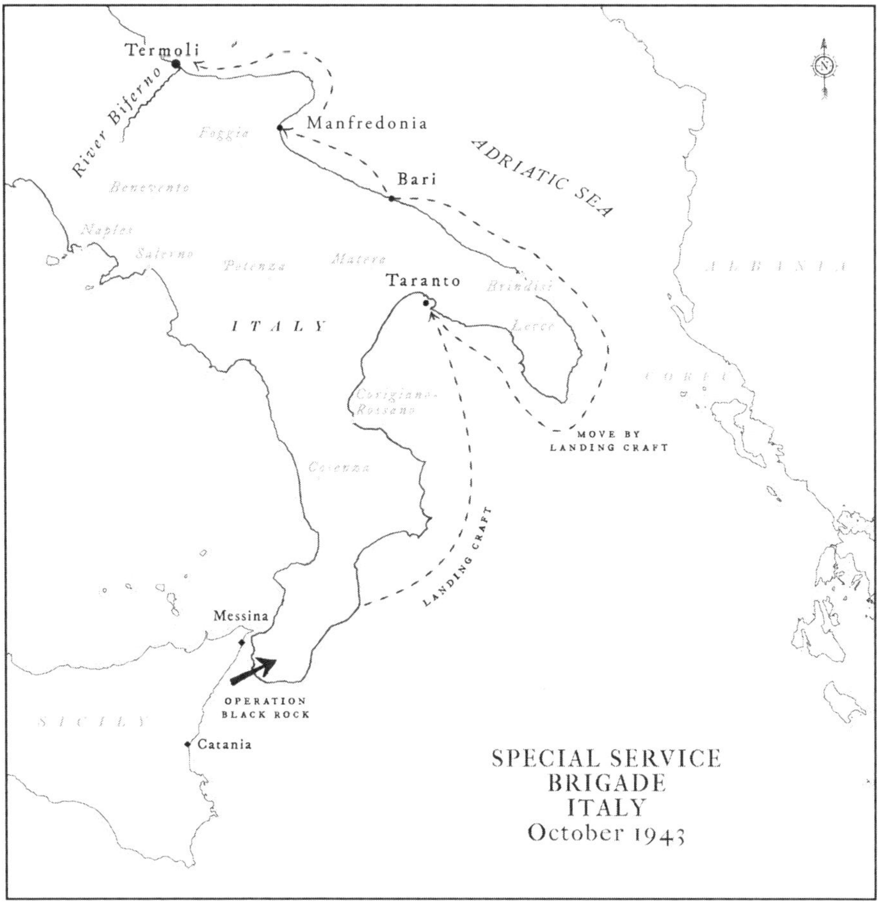

town, the intersection of highways 16 and 87, the main link between Naples and Termoli.

Brian produced the operation order on one sheet of paper. In a conventional brigade, an operation order for this type of operation would have run to at least ten pages with many annexes. Brian's task in preparing for these operations was made much easier because the units were highly professional, with considerable combat experience and comprehensive, well-practised Standard Operating Procedures (SOPs) which enabled slick battle procedure prior to and during operations. He was also helped by the excellent relationship the brigade had formed with their landing craft flotilla commanded by the very efficient Lieutenant Commander Frank Lammert RNVR. This enabled Brian to produce the assault landing order for the Navy on half a sheet of paper.

First of all the brigade had to get to Bari by sea. It embarked for Taranto on the first leg of their trip on the 26th of September, arriving two days later. The operation was scheduled for the night of the 1st/2nd of October. The next two days at sea were horrendous. The weather was appalling and there was a shortage of drinking water in the landing craft. They had been due to go straight on from Bari, a further 120 miles to Termoli. Brian met Durnford-Slater on the quay at Bari and told him: '*We can't operate tonight. The men have had no sleep for four days, and had a very rough passage. They are in no condition to fight. You must get the thing put off for a day*.'

To add to their difficulties, the chief naval officer at Bari knew nothing about the operation, and refused to sign the necessary order for their onward passage. Durnford-Slater decided to adopt the Nelson approach, and ignore him. So Brian drafted a sailing order, and Durnford-Slater signed it. They sent it to the chief naval officer and left before anyone could stop them, heading full speed for a staging point that they had picked off the map, Manfredonia, a small port where they could recover for 24 hours. To make sure Manfredonia was clear of enemy and more importantly that the harbour was clear of mines, Brian sent a road party commanded by Captain David Barclay, the adjutant of 40 Commando, to secure the town.

Manfredonia was clear and the brigade moved in on the 1st of October. DEVON was confirmed for the following night. A patrol from Phantom joined the brigade headquarters and Brian was delighted to find some familiar faces among them.

At 0900hrs on the 2nd of October, Brian received the 'go' signal for Operation DEVON, and they set sail at midday. The weather was excellent and they enjoyed the sunshine and scenery, uninterrupted by the enemy. However, soon after last light, ominous storm clouds built up and it became pitch-black. As they neared the mouth of the Biferno they ran aground. The mouth of the river had silted up and

En route to Termoli

this did not appear on their charts. It was an uneasy feeling being aground close to the enemy coast but the heavy rain helped cover their presence and within 30 minutes the naval crews had them moving again.

They reached the jumping-off point for the landing, cross decked into the smaller landing craft, and made the final run in on time, just as the rain lifted. Their Navy friends had done an excellent job landing them in exactly the right place at exactly the right time at 0215hrs on the 3rd of October. The brigade headquarters was in one of the first landing craft. Durnford-Slater and Brian ran up the beach, closely followed by the Phantom signals detachment and the rest of the small headquarters team. Phantom's role was to relay essential information direct to General Dempsey's HQ 30 miles away, and to enable Brian to co-ordinate fire support from the corps artillery, naval gunfire and RAF attack aircraft.

3 Commando seized the beachhead undetected. It was then the turn of 40 Commando, and the SRS to come ashore, and quickly pass through the beachhead to secure their objectives. Unfortunately, on the way in, their landing craft became stuck on a sandbar also not marked on the charts. Brian turned to the young naval liaison officer on the beach and told him to get it sorted. Again the Navy worked its magic and soon 40 Commando and the SRS were on the move into the town. Suddenly all hell broke loose and very brisk close-quarters

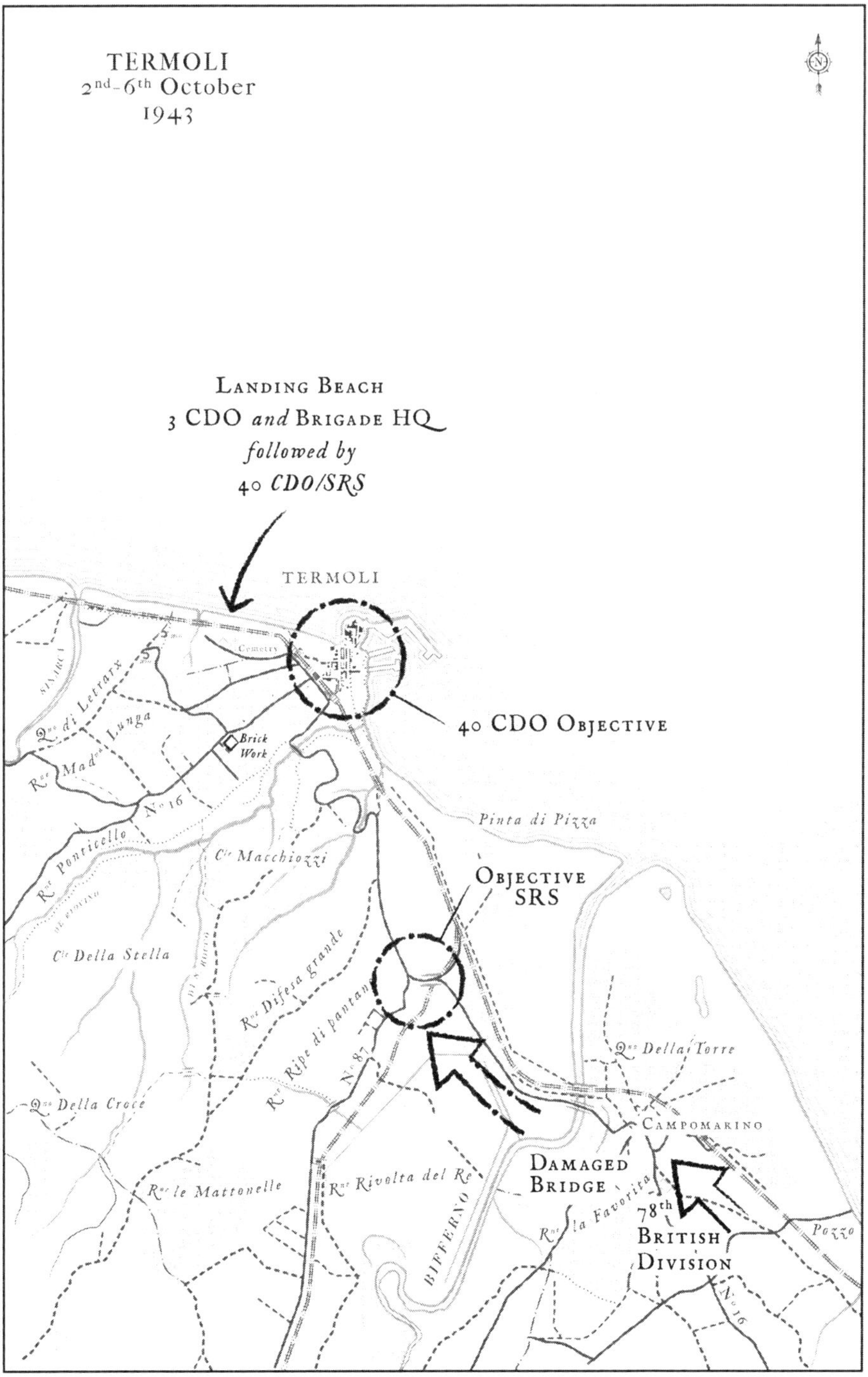
TERMOLI
2nd-6th October
1943
LANDING BEACH
3 CDO and BRIGADE HQ
followed by
40 CDO/SRS
TERMOLI
Cemetry
Brick Work
40 CDO OBJECTIVE
Pinta di Pizza
OBJECTIVE
SRS
DAMAGED
BRIDGE
CAMPOMARINO
78th
BRITISH
DIVISION
BIFFERNO
No 16
No 87

Termoli railway station

fighting erupted. The Germans were taken completely by surprise, but being paratroops from Kampfgruppe[59] Rau, a mixed detachment of infantry engineers and flak[60] guns, under command of Major Rau, they reacted swiftly but too late. By 0800hrs 40 Commando had secured the town and the SRS its crossroads. The unfortunate Major Rau was captured wearing his pyjamas.

The brigade headquarters moved into the town hot on the heels of 40 Commando. They were heading for the railway station to set up their headquarters. When they got there they saw a train getting up steam, intending to make a quick getaway. Quick as a flash Brian drew his Colt .45, and jumped into the cab: '*Hande hoch!*' ('*Hands up!*') he said to the driver. The driver did as he was told. The coaches behind the engine were loaded with German troops, fast asleep. They were woken up and taken prisoner, scarcely believing what was happening. They thought they were safe 30 miles behind the frontline.

Brian set up the headquarters in a house near the station. The signals detachment was then on the move to join them so Brian ordered the release of a couple of carrier pigeons with news of their progress. The pigeons merely circled and landed again. '*Those damn Italian birds*,' said Brian in utter disgust, '*they're no better than their troops!*'

The Germans had been caught out and were in some disarray. The parachute division commander had been in the town visiting Rau, but

59 Kampfgruppe – battle group.
60 Flak: Flugabwehrkanone – anti-aircraft guns.

managed to slip away on foot, leaving his Horch staff car as a present for the brigade headquarters. Also news of the capture of Termoli didn't seem to have spread quickly among the Germans, as supply convoys continued to bumble into the town, only to be shot up or captured by the Commandos.

Gradually the situation calmed down. There were 70 German prisoners, and many captured supply trucks. The booty included a large number of very welcome British cigarettes. 40 Commando and the SRS were withdrawn into the town to rest and resupply. Allan Peile secured the best house in the town, a large villa overlooking the harbour, for the headquarters. The house had belonged to a notorious Fascist, who had left with his wife in a hurry. The butler, who had been left in charge, was very obstructive and had locked up all the best rooms and hidden the keys. Brian told Allan to lock him in the cellar until he became more co-operative. Basil Bennett was soon to arrive, making sure all was in order. Also arriving with the follow-on landings was a pompous colonel in the Royal Army Medical Corps who started berating Durnford-Slater about his use of the field surgical team that had accompanied the operation. Brian intervened and the fellow was given short shrift and quietly disappeared. The peace and quiet was not to last. The German 16th Panzer Division was ordered to retake the town. For the next three days the Commandos, reinforced by troops from the 78th Division, held off combined infantry and armoured assaults. The fighting became very fierce.

The next day, the 4th of October, began quietly and although reinforcements from 78th Division were arriving later in the morning, sniping increased, and accurate artillery fire started to land among their positions. John Durnford-Slater was having lunch when he received a report that German tanks were approaching the perimeter. The attack didn't materialise but it was only a matter of time. Over 18 hours of constant rain had raised the level of the River Biferno and washed away the Royal Engineers' Bailey bridge. This severed the resupply and reinforcement route to Termoli so the defenders would be isolated, except from the sea, until it was repaired. Shelling intensified all day and Brian was tasked with getting the SRS and 40 Commando into a tight defensive perimeter around the town.

Biferno bridge and Royal Engineers' Bailey bridge

Roy Farran had arrived with a detachment of 2 SAS, whose orders were to move out of Termoli to conduct a sabotage operation on rail lines further north. They were resting down near the port when Sandy Scratchley,[61] the SRS Second-in-Command, told him to '*stop skulking like a rat*' and report to Brian Franks at brigade headquarters. When he got there he found it was in some turmoil as it had just been hit by an 88mm artillery round.

Brian was talking to Durnford-Slater in his office when the shell burst in the next-door room. Luckily the villa's walls were very solid and the explosion was contained. Brian opened the door and went in first. '*Keep back, Brigadier, things are not good.*' Tim Lease, one of the staff captains, and RSM Stoneham were dead. Allan Peile, the intelligence officer, had been blown out of the window and was hanging on the ledge seriously concussed. He was hauled in and the survivors moved to the ground floor. The barrage continued. Farran and his crew were ordered to shelter in the cellar until things were sorted out. Later with the shelling continuing Brian took Scratchley and Farran on a tour of the town pointing out where they were to take up positions. Farran takes up the story: '*Shells were crashing around us and every time one went over or exploded nearby I ducked for cover. Brian Franks and Sandy Scratchley ignored them and didn't flinch once. Franks struck me as being incredibly cool amongst it all. He walked on as if nothing had happened.*'

61 Farran and Scratchley will appear later as stalwarts of 2 SAS.

The shelling intensified throughout the day and was supplemented by two aerial bombing raids. It was clear from the accuracy of the shelling that it was being co-ordinated by an observer. Eventually by the late afternoon of the 4th of October, he was pinpointed in a church tower. He was invited to surrender but chose to shoot it out and was killed next to his radio set. The next morning began with a full-on German attack. The Commandos and the SRS held on to their positions. Early the next morning, Brigadier Arbuthnot Commanding 38 Infantry Brigade arrived at brigade headquarters with an over-excited officer from the 78th Division Recce Regiment. He was raving that '*the Commandos were withdrawing on the right ...*' Brian had just returned from 3 Commando and assured him this wasn't the case. Arbuthnot wasn't satisfied, so Brian at great risk returned to the sector. He found that an SRS mortar team had run out of ammunition and withdrawn 20 yards to better cover while they waited for a resupply. German attacks continued all day and into the night. The SRS deployed along the railway embankment alongside 40 Commando and spent a very uncomfortable night.

Things were better at brigade headquarters; Durnford-Slater:

> *The butler who had earlier been confined to the cellar was released from time to time to attend to my headquarters officers and men. He was in a much chastened mood, and produced hitherto undivulged stores of food and wine. We had kept the house clean and tidy throughout the battle. There was never any excitement, shouting or confusion in Commando Brigade headquarters. I think that during the Termoli battle, all our headquarters staff did their job well.*

The morning of the 6th of October saw an intense finale to the battle, with the Commando Brigade and reinforcement from 38 Infantry Brigade, who had arrived during the night, firing everything they had at the Germans. Brian, together with the artillery staff at brigade headquarters, co-ordinated fire mission after fire mission and eventually the Germans broke and withdrew, and by midday the battle for Termoli was over.

SRS after the battle

Sandy Scratchley (left) and Roy Farran

On the 9th of October Lieutenant General Allfrey visited Termoli and congratulated all members of the brigade. This visit was followed by Lieutenant General Dempsey on the 10th of October and Montgomery the next day.

General Dempsey, in addressing the SRS, said: '*in all my military career, and in my time I have commanded many units, I have never yet met a unit in which I had such confidence as I have in yours. And I mean that!*' He expressed regret that the association of 13 Corps and SRS was at an end but '*I hope that the association may be renewed at some later date.*'[62]

Montgomery, usually austere and prudish, told Durnford-Slater '*to take his brigade back to Bari where there is plenty of wine and plenty of girls. They deserve it.*' No further encouragement was needed. Operation DEVON was a success. It had captured a valuable harbour and held it against very determined attacks. It forced the Germans to abandon their plans for a defence line on the Biferno and denied them the important lateral road to Naples. David Stirling, when interviewed after the war, said: '*The battle for Termoli was a marvellous example of sheer fighting spirit and great shrewdness.*' It involved intense close-quarters fighting and was not without considerable cost: three officers and 29 other ranks killed, seven officers and 78 other ranks wounded and one officer and 22 other ranks missing.

62 Miles Dempsey would become Colonel Commandant of the SAS in February 1951, suggested for the job by Brian Franks.

John Durnford-Slater, Montgomery, Miles Dempsey

The missing officer was John Tonkin of the SRS, who subsequently escaped and eventually returned to the SAS in time for D-DAY.[63]

In early November the Commando Brigade was reorganised with Tom Churchill as brigade commander and John Durnford-Slater as deputy. Brian spent a few weeks at Molfetta, where he wrote some quite pithy private reports to Tom Churchill and Bob Laycock, one in particular about General Allfrey commanding 5 Corps. For his actions at Termoli Brian was put up for a DSO, but this was downgraded to an MC[64] by Montgomery, in spite of a full endorsement for a DSO by John Durnford-Slater and General Dempsey. Perhaps Montgomery got wind of Brian's frankness and ability to criticise senior officers, particularly when they deserved it. Brian was back in Britain by the end of November 1943, summoned by Bob Laycock for a very important mission.

*

Brian was given a few days' leave before reporting to Combined Operations Headquarters in Richmond Terrace near the War Office. He was ushered in to see his old friend Bob Laycock, who was now Chief of Combined Operations. Bob got straight to the point: '*I'm very glad to have you back. There is something I want you to do that is*

63 After capture he was invited to dinner by a German general, and was advised, in veiled speech, to escape as the Army were obliged to hand him over to the Gestapo and he would then be shot.
64 The citation is at Annex C.

very, very sensitive. I have arranged for you to have a BIGOT security clearance.' Brian started to laugh, but Bob interjected, '*It's not what you think, although there are quite a few bigots around here. BIGOT is the highest level of classified security clearance surrounding our plans for the cross-Channel invasion – British Invasion of German Occupied Territory.*'

Bob went on to explain that Combined Operations had set up a number of COPPs, Combined Operations Pilotage Parties, which would recce the beaches for the coming invasion. These teams were the result of some of the early work done on beach reconnaissance for raids and amphibious landings since 1941. This had been pioneered by Lieutenant Commander Nigel Clogstoun-Willmott when he realised at the time of the planned invasion of Rhodes in 1941 – Operation CORDITE – that visual observation by submarine was not good enough, and that each beach must be visited by a clandestine recce team. He had originally pitched the idea to Bob Laycock when he was commanding LAYFORCE. Bob introduced him to Roger Courtney of the Special Boat Section (SBS). The two of them began working together and laying down the foundations of what would become COPPs.

The COPP programme would develop into a highly sophisticated scientific analysis of potential invasion beaches based on the data of currents, tides, gradient, samples of sand and gravel collected from the beaches, and obstacles both natural and man-made. COPPs were first used in the invasion of North Africa, and later in Sicily. They would be essential for the invasion of Normandy. It was dangerous, high-risk work, involving one or two individuals being put ashore from a submerged submarine on to a heavily fortified beach in order to collect the necessary data and samples. Individuals would have to work incredibly stealthily and it was essential they remained undetected. Capture would not only mean extremely unpleasant torture and certain death, but would also blow the cover of the landing locations. By late 1943 the sensitivity of these operations was on a par with ENIGMA.

Bob outlined Brian's role: '*I want you to be my liaison officer with COPPs, and in particular I want you to work with a COPP commanded*

Scotty

Sergeant Bruce Ogden-Smith

by Major Logan Scott-Bowden, 'Scotty', who is going to conduct the primary reconnaissance for Normandy.'

The COPPs were based at Hayling Island Yacht Club on the south coast, and Brian was soon off down there to be indoctrinated and briefed on their capabilities. Detailed planning would take place in Richmond Terrace. 21st Army Group were desperate to get the beach intelligence as quickly as possible so it could be fed into the plan for OVERLORD – the invasion. Until these operations had been carried out successfully and with no compromise, finalised planning – the confirmation of beaches, viability for landing craft and armour, assault loading tables, obstacle breaching – would all have to wait.

This urgent requirement was transmitted to Combined Operations and hence to Brian. A plan was made for the first operation to take place on the night of the 31st of December 1943/1st of January 1944, New Year's Eve, when not only were the tides and moon right, but it was felt that patrols and sentries might be less vigilant. A rehearsal would take place on the night of the 22nd/23rd of December 1943 at Brancaster Beach in Norfolk where the slope of the beach, the geological structure, and tidal flows were similar to those in Normandy.

The rehearsals, watched by Brian and two marine scientific experts, Doctor Schofield, and Professor Bernal, as well as Colonel Dove and Lieutenant Colonel Johnson from the invasion planning staff, were a success. A final briefing for the operation would take place at 21st Army Group on the 24th of December. On the 28th of

December an officer from MI9[65] would brief Scott-Bowden and his other team member Sergeant Bruce Ogden-Smith on a cover story and an escape and evasion contingency plan at HMS *Dolphin*, the submarine base in Portsmouth harbour. This would include escape routes, contacts and safe houses, as well as giving them French francs, and escape and evasion equipment such as button compasses, silk maps and hacksaw blades.

On the 21st of December an emergency meeting was called at 21st Army Group. Brian attended and a possible postponement of the operation until the 20th of January 1944 was discussed. After the meeting, Brian immediately circulated the following report:

1 By reason of the landward approaches to the beach, and the fact that the 'X' craft draws 8'6", it can only be done with the tide at mean level. Much of the information required can only be obtained below mean level.
2 In the next dark period it will be possible to land at low tide and recover Scott-Bowden after six hours ashore.
3 Two reconnaissances are undesirable for security reasons.
4 Bernal stated that more definite information would be available for briefing by 20th January.
5 There will be more opportunity for developing the technique and instruments to be used.
6 Lt Cmdr Willmott stated that he thought it doubtful whether the crew would be able to stand up to two operations so close together.

Against postponement

1 The information is urgently required for planning.
2 COPP are most anxious to gain operational experience.
3 Admiralty are anxious to have a report on the 'X' craft under actual operational conditions.
4 It might mean postponement of the proposed reconnaissance of the American beaches.

65 MI9: Military Intelligence section responsible for helping Allied POWs and airmen evade capture and escape from occupied Europe, establishing clandestine communications systems and employing ingenious tactics and secret escape routes. See *A Dangerous Enterprise*.

21 Army Group will make a decision by 22nd December, 1943. The Brancaster trials are not affected.

On the 24th of December yet another meeting:

COPP RECONNAISSANCE

I attended a further meeting at 21 Army Group today at which the following decisions were made:

1 The reconnaissance would take place as originally planned.
2 They will sail on the 30th Dec. and it is hoped that they will stay for three nights, working two nights and possibly three.
3 The priority of exits was again discussed. Exit 5 remains as first priority, exit 6 as second priority, and exit 4 provisionally as third priority.
4 The photographs and other intelligence seemed very satisfactory.
5 The trials at Brancaster are reported to have been very satisfactory. Colonel Dove and Professor Bernal were present and can therefore give any further information if required.

The operation codenamed BELL PUSH ABEL went ahead as planned. At one minute to midnight on the 31st of December 1943 Scott-Bowden and Ogden-Smith swam ashore from a landing craft anchored 400 yards offshore. They swam quietly into the beach at Ver-sur-Mer which was to be GOLD beach in the British sector of the invasion. Each carried a Colt .45, a commando knife, wire cutters, wrist compass, emergency rations, waterproof torch and an earth auger for testing the bearing capacity of the beach. The objective of their mission was to determine whether the landing area would stand up to the weight of heavy vehicles disembarking in great numbers. If armour and supply vehicles became bogged down in an undetected substratum of clay or peat bog, it would put the whole operation in jeopardy.

As they moved along the beach, they had to flatten themselves on the ground every few minutes as the beam from the local lighthouse swept over them. Heavy rain arrived to provide some very welcome

X-craft midget submarine

cover and, encouraged by the sounds of New Year celebrations by the Germans, the pair spent several hours collecting samples. Heavily laden by the time they attempted the return journey, they were thrown back many times by the rough sea before they managed to get through the surf. Scott-Bowden thought that his companion was in trouble when he heard him shouting, but when he turned to help he found Ogden-Smith wishing him a Happy New Year. Scott-Bowden responded, '*Swim you bastard or we'll be back on the beach.*'

On their return, the samples were rushed to scientists for assessment. Scott-Bowden was awarded an MC and Ogden-Smith an MM. On the 3rd of January 1944 Brian circulated a report that the operation had been a total success, and that GOLD beach was considered suitable.

Their next operation took place between the 17th and 21st of January, in an X-craft midget submarine commanded by Nigel Willmott. Codenamed POSTAGE ABEL, the task was to survey the beach, near Vierville-sur-Mer which was to be OMAHA beach within the American sector. After boarding at Gosport, where they were seen off by Brian, they were towed to mid-Channel by an armed trawler before starting their diesel engine and travelling on the surface during the hours of darkness. At dawn on the 18th of January 1944, they submerged but soon found their way partly blocked by a French fishing fleet with armed guards. As they threaded their way through the nets, they raised the periscope. Scott-Bowden found himself staring at the face of a German soldier perched on the stern of a boat, puffing away at his pipe, completely oblivious of their presence. They beached at periscope depth in seven feet of water off the beach. Scott-Bowden snatched a look through the periscope and saw hundreds of German soldiers at work preparing a strong defensive position. The submarine withdrew offshore using its electric motor, surfaced and recharged its batteries. For the night reconnaissance, the eastern sector of the beach was chosen. Scott-Bowden and Ogden-Smith swam ashore. They checked for obstacles and mines above the high-water mark. A patrol passed nearby but they were not interrupted. They withdrew to the X-craft and spent the day submerged on the bottom. At nightfall the two men made another sortie, this time to the adjoining sector. As they reached shallow water, a powerful torch was beamed straight at them. They kept their faces down and, after a nerve-racking wait, the sentry switched it off. They swam away to the east and examined another beach. Stones from a shingle bank that might cause problems to tanks were retrieved and the locations of wire and a suspected minefield noted. They had spent three nights on the beaches and four days on the seabed. Scott-Bowden was awarded a DSO for the operation, Ogden-Smith a DCM.

After returning to Britain, Scott-Bowden was summoned to Norfolk House[66] in St James's Square to a briefing with General Omar Bradley. After the debrief Scott-Bowden had a private word with Bradley, '*Sir, I hope you don't mind me saying it, but this beach is a very formidable proposition indeed and there are bound to be tremendous casualties.*' Bradley put his hand on his shoulder and replied, '*I know, my boy. I know.*' Scott-Bowden, Ogden-Smith and Willmott made a total of 30 reconnaissance trips. On D-DAY they assisted in piloting in the first wave of the American landings on Omaha Beach.

Bob Laycock was both glad he had appointed Brian to oversee this important and sensitive operation, and very pleased with the results, as were Generals Eisenhower, Montgomery and Bradley. He knew that Brian was angling to get back into the action for the coming invasion. The various components of the SAS were being brought back to

66 Norfolk House, 31 St James's Square: General Eisenhower's headquarters for Operation OVERLORD, the invasion of Europe.

Britain to be formed into an SAS brigade for the Normandy landings. 2 SAS needed a Second-in-Command. The whole regiment was short of manpower and had to be brought up to strength in a hurry. Bob felt that Brian was just the man to help Bill Stirling do this. David Stirling had tried to recruit Brian for the first iteration of the SAS in 1941: '*From the beginning I subjected Brian to pep talks on SAS principles – after I'd come out of hospital and was telling him what I was trying to do, and trying to recruit him, but he was too ill. Franks was one of my top chums. I adored Brian and we were very close.*' Already having the 'Stirling imprimatur', Brian had also enlisted the help of Paddy Mayne, whose SRS had now been redesignated 1 SAS. They knew and respected each other from the Termoli battle. Brian wrote to Paddy on the 12th of January 1944, after he had got the backing of Bob Laycock:

> *32 Drayton Court*
> *Drayton Gardens*
> *SW10*
>
> *Dear Paddy*
> *I tried to get hold of you on the telephone today but failed. I gathered you would be back late! I am off for three days early tomorrow and expect that you will be away when I get back. I have leaped the first hurdle today in the shape of the great man (CCO), who I felt I should speak to first as I have been his employee for so long. I am going off with John Durnford-Slater tomorrow so will have a good chance of getting a crack at him, and I anticipate no great difficulty. I would like to get hold of you when I get back (Monday) and will try to do so through Ian Collins, so perhaps you will let him know how I can contact you and let you know how I have prospered.*
>
> *I am very excited at last having what looks like a proper job of work to do and I hope that you will not regret it – I will do my best to see you don't.*
>
> *This telephone no. will know where I am if you want me.*
> *Yours ever*
> *Brian*

CHAPTER 6 – STIRLING AND STIRLING

'Doesn't it make you sure you were right, to see all the General Staff opposing you?'

T. E. Lawrence

Brian was successful in his manoeuvring, having the full support of Bob Laycock, John Durnford-Slater and Paddy Mayne, and was posted to 2 SAS as Second-in-Command on the 21st of February 1944. He would soon prove ideally suited to the SAS. His early experiences in the war had turned him into a thoroughly professional soldier, but the SAS required more than just military skills. It required the right temperament and mental aptitude combined with a disciplined individualism, imagination and initiative.

A lot had happened to 2 SAS in the months leading up to Brian's appointment. William (Bill) Stirling, the elder brother of David, Scottish aristocrats, had both joined the Scots Guards, where they served alongside their cousin Simon Fraser – 'Shimi' – who was also to make his name as an unorthodox commando soldier. [67] Bill had been to Sandhurst and become a professional soldier in the 1930s, before transferring to the reserve in 1936. David did not join the Scots Guards until the outbreak of war. Both served briefly in the 5th Battalion – a ski battalion formed for a planned Anglo-French expedition to Finland to help them fight the Russians in what was known as 'The Winter War'.[68] It was largely composed of officers – 167 of them – those who could ski and had a taste for adventure. The unit was short-lived and disbanded in March 1940 after the armistice between Finland and Russia. Both Stirlings joined Bob Laycock's 8 Commando, 'The White's Commando'. Brian had known both Stirling brothers before the war. In Cairo David had tried to get him to join

67 Simon Fraser, Master of Lovat, 15th Lord Lovat. Commander of the Special Service Brigade on D-DAY. Winston Churchill said of him, 'He was the most handsome of men to slit a throat.'

68 The Soviet Union invaded Finland on the 30th of November 1939, three months after the outbreak of World War II. The Russians were effectively defeated by the Finns and the war ended three months later, on the 13th of March 1940.

Bill (left) and David Stirling

the embryonic SAS L Detachment, which Brian would have eagerly done had he not been very ill and invalided home.

Both brothers believed in the great strategic opportunities provided by unconventional warfare deep behind enemy lines, to interdict lines of communication, logistics, and to attack headquarters with the aim of killing senior enemy commanders, all with the purpose of unbalancing the enemy, tying down troops to protect rear areas, and disrupting command and control, without becoming embroiled in pitched battles.

Of the two brothers, Bill was the more measured, David being more impulsive. Evelyn Waugh described Bill as '*vague, mystical, imaginative, aristocratic*'. He soon joined SOE, but he found the organisation and training not nearly as good as it should be for clandestine operations. He suggested to the War Office that there was a need for a dedicated training centre for unconventional warfare. This idea caught the attention of Winston Churchill (prompted by Bill) and as a result, the War Office took over Inverailort House on the west coast of Scotland, named it Special Training Centre I and made Bill the chief instructor. Among its early attendees were David Stirling, Paddy Mayne and David Niven. Brian had attended a week's course there in 1942; STC-I would be the forerunner of the numerous SOE training schools, and the Commando training centre.

After setting up and commanding the school for six months, Bill returned to SOE in Cairo. After another round of ineffective operations, he moved to the GHQ Middle East as military assistant to Lieutenant General Arthur Smith. David was pushing his idea for the SAS and it is generally believed that it was he who got the idea through. It was in fact a joint effort, with Bill working behind the scenes to help David get his concept in front of General Neil Ritchie.[69] When the SAS was formed under David's command, Bill returned to Britain and took a four-month break, before being appointed to command the Small Scale Raiding Force (SSRF) on the 17th of October 1942. SSRF was soon renamed 62 Commando and headed to North Africa, arriving there in February 1943. On arrival Bill was given the news that his brother had been captured in Tunisia in January. Paddy Mayne took over command of the SAS – now temporarily renamed the Special Raiding Squadron (SRS). In May 1943 Bill was given authority to raise a second SAS regiment from the nucleus of 62 Commando, and was appointed Commanding Officer on the 13th of May. SRS would focus on amphibious raiding, while 2 SAS would continue to develop the original SAS concept of small teams operating deep behind enemy lines. Bill was about to become frustrated with the lack of imagination of the staff hierarchy in the Middle East and Italy.

2 SAS was established at Philippeville,[70] a coastal port in north-eastern Algeria. They set up camp near the beach, which to all intents and purposes was an ideal place to train. Unfortunately it was close to a swamp which was home to malarial mosquitoes. Soon there were many cases and its recurrent strain was to dog the regiment in Italy and later in France and Germany.

The regiment was lucky to get some very experienced officers

69 General Neil Ritchie GBE, KCB, DSO, MC was Deputy Chief of Staff to General Warrell, the Commander-in-Chief Middle East Command, succeeded by General Auchinleck.
70 Now called Skikda.

Bill Barkworth

posted in: Sandy Scratchley as ops officer, Roy Farran as a squadron commander and Eric 'Bill' Barkworth as intelligence officer, in addition to some excellent NCOs such as Harold 'Tanky' Challenor and Fred Rhodes. Training was hard, lots of physical work, map reading, sharpening of small unit tactics, and shooting.

Close-quarter battle shooting was taught by Hector Grant-Taylor[71] known as 'Tack tack' because of his insistence on firing two shots or a 'double tap', at each target. Roy Farran loved him – particularly his style of instruction, his trademark '*Good morning gentlemen. First I must tell you that murder is my business*.' He also taught the submachine gun, particularly the SAS favourite, the German MP40 Schmeisser, which he told them '*must be played like a musical instrument in short bursts to maintain accuracy*'. The 'tack, tack' system would save the lives of many members of 2 SAS. It was used to particularly good effect by SQMS Jack Alcock on Operation PISTOL[72] when he dispatched several Germans in a farmhouse kitchen in very short order.

71 Leonard Hector Grant-Taylor (1891–1950), after graduating from Cambridge University, served in the First World War. Subsequently he worked as a Home Office lecturer and physical training instructor. Re-enlisting in 1940, he was commissioned into the 8th Battalion, Queen's Own Royal West Kent Regiment and soon transferred to the SOE. He served as adjutant and quartermaster at STS 22, Morar, later as instructor at STS 102, Haifa (Palestine), and from February 1943 acted as SOE liaison officer with the War Office. During the North African campaign he served at Philippeville with 2 SAS.
72 Operation PISTOL – see Chapter 9.

While 2 SAS was being forged into a fighting unit Bill Stirling was trying to get the planning staff at 15 Army Group to listen to his ideas for the most effective way of using them in the forthcoming invasion of Italy. He had written a paper which concluded: '*SAS troops will normally be employed where vital tasks exist which cannot be tackled by regular formations and more particularly which are far behind enemy lines*.' He envisaged his regiment being used in northern Italy hundreds of miles from the landings in the south, being parachuted in in small groups to conduct sabotage of railways and other transport, logistic stockpiles, airfields and enemy headquarters. They would also link up with and conduct operations with local partisans. Jeeps could be parachuted in later to enhance mobility and firepower.

Initially he was allowed to carry out one operation in northern Italy: Operation SPEEDWELL, which ended up destroying ten trains, railway tunnels and other infrastructure, which rather proved his point. To quote Roy Farran: '*But think how much more could have been done*.' This was Bill Stirling's vision but he constantly found himself '*fighting against the dead weight of staff officers to keep his unit going*', in other words '*the fossilised layers of shit*' as his brother put it so eloquently. He was exasperated that the bulk of 2 SAS came ashore as part of the 1st Airborne Division at Taranto on the 10th of September doing a job that could have been done by any reconnaissance unit and was a total waste of highly trained SAS talent. This was the catalyst for a turn of events that would unfold over the next six months. Bill felt his small-team operations concept had been proven, in spite of attempts to stymie them, and there had been some quite successful small operations: POMEGRANATE, MAPLE, THISTLEDOWN, DRIFTWOOD and BAOBOB, but nothing on the scale that he had hoped for.

Bill Stirling went home on leave in September 1943. He was keen to continue to develop his ideas and in particular he wanted to establish an SAS brigade including 1 and 2 SAS together with the two French SAS units 3 and 4, and the Belgian SAS company. He still believed that if used properly and commanded at the highest level by someone who understood the SAS ethos and methodology, they would be a huge force multiplier in the forthcoming invasion

Members of 2 SAS at Sorn Castle

of France. He intended to enlist powerful friends like Bob Laycock and Winston Churchill to support him. He also bumped into Evelyn Waugh in the bar of White's, who was desperate to come to the SAS. Bill knew that his ability to write, and his excellent staff work, would be of great value, in helping formulate his plans for the future of the regiment, so promised him a job. This in turn would provide a small drama for Brian when he took over command. Bill also saw Brian at White's and Brian elicited a promise from Bill that he would find him a slot if he could get himself released from Combined Operations.

2 SAS was ordered home from Italy in mid-March 1944 to join 1 SAS in Scotland. On the troop ship home a rather difficult and unpleasant event unfolded which divided the officers of 2 SAS. A faction of what Roy Farran described as '*the half-arsed*' officers tried to mount a mutiny to oust Bill Stirling. The plotters were Oswald Cary-Elwes, Esmond Baring, Potter Miller-Mundy and Philip York. The ringleader was Toby Milbank. Their complaint was that Bill had never been on an operation since the regiment was formed. They had perhaps forgotten that Bill was rather busy trying to ensure the survival of the regiment, and its proper use on operations. Bill also knew an awful lot about the clandestine world, including SOE, with whom he had worked twice, and he would have been a great catch for the Gestapo.

Ranged against the mutineers were the voices of Sandy Scratchley, Roy Farran, Tony Greville-Bell and Alastair McGregor, all with impeccable operational records, and the medals to prove it. Eventually the mutiny was quelled and some of the miscreants were RTU'd[73] on arrival back in Britain, and others were posted away from 2 SAS.

*

In spite of his successful lobbying to get to the SAS, Brian didn't join them in Italy as they were about to return to Scotland. In the interim he got himself parachute qualified along with others like Christopher Sykes waiting to join 2 SAS. Most parachute training was done by airborne forces parachute school at Ringway near Manchester.[74] Course places were tight due to the demand for trained parachutists for Normandy. Brian and Christopher Sykes arranged to go on a separate SOE jump course at Tatton Park. Brian also spent time with Zoe and young daughter Valerie and refreshed his ties with the Hyde Park Hotel, arranging with them that, as his new job was likely to involve much travelling from Scotland to London and southern England, he would need a secure office from time to time, as would some of his officers like Eric Barkworth and Christopher Sykes. He also ensured Evelyn Waugh would be welcomed there.

Bill Stirling arrived back in Scotland in March 1944 after a somewhat fraught journey home to find that while his plan to have an SAS brigade in the Order of Battle for D-DAY had been agreed, it was to be under command of the 1st Airborne Corps commanded by General 'Boy' Browning. Browning was a professional soldier, commissioned into the Grenadier Guards in 1915. He had already commanded the 1st Airborne Division, but had no experience of the SAS or how to use them. To make matters worse the SAS brigade was to be commanded by Brigadier Roderick Macleod, a traditional soldier from the Royal Artillery. Bill must have felt a degree of disappointment at not being chosen to command the brigade himself, given his experience and that it had been his idea in the first place. He was also more

73 RTU – Return to Unit – the ultimate punishment for an SAS soldier.
74 No.1 Parachute Training Centre, established in June 1940 at RAF Ringway, now the site of Manchester Airport.

Christopher Sykes

suited to the role than Paddy Mayne, the other obvious choice. This was further compounded by the petty and insensitive direction from Browning that the SAS were to give up their sand-coloured berets and wear the red beret of Airborne forces, although they could retain the winged dagger insignia. Most of 1 SAS and in particular their Commanding Officer chose to ignore the order, as they felt rather attached to their sand-coloured berets.

However that was trivial in comparison with what was to come next. On the 4th of April the SAS brigade was issued with an operational order by 21st Army Group, responsible for planning the invasion of France. It stated that the primary task of the SAS would be '*attacks on suitable types of objectives in the concentration areas of hostile mobile strategic reserves behind the length of the French Channel coast*'. In effect, the SAS would parachute in only about 40 miles ahead of the frontline to act as a blocking force when the German reserves of three Panzer divisions were identified moving towards the beachhead. This was clearly madness, and would have been a death sentence for lightly armed forces trying to stop armoured divisions.

Bill Stirling viewed this as a total misunderstanding of the purpose of the SAS, which would result in the brigade being decimated. He dug in his heels and demanded a return to strategic employment deep in enemy territory, where they would establish secret operating bases to attack lines of communication and high-value targets-of-opportunity, and also assist with arming, training and stiffening local Resistance groups. This was the same argument he had had in Italy the previous year, where he had been ignored or overruled, but had ultimately been shown to be right. It only made his determination stronger that there should be no repeat. His officers shared his view and within days there was something close to mutiny in the air. Roy Farran pointed out that it '*proved such lack of understanding of our role that our confidence in the new command was severely shaken*', and it seemed like clear evidence that the freedom of action which the SAS had enjoyed in the early days, and which had been steadily eroded since late 1942, was now about to disappear completely.

Lightly armed as they would be, the SAS's only advantage would be the element of surprise, but the chances of parachuting into enemy territory just ahead of the frontline without being seen were very slim. In the immortal words of 'Tanky' Challenor, '*We would stand out like a sixpence on a sweep's arse.*'

Bill Stirling and Paddy Mayne were incandescent at their orders, exasperated that once more the SAS was to be used tactically and not strategically. Brigadier Macleod had a nervous relationship with the SAS. He knew he was not the man who should have been chosen to command them, but he made every effort to understand their ethos, how they operated, and adapt to it. He had first come across them in Italy, where he described them as '*colourful and curiously dressed ruffians*'. He also knew that they '*regarded my HQ as a necessary evil that should be humoured providing it did not interfere with what the regiment thought should be done*'. A perceptive chap, he would become one of their greatest champions.

The operational directive for D-DAY was clearly absurd. It became known inside the SAS as Operation BRIDES IN THE BATH, after the famous 1915 murder case,[75] which became a *cause célèbre*, and in Evelyn Waugh's *Unconditional Surrender* the character of General Whale (Browning?) is referred to as 'General Brides in the Bath' because all the operations he planned seemed to require the death of all involved.

75 George Smith, a serial killer, murdered three women in 1915, for which he was hanged.

It was so obviously ludicrous that even Brigadier Macleod took issue with it. Bill Stirling decided it was time to take a stand, and he drafted a letter to Browning stating in forthright terms that he had no confidence in the new command structure or their operational planning concepts. Eventually he was persuaded, by Farran and others, to delay sending the letter until every possibility of the plan being amended had been explored. In fact, it was subsequently changed, along lines Browning suggested in a letter he wrote to 21st Army Group's Chief of Staff on the 8th of May, though in it he stated that *'The delay in formation, mobilisation, providing reinforcement, equipping and training of SAS troops and the shortage of intelligence, signal and other specialised personnel'* was the reason for the modification, not any objections made to the original plan by Bill Stirling. The updated plan, which substituted harassing enemy lines of communication and assisting Resistance groups for a head-on battle with enemy Panzer divisions, was much better, and more in tune with SAS operational philosophy, but Bill decided to send his letter anyway.

As one might have suspected, this caused a furore and Browning summoned him for a meeting at Sorn Castle in Ayrshire, the headquarters of the SAS brigade, on the 3rd of June 1944. It was very much what in the military is known as *'the interview without coffee'*, which implies an extremely frosty atmosphere. The meeting took place in one of the rooms of the castle, and what exactly happened is not recorded. Bill Barkworth and Sergeant Fred Rhodes were briefing Browning and his ADC on the planning of operations in France. Bill Stirling arrived and things started to get heated. Rhodes left: *'Once Bill Stirling had decided he would oppose Browning's proposals, as a non-commissioned officer, it was time I did a quick disappearing act, because it wasn't on for a sergeant to be present when a general and a Commanding Officer were having a ding-dong.'* It is not known if Barkworth stayed throughout the meeting, but he told Rhodes immediately afterwards that Bill had been sacked.

It is likely that Boy Browning asked Stirling to withdraw his letter and its criticisms in the light of the change in plan. Stirling stuck to his guns and refused, telling Browning that he had no confidence in him as a commander, and that he had no idea about the use of the

SAS. This created an impasse. There was only one way that the meeting was going to end ... either he would be fired or invited to submit his resignation. The result was the same: he was out. Although Browning had fired him, he most likely allowed Bill a dignified exit and Bill submitted a letter of resignation from command of 2 SAS but not from the Army.[76]

Back in Monkton, the 2 SAS base in Ayrshire, word spread fast. There was fury among the officers and men alike. Tony Greville-Bell, by now a captain with a DSO, said, '*We were in absolute agreement with his decision because of that thick-headed idiot Boy Browning.*' Bill Stirling got all the officers together and told them what had happened and furthermore that they were not to resign. '*I won't forgive any one of you if you don't back up Brian.*' Brian as Second-in-Command was to step up and take command on the 4th of June 1944.

Stalwarts such as Roy Farran and Eric Barkworth lobbied their fellow officers to stay and support Brian. Roy Farran was unequivocal: '*I agreed to stay and have never regretted it since. Brian Franks proved to be the best Commanding Officer you could wish for, and we knew that we were finally to be employed in the way Bill Stirling had visualised.*' Tony Greville-Bell agreed: '*We were lucky to get Brian Franks. He was a brilliant officer.*'

Brian (left), Hannah Stirling's godfather, Hannah, Sister 'A', Bill Stirling, Christopher Sykes

76 It had the same effect. He went home to Keir and took no further part in the war, being eventually struck off strength of the Scots Guards in 1945.

CHAPTER 7 – THE GAME IS AFOOT

> 'Never tell people how to do things. Tell them what to do and they will surprise you with their ingenuity.'
>
> General George Patton

When Brian took over command he showed a lot of compassion for the mood of some of the dissidents. He knew he needed to tread lightly but he realised that he had quickly to mould his officers and men into an effective team if they wanted to be in on the action. John Hislop, who had just joined 2 SAS as their Phantom detachment commander, found Brian an excellent commander: '*In build tall, lean and athletic, he was by nature cheerful, understanding, full of initiative and brave*.' His job was made easier by the fact that he was already held in respect by all his highly individualistic officers and men. This was no mean feat, for apart from the squadron commanders, who were accustomed to taking their own decisions in guerrilla operations, the ranks of 2 SAS included many foreigners, French, Spaniards, Poles and even Germans, as well as tough, combat-experienced NCOs and soldiers from British units. They were proper adventurers and hard fighting soldiers, intensely loyal to their proven officers. Brian wielded just the right blend of discipline and tolerance to bring out the best of all under his command, rough diamonds that they were. He could deliver a serious 'bollocking' that put the fear of God into any miscreant officer or soldier, but there was no ill-discipline. Although relations between officers and men were more relaxed in the SAS, Brian was always referred to, and known as, 'The Colonel'. Now firmly established in command, Brian needed to get them ready for operations.

He had three problems to deal with immediately: bringing the regiment up to strength, ensuring it was battle ready, and then developing operational plans to ensure that they were fully and correctly employed in post D-DAY operations. Many of the problems that

Brian was about to encounter could have been avoided by more understanding and a more flexible approach at SHAEF. Bill Stirling's departure was a sad waste of a brilliant strategic thinker who understood the business of Special Forces operations better than most. If there had been less intransigence, and both Bill and Browning had taken a pace backwards, the ideal solution would have been to have Bill set up an SF planning cell at SHAEF, to advise Eisenhower on the proper strategic co-ordinated employment of SAS, SOE and the Jedburgh teams, which would wear uniform and organise the reception of parachuted weapons and supplies, as well as providing training and operational support to the Resistance groups, after D-DAY. The planning cell would read the battle as it unfolded, advise on strategic targeting, co-ordinate resources, timings and deconfliction as ground operations developed. However it would need the authority to cut through layers of command, to allocate resources and give orders.

As it stood it was left to Brian to fend for himself working with a brigadier who tried his best to help but lacked the knowledge and seniority to be effective. Matters were not helped by the Airborne Corps losing interest and turning their attention to Operation MARKET GARDEN, which would take place in a little over three months' time, on the 15th of September, and taking up the resources that were needed to support Operation LOYTON.

Brian was lucky in that he had some outstanding and experienced officers. Sandy Scratchley stepped up to be Second-in-Command, Roy Farran, Tony Greville-Bell and Alastair McGregor were all experienced and knew their business, as did Eric Barkworth, the intelligence officer. Tom Burt was the best quartermaster you could find and more importantly he also understood that his Commanding Officer hated the minutiae of admin.[77] This was an excellent bedrock on which to build. They were joined by some sound 'new blood'. Christopher Sykes joined the intelligence team and John Hislop was in command of the Phantom detachment. Brian told his officers to '*put out the word*' and used his own connections to seek people out.

77 He had been recruited by Bill Stirling, who had given him a lift in his staff car and was so impressed that he recruited him there and then. Tom Burt had enlisted in the Royal East Kent Regiment as a boy bugler in 1914.

Tom Burt

One new officer recruit was the young 22-year-old Lord John Manners, who Brian found lurking in the bar at White's. Asked what he was up to, Manners explained that he had had a falling out with his regiment, the Life Guards, and was at a loose end. Brian recruited him on the spot and he went on to be both a brave and effective officer, earning himself the nickname 'Machine Gun Manners' on Operations WALLACE and LOYTON. 'Tanky' Challenor would report that in spite of being the son of the Duke of Rutland, '*He slotted in perfectly, without sacrificing an ounce of respect; he mixed and drank with the lads while his barrack room vocabulary could make old sweats nod approvingly. Our admiration and affection were boundless, and thanks to his nonchalant bravery we owe him our survival.*'

Bob Walker-Brown saw an officer from 2 SAS in the Caledonian Hotel in Aberdeen looking suitably exotic, so asked him for his Commanding Officer's name and phone number. He phoned Brian and asked to join. Once the adjutant had checked out his impressive war record, he was taken on.

Another interesting character who joined was Captain Raymond Lee, real name Raymond Couraud. Lee was a bit of a mystery, with a French father and an American mother. He had joined the French Foreign Legion in 1938. Before that he had operated as a soldier of fortune for the Chinese warlord Zhang Zuolin in Manchuria, and then for the Ethiopian Army. His regiment took part in the Norway campaign in 1940 and he was awarded the Croix de Guerre.

He returned to France but didn't want to serve the Vichy government so deserted and went 'underground' in Marseille. He was involved with the Marseille mafia and became the lover of a rich American heiress, Mary Jayne Gold,[78] who had lived in Paris during 'Les Années Folles' and in 1940 moved to the south of France. She used her money to fund an escape line, the Emergency Rescue Committee, which helped mostly Jewish artists, doctors, and scientists to escape from France, including Marc Chagal, Marcel Duchamp, Max Ernst, sculptor Jacques Lipchitz, and Nobel Prize-winning biochemist Otto Meyerhof.

In April 1941 Lee escaped himself before he had his collar felt by the Gestapo. He made his way to Britain and, introduced by Lord Louis Mountbatten, was recruited by SOE and given the alias Raymond Jack William Lee. He was attached to the Commandos for the St Nazaire raid in 1942 and was wounded. Once he had recovered he went on an SOE operation in the south of France[79] and again escaped through Spain where he fell out with the SOE station in Madrid. Back in England his love of the high life was beginning to catch up with him and that, combined with his unpopularity in SOE, led to his being fired on the 21st of December 1942.

Although considered no longer suitable for SOE, he was described in his file as '*a lion, full of enterprise and daring*', and as they did not want his aptitude for clandestine warfare to go to waste he was posted to Bill Stirling's 62 Commando at Philippeville, where he was given command of their 'foreigners', which is how 2 SAS inherited him. We will hear a lot more about Raymond Lee shortly.

By far the luckiest chance encounter came in April, when Brian, travelling back from London on a train, found himself in a compartment with another officer, who was on his way to do a refresher parachute course. Brian started to chat to him and found out he had been seconded to SIS because of his linguistic skills: French, Dutch and Flemish. He had been captured by the Gestapo in Holland but

78 Mary Jayne Gold. Born in Chicago 1909. She was the granddaughter of the man who invented the cast-iron radiator. Extremely wealthy, she moved to Paris in 1932, where she became a close friend of Josephine Baker and Biffy Dunderdale.

79 Operation SNOWDROP – the assassination of Gestapo informers.

Lee, second from right, Jane Gold, third from right, with members of the emergency rescue committee, Marseille 1940

Henry Druce

escaped and made his way through France on foot, to the Pyrenees and then through Spain and Portugal, back to Britain. He told Brian he was unemployed because his cover had been blown, as he had been betrayed by a double agent. Brian recruited him on the spot. His name was Henry Druce.

There was, however, one recurring officer problem: Evelyn Waugh. Bill Stirling had met Waugh in White's back in December 1943. He had told him to get himself parachute trained but Waugh had injured his knee. Stirling gave him six weeks' leave to recover (and finish *Brideshead Revisited*). Once Evelyn had finished and recovered, Bill Stirling had gone, and Brian was now Evelyn's Commanding Officer once again. He reported in by letter, saying that he wished to get back to active service as soon as possible, and what were Brian's orders?

Christopher Sykes takes up the story:

I was with Brian Franks when he received the letter at his headquarters at Ardchullery Lodge, a property of Bill Stirling's in Perthshire. Brian was dismayed. 'What on earth shall I do with him?' he groaned. 'I can't very well tell him to take another three months' leave and write another book, which is what I would like to do.' We all bent our minds to the problem, which was not an easy one, for Brian had set an absolute condition on any solution. 'I'm not going to allow him near the men,' he had asserted. 'Get him up here and see what he wants to do,' someone suggested.

'I know exactly what he wants to do,' said Brian. 'He wants to mess up the men, and the regiment, and the brigade, and Airborne Corps if possible.' I was described at the time as the operational intelligence officer and I suggested that with the second front opened and voluminous enemy documentation becoming available, Evelyn might be useful as an addition to the intelligence staff. The chief intelligence officer, Bill Barkworth, turned pale at this suggestion but admitted that paperwork was likely to grow beyond the capacity of the present staff. Nothing was decided, but Brian Franks sent a telegram to Evelyn ordering him to report to Ardchullery at his earliest convenience. He arrived with Basil Bennett on 23 June.

Evelyn soon understood the situation. He wrote in his diary that '*Brian was so shy of having me under command as to be almost hostile. I was in some doubt as to my future.*' Brian had told him quite forcefully that he was not allowed to have anything to do with soldiers.

Luckily a mutually beneficial solution was about to appear. Christopher Sykes again:

Though I delighted in Evelyn's companionship my sympathies were entirely with my colonel. To fit Evelyn into the humblest military organisation was an impossible task. As an intelligence officer I was often used as a liaison officer in matters which could be more easily thrashed out in conversation than in lengthy correspondence. I was used thus in the frequent negotiations between Airborne Corps, Combined Operations Headquarters and SAS Brigade. I remember being seen off from Glasgow on the night train to Euston by Evelyn and Basil one evening in the last days of June. It was a hectic time for us, as the SAS role changed daily with the general military situation. On 28 June I spent a busy morning at Combined Operations Headquarters, and at the end of it went to White's for refreshment and relaxation. I had not been there many minutes before I heard the loud and unmistakable voice of Randolph Churchill at the bar, saying: 'Where the hell is

Evelyn Waugh? I've tried everywhere! No one can tell me! I need him immediately!'

I went quickly to the bar. I said, 'Randolph, did you say you want Evelyn? I think I can help you. What's it for?'

'I've spent the morning with my father,' he explained, 'and it's now all fixed; I've been commissioned to undertake a subordinate mission under Fitzroy Maclean[80] in Yugoslavia. I told Fitz before I left that I must have officers I can talk to and he agreed with me that Evelyn was just the chap for me. It's all very secret,' he added, his voice rising in volume, 'so don't tell anyone. But where the hell is Evelyn? How can I get him? I've asked everyone I can bloody well think of. No one seems to know.'

I said, 'Randolph, if you just stay where you are, I think I can get him for you. Don't go for five minutes. Where are you staying?' He told me he was at the Dorchester Hotel.

I put through a 'priority call', as it was known then, to Ardchullery. I told Brian the bare fact that Randolph wished to see Evelyn in London, the next day if possible, regarding a likely and important appointment. The note of relief excited by my words was fully audible over the telephone. I rushed back to the bar and told Randolph that Evelyn would be with him at the Dorchester Hotel the following morning. In gratitude he gave me a drink, which I had certainly earned. Evelyn came down on the night train. I did not see him again until after the war.

A late arrival in 2 SAS was Joe Patterson, who volunteered to be their medical officer. When he arrived at the end of July he noted that Brian now held the respect of all of his highly individualistic officers and men. The soldiers were a mixed bunch, many experienced NCOs and soldiers, but also some not yet tested in battle. Among the more experienced were the 'Foreign Legion', commanded by Raymond Lee: Spaniards who had fought in the Civil War, Frenchmen who had

80 Sir Fitzroy Maclean. Unionist MP 1941–74. Joined the Army as a private in 1940. Finished the war as a brigadier. At Eton with Brian. Diplomatic service: Paris Embassy with Biffy Dunderdale. Early member of the SAS. Personally chosen by Winston Churchill to lead a mission to Tito's partisans in Yugoslavia.

served in the French Foreign Legion or who had escaped from France and some anti-Nazi Germans. Brian was as good with his soldiers as with his officers. In spite of the hellish pace of training and the fact that Brian was desperately trying to get the regiment deployed into France, there was still room for compassionate leave for (among other things) getting married. One morning one of the French soldiers appeared on Commanding Officer's orders requesting permission to get married before they deployed. Brian granted permission and then asked him: *'You intend to spend your honeymoon in London. Tell me, have you arranged a place to stay?'*

'No sir, I am still trying to find a suitable hotel that isn't too expensive.'

'It so happens, Corporal, that I have some connections in the hotel business in London, and I'm sure that I could help you, should you wish.'

'That is very kind of you, Sir. Thank you.'

So the French corporal and his bride spent a week in the bridal suite at the Hyde Park Hotel, entertained as only the Hyde Park could entertain. And there was no charge whatsoever. Such was Brian's style of command, summed up by Robert Laycock: *'He was dedicated to the training and welfare of his men, and judged others by the standards he set himself.'*

*

While the manpower recruitment and training continued apace, Brian's real challenge was to get his regiment into the fight in France. Because 1 SAS had arrived back in January, they had had more time to recruit and train, and were therefore ready to go. Also they had not had a run-in with the brigade and corps headquarters, whom they largely ignored, necessitating a last-minute change in command. The headquarters staff were also somewhat in awe of Paddy Mayne – by now the holder of two DSOs. However, Brian rose to the occasion, lobbying hard for early deployment of 2 SAS. The first few weeks following his appointment were intensely frustrating for him.

He continued to travel up and down the country from Scotland to London to visit SAS brigade headquarters at Moor Park, and

SOE headquarters in Baker Street and Montague Mansions. Luckily he had organised a secure office at the Hyde Park Hotel. This was also used by Bill Barkworth and Sergeant Fred Rhodes. As if there wasn't enough friction around 2 SAS, the use of this office caused some more. On the 29th of May 1944, Brigadier Macleod wrote to Bill Stirling: '*It has been reported that at some time during the last week a room in the Hyde Park Hotel was being used by Major Barkworth for planning purposes and that maps and other information were displayed in a way which was insecure. Please forward a report on this matter as soon as possible.*'

The background was later explained to Brian in another letter dated the 9th of August:

> *At a time when Bill Barkworth was using a room at the Hyde Park Hotel as a London office, a good number of Top Secret documents were borrowed by them from Combined Ops. The security branch at Combined Ops was asked whether it was all right to let these documents out under these conditions.*
>
> *Simultaneously it was reported that the room at the hotel was in fact being used as an office and that they were not quite happy about it, although, admittedly, the room was properly locked in the absence of any of the regimental staff.*
>
> *The security staff at COHQ considered that the matter required investigation.*
>
> *Meanwhile a very serious breach was suspected somewhere since a French officer was reported by David Astor to have put his finger on the NEPTUNE[81] area on a map, and discussed French reactions in a way which suggested that he knew exactly where the invasion was to take place. This was immediately reported and raised a big flap. SFHQ were very worried as to whether he had any special information to which he was not entitled. 21 Army Group became more than interested and every contact which he had had with British officers during the previous week or so was investigated. In the course of this investigation it became known*

81 NEPTUNE – the codename for the Naval plan for D-DAY, OVERLORD being the codename for the landing operation.

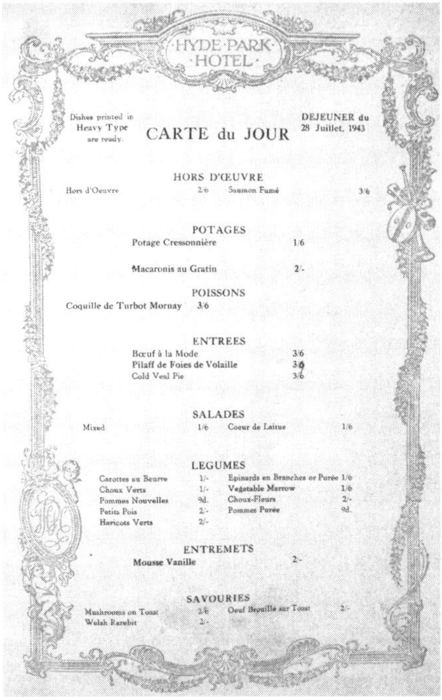

HYDE PARK HOTEL

Dishes printed in Heavy Type are ready.

CARTE du JOUR

DEJEUNER du 28 Juillet, 1943

HORS D'ŒUVRE

Hors d'Oeuvre 2/6 Saumon Fumé 3/6

POTAGES

Potage Cressonnière 1/6

Macaronis au Gratin 2/-

POISSONS

Coquille de Turbot Mornay 3/6

ENTREES

Bœuf à la Mode 3/6
Pilaff de Foies de Volaille 3/6
Cold Veal Pie 3/6

SALADES

Mixed 1/6 Coeur de Laitue 1/6

LEGUMES

Carottes au Beurre 1/-
Choux Verts 1/-
Pommes Nouvelles 9d.
Petits Pois 2/-
Haricots Verts 2/-
Epinards en Branches or Purée 1/6
Vegetable Marrow 1/6
Choux-Fleurs 2/-
Pommes Purée 9d.

ENTREMETS

Mousse Vanille 2/-

SAVOURIES

Mushrooms on Toast 2/6
Welsh Rarebit 2/-
Oeuf Brouillé sur Toast 2/-

July 1943 lunch menu, Hyde Park Hotel

that he had lunched with Bill Stirling at Claridge's a few days previously.

The security birds immediately connected this with the question which had already been raised to them about the hotel, and I was asked for an immediate report, hence my original letter to you.

The explanation was accepted and as far as I am concerned that is the end of the matter. Tell Barkworth there is nothing to worry about.

The Hyde Park also had other uses. Brian regularly entertained friends and important contacts there. Fred Rhodes recalls that when he was working in the office one day just after the invasion, he took a break for lunch:

About lunchtime I went down into the basement and 20–30 high-ranking people were having drinks and lunch with the colonel, and one of them was Winston Churchill. I always remember that, because when I went to the bar for a beer, the barman wouldn't serve me a pint – it had to be half a pint. Colonel Franks heard the barman say I couldn't have a pint, and he said: 'If Sgt Rhodes wants a pint of beer, you bloody well get him one.' That was it. But then I was away – a sergeant doesn't mix with generals.

*

After the Stirling furore Brian quite rightly focused on operational deployments as early as possible. On the 17th of May a signal from brigade headquarters had been sent to all SAS units: '*Operational Instruction No. 2 cancelled. All copies are to be destroyed.*' This was a step in the right direction. A new directive for the use of the SAS followed. The new concept was to drop small advance parties deep inside France where they would link up with local Maquis groups and establish a base. Into those bases, more men, weapons and Jeeps would be dropped, enabling enemy communications to be disrupted over a wide area. Brian and his team were already studying the map and rightly identified an area in which 2 SAS could operate.

Brian had the vision to see how the battle might go. Following a breakout from the Normandy beachhead, the Allies would attempt to advance rapidly, keeping the enemy on the hop and not allowing them to pause long enough to establish strong defence lines to halt the advance. This breakout would be co-ordinated with air power, both tactically and in depth, and would eventually be supported by the landings in the south of France. Brian quite rightly identified that the Belfort Gap would be the confluence of two withdrawing German armies and that the Vosges Mountains and passes through them would be a natural place for the SAS to operate. At that time, the Vosges were sufficiently far from the frontline as to be perfect for interdiction of logistic supply, attacks on headquarters and the causing of general mayhem. If these operations could be co-ordinated with Resistance groups, so much the better. The development of this concept would involve a mobile operation advancing out of the Normandy/Brittany area striking towards Metz, and a

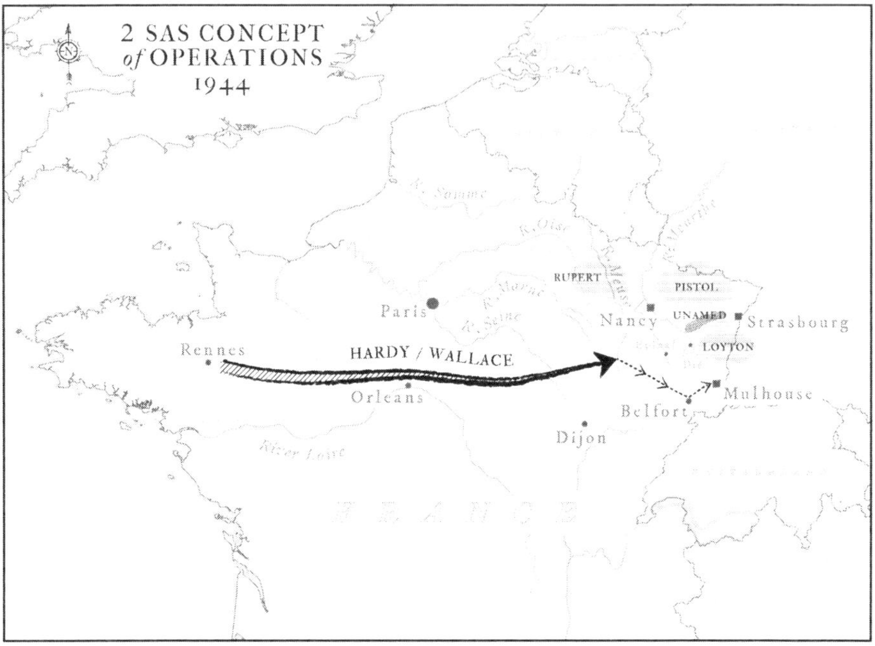

parachute delivery operation in the Vosges and Belfort Gap area. This was the genesis of what would become Operations HARDY/WALLACE and LOYTON.

All this was set out in a letter to Brigadier Macleod on the 15th of July:

> *There is therefore a third alternative which I suggest would achieve the best results. This is for the area covered by the triangle LOYTON–RUPERT–HARDY to be considered a regimental area into which this regiment should be infiltrated. Three squadron bases could be built up with a main base at LOYTON. Minor tasks would be carried out from all bases taking care not to attract too much attention. E.g.*
>
> i Cutting and keeping cut main railways.
> ii Small attacks on dumps.
> iii Attacks on airfields.
> iv Attacks on Gestapo and other enemy personnel.

Major tasks would not start until instructions were received from here. These would be based on the main army's tactical plan. In fact the regiment would remain temporarily inactive until the word were given from here. It seems probable that this area may become an important one should the enemy decide to withdraw from France.

Our relationship with the Maquis would be:

i To explain that we had certain specific tasks to perform.
ii To prevent them rallying round us but to use a few as required.
iii Not to promise supplies but to report upon their deficiencies.

This plan would involve RHQ and six squadrons. The remaining squadron would be earmarked for special tasks inside or outside the bridgehead.

SHAEF Headquarters would eventually concur.

*

In the interim there were many difficulties to overcome as the battle for France developed. While the new directive for SAS operations laid down three types of operations: first, arm and train the French Resistance, to allow them to be more aggressive, and to play their part in delaying German reinforcements moving up to the main battle area; second, aggressive operations by the SAS acting on their own in armoured Jeeps dropped or flown in to them; third, locating targets for the RAF: railway stock, tunnels and bridges. These would also be attacked by the SAS themselves.

The practicalities were somewhat different. It was difficult to predict the rate of advance from the beachhead, measured against the planning cycle for SAS operations. A fast rate of advance and the planned operation might be overtaken by events, a slow advance might prevent a speedy linkup, forcing SAS troops from offensive action to survival mode. Speed of decision-making was essential. Detailed planning was frequently delayed to the last minute as information about the main battle plan took time to trickle down to SAS HQ.

To mount an operation involved the following cumbersome procedure: first, SHAEF had to approve the project. This was the most difficult stage of all; G3 (Special Operations) Division of SHAEF, which had the last word on all SAS tasks, was a newly-formed branch and complex co-ordination between it, 21st Army Group, airborne troops and SAS troops was needed before an operation could be approved. This was compounded by a total lack of understanding of SAS capabilities.

The operation order was then issued to the unit concerned. Stage three involved the provision of intelligence. Stage four was the arrangement of reception in the field and, as we shall see, embroiled the planners in endless controversy. The fifth stage was the allotment of aircraft, which could be confirmed only on the morning of the actual drop. The final two stages were the collection and loading of equipment and stores, and finally the briefing and orders. All this before the operation started. Resupply would also prove to be a critical factor.

This extremely cumbersome process could have been overcome had Bill Stirling been allowed to set up a special operations planning call at SHAEF headquarters working directly with General Eisenhower, and the staff at the highest level.

Another problem was the relationships between the SAS and SOE, which became apparent as soon as the new operating priorities were laid down. SOE regarded itself as the final authority on all matters concerning the French Resistance. That was what they had been doing throughout the war and their agents had operated with considerable but not universal success. As far as arming and training the Resistance was concerned, SOE was preparing to drop small liaison parties into France as soon as the invasion started as part of Plan SUSSEX.[82] SOE was naturally unamused to learn that it was proposed to send teams of SAS, outside its control, to do exactly the same thing. This problem was to dog Brian through the whole campaign in France, but as we will see, particularly applied to

82 Plan SUSSEX: A plan to drop teams into France after the invasion to work with the Maquis and conduct sabotage and intelligence-gathering operations. Known as 'Jedburgh' teams, each team would consist of an American (OSS), British (SIS/SOE) and French (BCRA) officer.

Operation LOYTON. Superimpose on all these internal problems a battle-hardened, aggressive and ruthless enemy, and you have a very difficult operating environment.

In spite of all this, Brian continued to badger SAS headquarters. On the 13th of June he wrote pointing out deficiencies in the targeting package:

> *It is noted that the following suitable SAS targets are not mentioned:*
>
> a) Centres of German control of occupied areas i.e. Gestapo Feldkommandantur etc.
> b) Grounded aircraft.
> c) RDF and night fighter control stations.
> d) W/T Stations.
> e) Petrol and Arm dumps.
>
> *It is particularly suggested that attacks on known enemy headquarters in the rear areas are very often possible for small parties with the object of creating confusion by killing staff officers.*
>
> *It is further considered that it is not beyond the bounds of possibility that SAS should capture a high-ranking officer of the Wehrmacht or Gestapo and bring him back to this country by Lysander or similar aircraft.*

It was clearly a very frustrating time for Brian and his team. The location of 2 SAS in Scotland did not help matters. It was ideal for training but over 400 miles from any airfield that could be used to deploy operations to France. This particular problem was solved when 2 SAS was moved to Shipton Bellinger on Salisbury Plain in late June. It wasn't only the physical separation in Scotland that was irritating. There were internal problems at SAS brigade HQ. In a letter to Brigadier Macleod in July 1944 Brian pointed out the lack of high-grade intelligence as well as poor admin:

On 10.5.44 I wrote a letter in which the supply of a few useful drawing instruments were requested. Captain Foot[83] *has twice been reminded, but so far nothing has arrived ... I also asked in April for some maps ... Despite frequent reminders and assurances these have also not arrived. When I was in London on 29.6.44, I told Captain Foot what maps we would need for RUPERT and HARDY. He made a note of this. When on 2.7.44 I telephoned Major Shaw, he told me Foot had gone on leave, and that he, Shaw, knew nothing about it. This appears to be inexcusable. I have made this sorry account as objective as possible, and I'm sure you will appreciate how I feel when I see such incompetence and mismanagement.*

Nevertheless operations began on the 19th of July with Operation DEFOE. 2 SAS's first deployment was a tactical intelligence-gathering operation. A team of 22 men were dropped into southern Normandy to set up OPs and report back tactical information. The operation lasted three weeks and proved completely pointless.

This was followed by Operation DUNHILL on the 5th of August, which again turned out to be utterly useless. There was a complete lack of co-ordination between SHAEF, airborne headquarters and 21st Army Group. By the time the operation was launched, the Germans had left the area. Commanded by Tony Greville-Bell, with 59 men, most of them landed in an area already liberated by the Americans. Their original mission now being superfluous, Greville-Bell used his initiative to assist downed Allied airmen, following a contact made with Airey Neave of MI9 at Le Mans on the 12th of August. The following day the party entered Forêt de Fréteval, where the airmen were concentrated, in a convoy made up of four buses, three Jeeps and three civilian cars. Dropping off small teams along the way to secure their route out, they escorted the evaders to safety. On the 17th of August Operation DUNHILL was officially terminated, and the men made their way back to the UK, arriving at Newhaven on the 20th of August. Greville-Bell summed things up: '*Everyone with*

83 Captain M. R. D. Foot. Wartime SAS officer and subsequent official SOE historian.

me made a great effort to save this operation from being completely valueless, but as far as offensive operations go we could do little as the Germans either avoided us or moved too fast.'

Hard on the heels of DUNHILL came Operation TRUEFORM, which consisted of a composite force of ten men from 1 SAS, 40 from 2 SAS and 62 Belgians from 5 SAS, with Brian commanding it from the Moor Park operations room. The SAS brigade's War Diary reports 101 all-ranks were dropped over the two nights, on to six DZs: '*Conditions were unsatisfactory for successful operations owing to the lack of accurate information about the enemy; the confused state of the battle and the need to operate immediately on arrival. The parties operated with moderate success for four or five days until reached by Allied forces.*'

The most successful of the early operations, and the most in-tune with SAS principles was Operation GAFF. The GAFF mission was '*To kill, or kidnap and remove to England, Field Marshal Rommel, or any senior members of his staff*'. The operation instruction goes on:

> *METHODOLOGY: This must be left to you and you will submit your detailed proposals as soon as possible to this HQ. The following points should be borne in mind: If it should prove possible to kidnap Rommel* and *bring him to this country the propaganda value would be immense and the inevitable avoided. Such a plan would involve finding and being prepared to hold for a short time if necessary, a suitable landing ground. To kill Rommel would obviously be easier than to kidnap him and it is preferable to ensure the former rather than to attempt and fail in the latter.*

The operation would be commanded by Captain Raymond Lee, he of the interesting past. His team were an equally eclectic bunch, including five other former legionnaires, an Englishman, a German using the alias Sergeant Mark, and a Russian. They dropped blind on the night of the 25th of July, but failed to find the container with their equipment. That was a severe blow but, undaunted, the party set off on foot carrying their personal weapons and rucksacks. Lee became ill during the first morning, with a severe attack of malaria picked up in Philippeville, and had to lie up in a farmhouse for two days. There, he heard that Rommel had been severely wounded when his staff car had been strafed by a fighter bomber on the 28th of July. Lee decided to make what he could of the operation and set out on a series of sabotage patrols on foot, derailing two trains and shooting up seven trucks and two staff cars.

On the 12th of August they found themselves in Mantes, and discovered from the locals that there was a German headquarters in a villa on the outskirts of the town. Lee decided to attack it that night. As soon as it was dark, he posted a cover group with a Bren gun, while the rest of the party hid in the garden close to the front door. Lee and Sergeant Mark knocked on the front door, which was opened by an orderly. Mark explained in German that his vehicle had broken down and he needed help. At that moment, the orderly was shot and the team stormed inside, clearing the rooms with grenades, while Lee ran from office to office grabbing papers and maps, and anything else of intelligence value.

German reinforcements arrived on the scene, but Mark shouted conflicting orders to them in German, which created confusion, and the Germans started shooting at each other. This enabled Lee and his team to slip away and return to their base in the woods. They heard later from the local Resistance that twelve bodies had been taken from the villa the following morning. By then, they were running short of ammunition and Lee decided to try and organise a resupply. Riding a bicycle, dressed as a gendarme, he left to contact the Americans, leaving his team hidden in the woods. His plan was to bring back reinforcements and a resupply to continue the operation. He passed through the lines and was taken to General Patton's headquarters at Le Mans, where they were grateful for the intelligence he had brought, but otherwise did not want to know. He was put on an aircraft back to Britain, and his men were overrun by the Americans a few days later.

GAFF was a classic example of the application of basic SAS principles. A determinedly led small group without vast technical back-up, speaking French fluently, had managed to operate with impunity behind enemy lines for the best part of a month. Lee showed the flexibility required of an SAS commander by switching his mission

Lee dressed as a gendarme

focus. They succeeded in destroying material vastly in excess of the resources employed to put them there and all returned safely. Lee's operational report contained some important pointers for future operations, including the need to have French and German speakers, in addition to the use of locals to recce approach routes to targets by day, allowing the SAS to move only at night.

Operation RUPERT began on the 4th of August. The mission was to sabotage rail lines in eastern France between Nancy and Châlons-sur-Marne. The advance party had left Fairford airfield on the night of the 23rd of July but crashed as it approached the DZ. It took two weeks to prepare and dispatch another advance party and the main body did not deploy until towards the end of August, by which time Patton's 3rd Army had overrun the operational area. Major 'Mickey' Rooney, commanding the operation, wanted to infiltrate through the American frontline to join up with Operation LOYTON but was prevented from doing so by a direct order from Patton. The RUPERT team was sent back to Britain, just when they would have been helpful to the LOYTON operation.

*

While this mixed bag of operations was taking place, Brian had continued to plan for the HARDY/WALLACE/LOYTON concept. One of the key points to emerge from the GAFF debrief was the important need to have native Frenchmen deployed on future SAS operations. Brian was ahead of the game. He had lunch with his old friend 'Biffy'

Robert de Lesseps (GOODFELLOW)

Dunderdale in Boodle's.[84] Biffy ran the ultra-secret A4 department of SIS, dealing with the Vichy Intelligence Service, and his own compartmentalised networks in France, which had been used in the preparation of the invasion.[85]

Brian explained his need for native Frenchmen with experience of clandestine work in France. SOE was an obvious source but there was already friction and mistrust between SAS and SOE, which would soon come to a head during Operation LOYTON. Could Biffy help?

Biffy gave it some thought and said that he might have a Frenchman who had worked for him since 1940, had been on several operations in France and would be happy to go back. His name was Robert de Lesseps – alias GOODFELLOW.[86] Brian gave Biffy an idea of his concept of future operations in France, and Biffy agreed to have a word with GOODFELLOW. The next day Biffy confirmed that GOODFELLOW could be released and was happy to go, but that Brian would have to square it with the War Office and have him transferred to the military. Brian agreed and arranged to meet Robert. There is a note in Brian's personal correspondence file showing meetings on the 10th of June: '*1200 Potter*[87] *at Boodles. 1800 Goodfellow at*

84 Many members of the special operations and intelligence world were members of both White's and Boodle's.

85 For a full account, see *A Suspicion of Spies*.

86 The grandson of Ferdinand de Lesseps.

87 Potter is Potter Miller-Mundy, who would run the SAS liaison with Patton's 3rd Army, during Operation LOYTON.

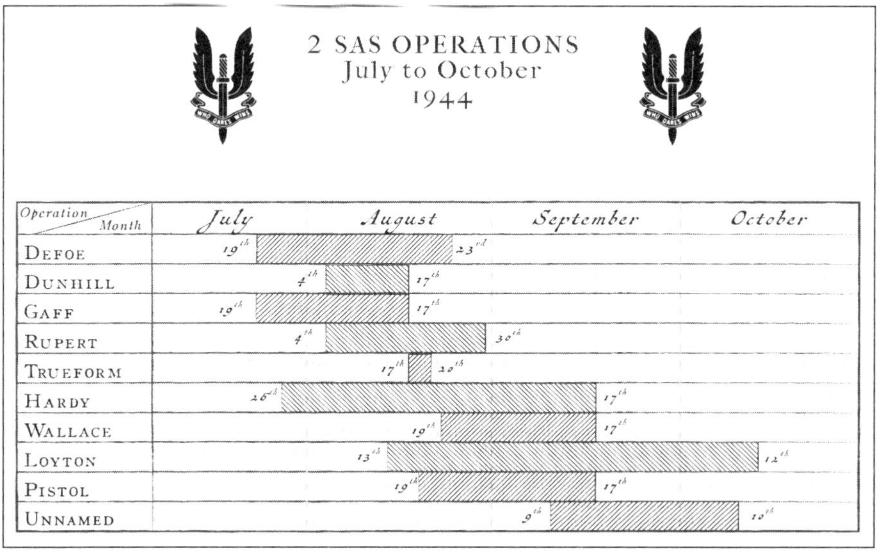

White's'. They met for a drink in the bar at White's and Robert said he would be delighted to join. Brian put the wheels in motion, writing to Captain Mike Mills at the War Office on the 13th of June:

> *Dear Mike,*
> *CAPTAIN R. E. R. GOODFELLOW*
> *I am enclosing a letter applying for an officer named Goodfellow, who as you will see I am most anxious to obtain. I am given to understand that the department for which he works at present are willing to let him go, either on attachment or posting, providing the case is put up by you.*
> *This is probably a rather unusual request, but he comes from an unusual department, and I have particularly not mentioned this fact in the official letter.*
> *The above named officer has certain qualifications which make it extremely desirable that he should be attached or posted to the regiment.*

On the 23rd of June the posting was approved and by the end of the month Robert had joined 2 SAS.

CHAPTER 8 – LIFE IN THE FAST LANE

'Impetuosity and audacity often achieve what ordinary means fail to achieve.'
Niccolo Machiavelli

'Crazy is our business.'
Paddy Mayne

Paddy Mayne and 1 SAS had got off to a flying start with a series of operations very much in line with the amended Operational Directive from SHAEF issued on the 19th of May for the use of SAS units after D-DAY. 1 SAS deployed most of the regiment on Operation HOUNDSWORTH in the Morvan hills to the west of Dijon and BULBASKET in the Vienne, south of Poitiers.

HOUNDSWORTH wound up on the 26th of September and together with its offshoots Operations KIPLING and HAGGARD, was considered a success. BULBASKET was not, and provided the first indication that captured SAS men, even though in uniform, would be executed in compliance with Hitler's Commando Order.[88] Paddy had himself deployed on the 7th of August as soon as the prohibition on SAS commanders doing so had been lifted. Brian on the other hand was becoming increasingly frustrated following the series of ineffective operations: DEFOE, DUNHILL, RUPERT and the partial success of GAFF, all mainly due to poor direction and co-ordination by 21st Army Group, HQ Airborne Forces, or difficulties with SOE. Brian was becoming exasperated with SOE or 'SFHQ' as it was referred to, and in particular Nick Boddington,[89] the Second-in-Command of F Section. On the 4th of August he wrote to Brigadier Macleod:

88 See Annex D for the Commando Order.
89 Boddington was associated with a number of controversial issues regarding SOE and the Germans. In 1942 he oversaw the evacuation of Mathilde Carré, a double agent. This operation was carried out with the full knowledge of the Germans. Boddington went ashore on the landing beach, a huge risk given his wide knowledge of intelligence matters. (See *A Dangerous Enterprise*.) Later he was involved in the controversial PROSPER network problems. He was investigated by MI5 at the end of the war with no specific conclusion.

As you know, I have been trying to mount the initial operations of this regiment, which in each case entailed the dropping of a reconnaissance party into areas to which you have ordered me to go. Although the personnel of these parties are perfectly prepared to drop blind, it is obviously preferable that in every case they should be received by a SFHQ reception committee. The difficulties and time wasted in endeavouring to arrange these reception committees satisfactorily has been appalling to say the least of it, and have necessitated constant journeys and considerable time spent at Baker Street. On the face of it, in view of the fact that there are five, and I believe now, a sixth SAS representative at SFHQ, it would appear that these journeys should be entirely unnecessary.

Brian then went on to cite various of his operations, including RUPERT:

I received the instructions to carry out this operation on 11th July, but the operation has been mooted for a long time prior to this date, and was held up, after considerable difficulties with SFHQ due to: a). Difficulty of finding suitable DZs and b). the fact that SFHQ had an operation of its own in the area under Boddington, who appeared to be much averse to having any SAS personnel in his area. The arrangements for the initial recce party were not satisfactory due to the fact that Boddington was not prepared to receive them, which he signified by making a signal that it would be 'criminally sadistic' to do so ... Finally a DZ was chosen, which having only a receiving set, confirmation that lights would be put out could not be received [by us]. The party therefore had instructions to drop on DZ if the lights were out, or to drop blind in an area about twenty miles away which had been carefully examined. The aircraft carrying this party did not return.

It is now 4 August. The replacement recce party is due to leave tonight. In spite of every effort and considerable discussion with SFHQ, the arrangements are the same as above except that the DZ is in a different area. While discussing this operation with Group Captain Hallmark at 38 Group on 31st July, I accidentally discovered that SFHQ had flown one, if not two, sorties recently to the exact area in RUPERT to which I had always signified I wished to go, and in fact to a reception committee within fifteen kilometres of the spot to which the party may now have to drop blind.

Brian next turned his attention to the projected Operation LOYTON, which had always formed part of his concept for the most effective use of his regiment. LOYTON had been under consideration since D-DAY as the second part of a two-phase operation of which part one would be HARDY/WALLACE. Brian wanted to know if anyone had been to the area recently. SFHQ prevaricated – probably because they had no one on the ground, and hadn't had for some time, in fact not since 1942. They had also been deceived by one of the great German deceptions or *Funkspiel*,[90] creating a false network ARCHDEACON which SOE believed to be genuine. It was not until June 1944 when A. V. Woerther, a French man, was inserted to set up the WOODCUTTER circuit and Octave Simon to set up PEDAGOGUE that SOE had a working presence in the LOYTON/PISTOL area, but it was too little, too late.

To make certain he then sent one of his officers to the French authorities to find out if they had anyone with local knowledge. They came up with a man who until four months before had been the Maquis leader in the area and was employed at the time at SOE HQ in Baker Street. '*Had this been left to official channels I should never have known of his existence.*'

Franks also discovered that some of the six possible dropping zones notified to him by SFHQ were in fact unsuitable for dropping men and that the Maquis in the area had not been supplied with anything since D-DAY. His plan had been to accompany his initial recce party with four aircraft carrying sufficient weapons and ammunition to arm the Maquis so that they could protect the dropping zones. However he discovered that SFHQ intended to drop these supplies in one of their own operations, using the DZs designated for 2 SAS,

90 *Funkspiel* – literally radio game. The use of captured radio operators working under duress to send false messages to SOE headquarters, some of which resulted in the delivery of additional agents into German ambushes, and their subsequent death or capture.

which could well have been compromised as a result. He summed up the attitude of SOE to the SAS as follows.

> *There is a prevalent view amongst some members of the staff at SOE, that uniform troops are not welcomed by the Maquis, and further, that in known Maquis areas, it is better to supply them with arms and explosives and let them do the tasks rather than send SAS to the area. This is in strict contradiction to the views of both French and British Maquis leaders who have returned recently to this country and with whom I have had the opportunity of discussing this question ... Their views are far more likely to represent those of the Maquis than the views of staff officers in London.*

Relations with resistance groups were to dog many of the operations carried out, and the success or failure of an individual mission often depended on the co-operation or lack of it from the Maquis on the ground. This was to have serious repercussions for LOYTON.

*

In the meantime, Brian was about to launch what has been considered the most effective SAS operation carried out in World War II, Operation WALLACE. The operation was to be in two phases. Phase one, Operation HARDY, would establish a firm operating base. Phase two, WALLACE, would conduct wide-ranging mobile operations in an easterly direction heading for the Belfort Gap where it was expected that the withdrawing 7th Army from Normandy and the 19th Army from the south of France would meet and try to establish a defensive stop line on the western side of the Vosges Mountains. It was also hoped WALLACE would be able to link up with the projected Operation LOYTON. The operation would be commanded by Roy Farran,[91] and last from the 27th of July until the 18th of September.

91 Farran had been captured in Crete but had escaped. Standard procedure for those who had been in German hands was to have a nom-de-guerre. Farran's was Paddy McGinty, taken from a traditional Irish song about a goat which ate five sticks of dynamite.

Farran commented: '*Our instructions were to create hell all across France, and to make for the Belfort Gap.*[92] *We were trying to link up with LOYTON, but I didn't quite get that far. Sorry about that. Germans became too dense for us to get through.*'

The operation started with the squadron Second-in-Command Grant Hibbert parachuting in to the 1 SAS HOUNDSWORTH base on the night of the 26th/27th of July with nine men to set up an operating base in the Fôret de Chatillon, north of Dijon, astride the main route from Normandy to Belfort, roughly in the centre of France. The establishment of the base conveniently coincided with the American breakout at Avranches. This created a fluid operating environment which the SAS could exploit, enabling them to infiltrate their 'Jeeping' parties to cause maximum chaos behind the withdrawing Germans. The operation could not have been better timed. On the 19th of August, 20 Jeeps were loaded into Dakotas at Brize Norton. Each aircraft carried a Jeep, and a crew of three men – 60 men in all. They landed on the newly captured Rennes Airfield. Within 24 hours the column of Jeeps was winding through the forest tracks north of Orléans, avoiding pockets of Germans, to the open country in the enemy rear. Farran had trained his squadron in 'Jeeping' very well. They knew exactly what they were doing. His only regret was that he didn't have more experienced officers so that he could have moved in smaller groups of three Jeeps rather than groups of nine: '*If sufficient troop leaders of high quality, reliability and experience had been available, I believe that more damage could have been inflicted on the enemy by widely dispersed troops, only regrouping periodically for resupply. Three Jeeps could have penetrated to areas impossible for a party of nine.*'

Farran pointed out that it was:

> *Not too difficult at all. I'd really been trained in that and had a good idea of how to look by day, listen by night, move slowly, take back routes. I had a pretty good idea how to do it. That's how I*

92 The Belfort Gap or Burgundian Gate is the area of relatively flat terrain in France between the Vosges Mountains to the north and the Jura Mountains to the south. It is strategically important and historically the invasion route in and out of France.

The Vickers K gun

crossed France, the broadest part of France. The way to do it, you take back routes, look at the map, cross the main roads where you can, where there's least likely to be traffic. France is a country with better roads than any in Europe. Napoleon made sure of that. They have roads of every description going in every direction. So it's ideal for Jeep operations. If we kept to the tangle of country lanes we were fairly safe, as the Germans kept mostly to the metalled roads.

He also laid down some clear guidance for Jeep ambushes of columns of vehicles. Every ambush must be well sited. Sacrificing concealment for surprise, employing devastating fire from the Jeeps' Vickers K guns,[93] supported by Bren guns, for a short sharp engagement followed by a very swift exit along a properly prepared escape route. The escape route was always a critical part of the plan. '*As soon as sufficient damage had been done the Jeeps must disappear. It is not necessary to stay long enough to count the bodies.*'

Grant Hibbert launched his part of the operation from 1 SAS's HOUNDSWORTH base where he had received much advice from squadron commander Major Bill Fraser, one of the SAS 'originals', and from Paddy Mayne who was visiting the base. Hibbert moved

93 The Vickers K gun, originally designed for aircraft, had a high rate of fire – 900 rounds per minute. Each gun had a magazine of 100 rounds but only 97 were ever loaded to prevent jamming. Each Jeep carried 20 magazines per gun.

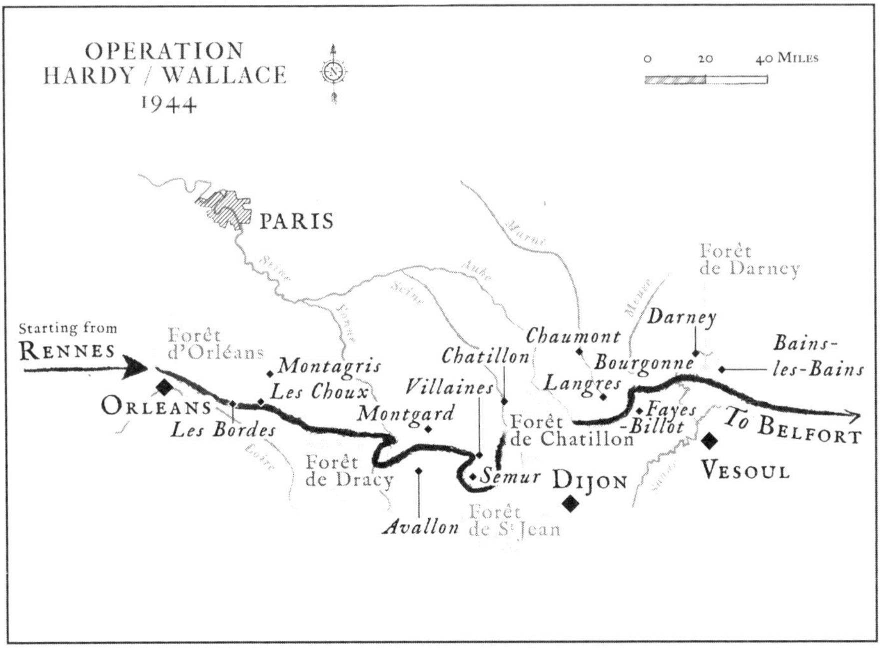

out and successfully established the HARDY base in the Fôret de Chatillon, where they made contact with the local Resistance, who warned him that the previous month a force of 2,000 Germans had swept the area and killed 37 Maquisards. Hibbert's orders were to establish and receive supply drops to create a stockpile for future mobile operations.

Hibbert needed to know what was going on in the surrounding area and carried out a series of reconnaissance patrols to determine the Germans' strength and dispositions. He also undertook some more aggressive operations against rail and road communications over which reinforcements could be moved. Crucially, they blew up a stretch of railway between Dijon and Langres and decimated a German convoy which was heading towards the Normandy front. Supply drops were successfully carried out on the 8th, 17th, 20th and 23rd of August. Communications with 2 SAS HQ were excellent and Brian, monitoring the operation from his operations room with Roy Farran, gave the go-ahead for the next phase, WALLACE.

Parme Souris Farm Tannerre-en-Puisaye, 22 August 1944

The journey from Rennes to Hibbert's position 200 miles behind German lines took Farran four days. The first 50 miles were uneventful, as local French Resistance fighters were able to help the SAS troopers avoid German positions. Things didn't always quite go according to plan. On the first day Sergeant Forrester's Jeep became separated from his column. However he used his initiative and knowing the RV in the Fôret de Chatillon made his own way there. He had a number of adventures en route including a head-on collision with a German staff car. The car came off worse and Forrester jumped out and shot four senior German officers.

The main body continued their journey, much to the delight of the local population along the route. Lieutenant Raymond Lee, of Operation GAFF fame, Farran's French-speaking officer, was invaluable in eliciting and sifting the conflicting information about German dispositions given to them by the locals. In a few days' time he would not be so popular.

Farran was keen to join up with Grant Hibbert without any major contact with the enemy. He split his squadron into three groups: five Jeeps under command of Raymond Lee, eight under Farran himself, and the remainder under Lieutenant David Leigh, another experienced officer. Each group was to leave at 30-minute intervals along the same route. Farran was clear in his orders: '*Bypass all opposition.*'

Unfortunately Lee's temperament got the better of him and, arriving at the village of Mailly-le-Château, he engaged the enemy on the east bank of the River Yonne, losing one Jeep in the process, although its crew escaped. Following on behind, Farran came under fire but managed to disengage, warn Leigh's troop and find another route through. All three groups met up at the next RV point in the Fôret de St Jean over 100 miles behind the front. Farran was furious with Lee for disobeying orders. He debated getting rid of him at the next available opportunity but, after consultation with Brian via radio, he decided to keep him as his French was so valuable, although he reduced his command to two Jeeps. The next morning they left before first light and had gone only about ten miles when Lee ran into the enemy again, in the village of Villaines-les-Prévôtes. These were experienced Afrika Korps troops and a serious battle ensued. Both of Lee's Jeeps were knocked out. Lee, as ever, fought bravely and escaped on foot but three of Farran's best men were killed.

Farran was moving up faster than he should have – assuming Lee would warn him of any opposition. Unaware of the battle in Villaines-les-Prévôtes, Farran turned the corner into the village and came face to face with a 75mm anti-tank gun blocking the road. It fired a shot at them from about 30 feet. Luckily they were so close that it roared over their heads. They had overturned their Jeep as they skidded to a halt, and were scrambling away when Farran remembered their codes and marked maps. Carpendale, the signals officer, crawled back and retrieved them. All hell was breaking loose around them. Farran reorganised his men and they were eventually able to break contact and get away on the remaining Jeeps cross country.

David Leigh had not been able to avoid the enemy. He was killed and his party sustained heavy casualties. The survivors got away and eventually joined up with Raymond Lee.

Next morning Farran found himself with only seven Jeeps out of his original 20. He was determined to press on as fast as possible to the Fôret de Chatillon base, and to report to Brian Franks on the next schedule. Just after first light they found themselves at a level crossing with a goods train approaching. They deployed the Jeeps quickly and raked the train, destroying the engine and killing the Germans on board.

By now they were close to Grant Hibbert's base. Farran sent two

Jeeps forward under Jim Mackie to make contact, which they did, but not before another skirmish in which they killed another 30 Germans.

Farran was relieved to make it through to join Grant Hibbert on the 24th of August, and they spent a few hours taking stock. Hibbert had set up an excellent camp, well concealed with fuel, food and ammunition dispersed over a wide area. He had established a link with a large Maquis group at Aignay-le-Duc about 15 miles away. Sensibly, because of the different operating styles, discipline and operational security, he kept them at arm's length. This was a very wise move, as will be seen later on during Operation LOYTON.

Hibbert had just started offensive action, attacking a number of vehicle convoys and the main rail line near Dijon. This had stirred up the Germans. That night Farran discussed the next move with Brian Franks on the radio. They agreed that Farran should move camp further east. They also discussed the need to have a static base as opposed to keeping mobile and arranging resupply by air. Brian told Farran that Operation LOYTON had been launched on the 12th/13th of August and was not going as well as he had hoped. He ordered Farran to expedite matters and push on to join up with LOYTON as soon as possible. He also explained that as he now had the bulk of the regiment deployed in France, he, like Paddy Mayne with 1 SAS, was going to parachute in to the LOYTON base within the next few days. He also brought him up to date with news of Raymond Lee.

*

Lee, having extracted from the fight at Villaines-les-Prévôtes, made his way with six Jeeps to the 1 SAS HOUNDSWORTH base. He intended to resupply, rearm and then make his way to join Farran.

On the 26th of August: '*Farran to Franks: Lee must hurry here.*' Lee dithered; news was coming in of the liberation of Paris, and at some point he decided to disobey orders, go absent without leave, and head for Paris with his Jeeps. His trail was picked up at Orléans and Brian signalled Farran: '*Franks to Farran: I'm furious with Lee making every effort to turn him east.*' Farran was livid. '*Farran to Franks: Put under close arrest.*'

On the 31st of August Farran was still expecting Lee and his Jeeps but by the 27th of August Lee had arrived in Paris, with four officers: Manners, Birtwistle, Gurney and Robinson, and 17 soldiers. They were probably the first British troops to enter Paris, driving up the Champs-Elysées to Fouquet's Brasserie where they intended to celebrate with a delicious lunch. Unfortunately there was no food but a very good cellar. They cooked up army rations on the floor and washed down their bully beef and biscuits with champagne. They then moved to the Hôtel Louvois.

On the 29th of August Lee revealed his hand. He took John Manners to the townhouse of the de Broglie family. There they met the Comte Alex de Castéja in whose château Lee had hidden on Operation GAFF. With the Comte were Jacqueline de Broglie and her husband Alfred Kraus,[94] an Austrian who had spent the war working for Siemens, thus dodging frontline military service. The FFI had him identified as an Abwehr agent responsible for the death of many Frenchmen and he was on their kill list.

Lee had a new lover back in London, Roseanne Gladstone, who was related to the de Broglies. Lee wanted to impress her by helping Kraus escape. Brian had put out an alert for Lee and he was soon tracked down in Paris and ordered to return immediately with his detachment to SAS headquarters in Britain. The whole thing then descended into farce. Lee told Kraus he would get him to Britain, where he could enlist in the SAS as they already had many foreigners including Germans in their ranks. To his detachment, Lee pretended Kraus was an important agent whom they had to get back to London.

After more deception, including dressing Kraus as an SAS soldier, and relieving him of a large amount of cash, Lee got Kraus back to England, and handed him over to his wife, who happened to work for

94 Alfred Ignaz Maria Kraus (1908–1978) was born in Sarajevo, Austria-Hungary. An Austrian-German electronics executive, he worked for Siemens and during World War II was linked to the Abwehr in a counter-espionage capacity. In October 1941 he married Princesse Jacqueline de Broglie, daughter of Prince Jean de Broglie and Daisy Fellowes, and entered the world of prominent Franco-British aristocratic circles in occupied France. Contemporary British security records indicate that he was regarded as a suspected intelligence agent figure and remained under Allied scrutiny. His situation showed the relationship which existed between industrial, social and intelligence networks during the Occupation. His marriage to Jacqueline ended in divorce.

the passport office. More shenanigans followed which would end in a court martial for Lee for leaving WALLACE and smuggling someone who was certainly a German agent back to London. The SAS officers reported back to Sandy Scratchley, who was in temporary command while Brian was deployed in the Vosges. Roy Farran had sent a signal wanting them court martialled for desertion in the face of the enemy, which could carry the death penalty. Their defence was that Lee was the senior, experienced officer, and they were following his orders. Sandy Scratchley agreed to a delay and returned them to the field following a flurry of signals to both Farran and Brian. Later, after LOYTON was concluded, Brian Franks agreed to drop any charges against Manners and Birtwistle. Sadly Gurney was dead.

*

Back in eastern France things were moving rapidly, or in the case of General Patton's 3rd Army, not so rapidly. On the 28th of August Farran received intelligence that there were a large number of Germans at the Château de Châtillon about to withdraw. After a full day of successful action, Farran had dinner with Colonel Claude, the commander of the local Maquis. The dinner was a splendid affair during which it was decided that they should put in a joint attack on the Germans at the château at first light. At 0630 hours the attack was opened with 3-inch mortar fire on the château; 48 mortar bombs were dropped on the designated targets. There was no sign of the Maquis and the SAS encountered strong resistance from the German troops in the town. A huge firefight broke out which destroyed several German vehicles and many were killed. Outside the town a reinforcement column of 30 vehicles full of troops was intercepted, and prevented from linking up with the garrison. After seven and a half hours of hard fighting, Farran ordered a withdrawal to their base. The operation was a major success for the SAS: around 100 Germans were killed and a considerable number wounded. In addition nine trucks, four cars and one motorcycle were destroyed. SAS casualties were very light – one killed and two wounded. After the fighting, the

2 SAS and local Resistance

Germans took 50 hostages, thinking that this attack had been carried out by the Resistance. However the discovery of the body of the one dead SAS trooper, William Holland, deliberately left by Farran, prevented their execution. The Battle of Châtillon was over.

On the 4th of September Farran got a signal saying the Germans were withdrawing en masse through the Belfort Gap and he was to do as much as he could to harass them.

Eventually, after some significant resupply drops, including the return of most of Lee's miscreants including Hugh Gurney, Edmund Birtwistle and 'Tanky' Challenor, more Jeeps, spares, ammunition and food, offensive operations were resumed. In an attack at Velorcey, Hugh Gurney was killed and after a very successful operation at Fontaine-lès-Luxeuil, Birtwistle was wounded, his team having killed upwards of 30 Germans.[95]

On the 8th of September twenty men under Lieutenant Bob Walker-Brown, acting on a tip-off from the Maquis, ambushed five German petrol bowsers en route from Langres to Dijon. A motorcycle and sidecar, and a troop carrier were allowed past the killing area before the lead and last vehicles were hit and the fuel bowsers systematically taken out. With all the bowsers destroyed, the SAS extracted themselves successfully.

95 Prior to this action Birtwistle had had a row with Roy Farran, who was still seething about Lee's departure. Birtwistle was tainted. For his action at Fontaine-lès-Luxeuil, Birtwistle should have been awarded an MC.

Edmund Birtwistle at home with his mother

The plan for WALLACE to link up with LOYTON was not to be. The retreating Germans were too thick on the ground. Eventually the WALLACE/HARDY team made contact with the advancing Americans on the 19th of September, who they were surprised to learn were from the 7th Army advancing from the south, not Patton's 3rd Army which had stalled on the line of the River Moselle.

The Germans were pouring into the area, intent on preventing the Allies' rapid advance to the Rhine. Unbeknownst to Farran his commanding officer was embroiled in a desperate struggle just a few miles away in the Vosges. Of the 116 that deployed on HARDY/WALLACE, seven were killed, two wounded, one was missing, and two were captured (though one subsequently escaped). Confirmed damage inflicted on the enemy amounted to approximately 500 killed or wounded, destruction of 23 staff cars, six motorcycles, and 36 miscellaneous vehicles including trucks, troop carriers and petrol bowsers. In addition a dump of 100,000 gallons of petrol and a goods train were destroyed. This was a significant achievement and proved again that 'Jeeping' was not only possible but easy when the enemy front is unstable and fluid, but as soon as the front becomes firm, such actions become much more difficult. The concentration of enemy troops on the line of the Moselle made penetration by vehicles very dangerous and prevented Farran from linking up with LOYTON.

WALLACE was the most successful operation of its type undertaken by 2 SAS, and probably of those of 1 SAS as well. Farran would claim that WALLACE was a perfect vindication of David Stirling's original principles of the SAS – that small units operating behind enemy lines brought a strategic advantage out of all proportion to the scale of the operation.

After linking up with American forces, Farran sent the squadron back to Paris and granted them a week's leave in the capital for some well-earned 'rest and recuperation'. For his outstanding leadership, Brian successfully recommended him for the Distinguished Service Order.

CHAPTER 9 – IN THE MOUTH OF THE WOLF

'A leader has got to dominate the events which surround him; he must never allow these events to get the better of him; he must allow nothing to divert him from his aim; he must always be on top of his job, and be prepared to accept responsibility.'

Field Marshal the Viscount Montgomery of Alamein

'I have always maintained that the men in a fighting unit must be led from the front by a commander they know is willing and able to do everything he asks them to do and probably more.'

Brigadier Mike Calvert

BBC nine o'clock news, Thursday the 10th of August 1944: *'Ici Londres. Les Français parlent aux Français. Voici quelques messages personnels: De Manicoco à Bamboula, l'Abbé Pellegrin visitera ce soir l'anatomie de Bamboula.'*[96]

This is the coded message the Maquis in the central Vosges had been waiting for. It meant that there would be a drop of British paratroops and weapons on to the drop zone codename ANATOMY, on the night of the 12th/13th of August. Operation LOYTON was a '*go*'.

The Vosges Mountains mark part of the north-eastern border between France and Germany bounded by the Moselle river valley to the north and west, the Meurthe river in the west and in the south by the strategically important Belfort Gap, a traditional invasion route into and out of France. On the southern side of the Belfort Gap are the Jura Mountains. The Vosges form the western boundary of the upper Rhine basin, and are divided into three: in the south the higher Vosges or 'Massif des Vosges' with peaks rising to over 4,000 feet. In the centre, the Middle Vosges, a lower range of hills running east from the Saint-Dié-des-Vosges valley towards the higher ground of

96 This is London. The French speaking to the French. Here are several personal messages from Manicoco to Bamboula. Father Pellegrin will visit the anatomy of Bamboula tonight.

The Vosges

Schirmeck and Natzwiller, and in the north a sandstone plateau with an average height of 1,200 feet.

The LOYTON area of operation is the central Vosges to the east of the Moselle and Meurthe rivers. The terrain consists of steep thickly forested hills, criss-crossed with deep ravines and streams. There are several narrow passes which lead to Strasbourg and the Rhine, and then directly towards the industrial heartland of Germany. These were the passes that Brian's men were to deny to the Germans, ahead of a thrust by Patton's 3rd Army.

The tricky terrain was compounded by ethnic allegiances and divided loyalties created by the region's chequered history. In 1870, after the French defeat in the Franco-Prussian War the provinces of Alsace and Lorraine were incorporated into Germany, and the new frontier ran along the crest of the Vosges. Forty-eight years later, after the German defeat in the First World War, Alsace-Lorraine was reincorporated into France. In 1940 it changed hands again. By 1944 the area in which 2 SAS was to operate was divided by an artificial frontier and inhabited by people who spoke both French and German. The majority regarded themselves as French and were intensely patriotic, although there was little organised resistance in the early part of the war. Others felt allegiance to Germany and were happy to betray members of the Resistance.

The terrain appeared ideal for concealment and ambushes, as the enemy was largely confined to the few available roads. East of Nancy

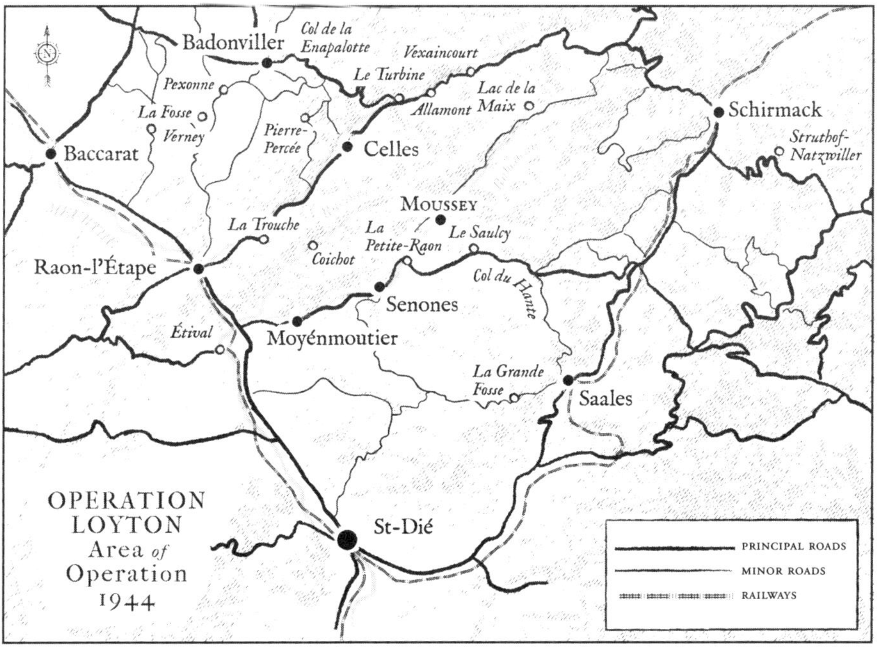

and Lunéville there were few towns of any size and the villages consisted of single streets of houses straggling along the valleys. In the wooded hills, the only habitations were isolated foresters' huts, sawmills, and the occasional small farm.

With the success of the Allied breakout from Normandy and the landings in the south of France, German forces were in retreat and heading for the Vosges from the west and from the south. All was looking good for an Allied pursuit, swift penetration through the Belfort Gap and the Vosges passes, and on into Germany. For the retreating German armies the defence of Alsace was based on both a military and political imperative. The Vosges are a natural defence line, which would allow the retreating troops to regroup and hold the Allied advance during the winter of 1944/1945. Hitler was determined that the Allies should not penetrate the territory of the Reich. He issued an order on the 25th of August to fight a defensive battle '*bis zum letzten Mann*' (to the last man) in front of the Reich's border. The plan was to establish the Schutzwall West, a double line of defence in depth, named Vorvogesenstellung (the Vosges Defence Line),[97] a forward line along the River Meurthe and on the western slopes of the Vosges, supported by a second line of anti-tank obstacles and strong points, on the ridgelines and making use of the old First World War fortifications.

*

After the Bill Stirling fracas, and in the amended planning for D-DAY, operations in depth were very much part of the overall concept for the liberation of France. Even before he had taken over command Brian had been discussing operations in the Vosges with Bill Stirling. SHAEF agreed but practical considerations meant it was put on hold. A decision was taken by the air staff at SHAEF on the 24th of May: *'It is not possible to implement LOYTON in the Vosges because the planes cannot fly that far during June. All preparations for launching LOYTON have to be cancelled.'*

Eventually, following the breakout from Normandy, LOYTON was back on, as part of a bigger overall concept of operations for the use of the SAS. 1 SAS had already been deployed on HOUNDSWORTH and BULBASKET.[98] 2 SAS would carry out Operation RUPERT between Verdun and Metz. HARDY/WALLACE, LOYTON, PISTOL and another unnamed operation would collectively be part of the plan to disrupt the enemy in the Vosges and enable a rapid advance across eastern France to the Rhine.

PISTOL would secure a northern bypass of the Vosges Mountains in the Metz Gap and the Col de Saverne. HARDY/WALLACE would aim for the Belfort Gap, and at the end of August 1944, OP ABEL, a 3 SAS operation, would operate further south in the Doubs. Finally, LOYTON would open the passes of the central Vosges, where the Germans were least expecting a major attack, or so the Allies thought.

SAS Operation Instruction Number 38 issued by Brigadier McLeod to Brian on the 3rd of August set out the intention for Operation

97 Schutzwall – protective wall.

98 HOUNDSWORTH centred on Dijon in Burgundy and BULBASKET to the east of Poitiers in the Vienne.

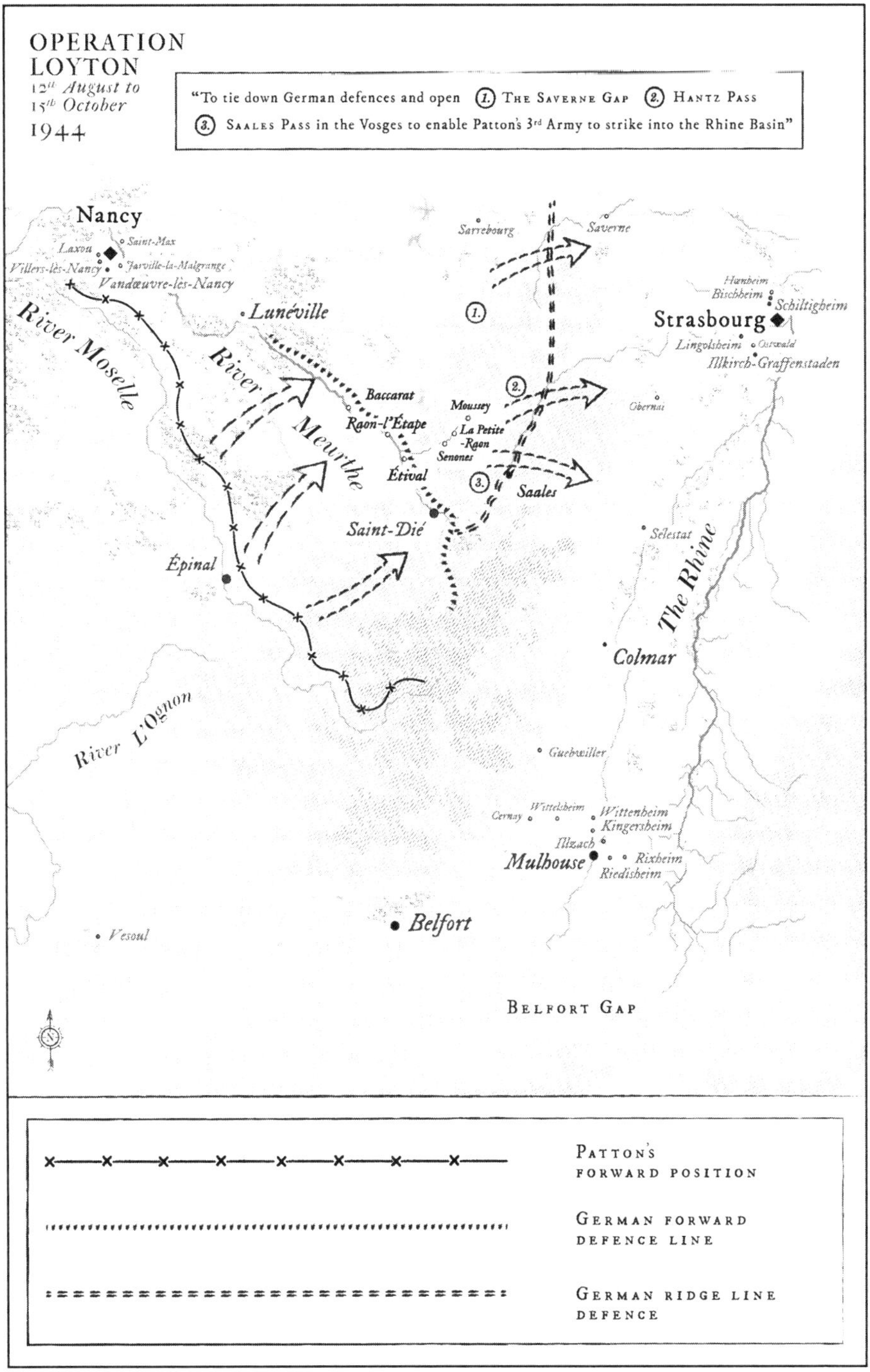
OPERATION
LOYTON
12th August to
15th October
1944
"To tie down German defences and open (1.) The Saverne Gap (2.) Hantz Pass
(3.) Saales Pass in the Vosges to enable Patton's 3rd Army to strike into the Rhine Basin"
Nancy
Laxou
Saint-Max
Villers-lès-Nancy
Jarville-la-Malgrange
Vandœuvre-lès-Nancy
River Moselle
Lunéville
River Meurthe
Baccarat
Raon-l'Étape
Étival
Saint-Dié
Épinal
Sarrebourg
Saverne
Moussey
La Petite -Raon
Senones
Saales
Hœnheim
Bischheim
Schiltigheim
Strasbourg
Lingolsheim
Ostwald
Illkirch-Graffenstaden
Obernai
Sélestat
The Rhine
Colmar
River L'Ognon
Guebwiller
Cernay
Wittelsheim
Wittenheim
Kingersheim
Illzach
Mulhouse
Rixheim
Riedisheim
Belfort
Vesoul
Belfort Gap
Patton's forward position
German forward defence line
German ridge line defence

LOYTON as follows: '*To co-operate with Resistance groups at first in clandestine, and later in overt offensive action in attacking enemy communications, installations, airfields and general harassing of the enemy. Also to assist Resistance groups in becoming organised and in their training. To report enemy movements, including ... a continuous watch on main roads and railways*'. It also pointed out two key factors which would have a big impact when the operation began: '*... the Resistance there does not appear to be fully organised and it has not been possible to send in any appreciable quantity of arms*' and '*... 38 Group anticipate that owing to the distance from bases and uncertain mountain weather, resupply may be difficult and intermittent*'.

It went on to confirm that as soon after the 5th of August as possible a ten-man recce party should be dropped in to a reception organised by SOE. The recce party would be joined by a Jedburgh team to work with the Maquis. Unfortunately a number of things beyond Brian's control were about to coincide, which would make life very tough for Operation LOYTON.

*

The advance party under command of Captain Henry Druce left RAF Fairford on the night of the 12th/13th of August. Druce was not the original commander of the team:

> *I was not supposed to go on LOYTON. The advance party had been set up with a troop commander whose name I can't remember ... At the last moment, I understand, this chap went to Franks and said: 'I really don't feel I can do this operation. I've lost my nerve.' He was indeed a most courageous man to have the guts to turn around and say: 'I can't do it.' So he dropped out literally on the morning they were due to leave for LOYTON, and Franks contacted me. I came rushing down to the airfield, and I was briefed there by Brian Franks and Eric Barkworth.*

The advance party was made up of Druce, using the *nom-de-guerre* 'Drake', his Second-in-Command Lieutenant Dill, Robert de Lesseps

– GOODFELLOW, the Frenchman 'borrowed' by Brian from SIS – and five men from 2 SAS together with a 'Phantom' wireless team of four under command of Captain John Hislop.[99]

The three-man Jedburgh team 'JACOB' was commanded by Captain Victor Gough, with Captain Baraud and Sergeant Seymour. Team JACOB's mission was to work with Colonel Henri Bourgeois – MAXIMUM – to arm and train a Maquis of 200 which was supposed to then support the offensive action of 2 SAS. In addition there was to be a drop of 40 containers of weapons, explosives and other supplies to enable team JACOB to arm the Maquis.

The drop took place at 0145. The DZ was marked by three large bonfires set out in a triangle. There were several small glitches which on their own were largely insignificant but when taken together would set the general tone for the whole operation. Henry Druce was concussed on landing, which put him off balance for the first 24 hours or so. Sergeant Seymour of team JACOB badly twisted his left ankle on landing and needed to be carried on a stretcher. All but one of the LOYTON and JACOB radios had been lost or damaged, which was also to have serious repercussions over the next few days. The Resistance reception team immediately appropriated the entire drop of containers. Brian Franks had briefed Druce to keep control of them until he knew where they were going. This was not to be, as the Maquis leader on the ground had instructions from Colonel MAXIMUM to grab the lot. It was not an entirely auspicious start.

While Druce was recovering, GOODFELLOW organised the removal of the containers and the move to the Maquis camp. The three bonfires used to mark the DZ were enormous and visible for miles from the surrounding high ground. While the Germans didn't attack the drop zone, they were fully aware of what was going on. John Hislop noted that while he was coming down on his parachute, the fires were bright and there was '*enough noise to wake the entire German force in the Vosges*'.

Colonel Gilbert Grandval (PLANETE) had delegated the running of the reception operation to Colonel Henri Bourgeois (MAXIMUM).

99 John Hislop MC. Regular soldier before the war, and friend of Brian's. Served in Jakie Astor's F Squadron Phantom. Outstanding jockey and horse breeder.

John Hislop

Albert Freine

He had assembled a mixed group of Maquis to receive the drop, unarmed men from his GMA[100] Vosges group, men recruited from nearby villages of Moussey and La Petite-Raon to help carry the containers and, by far the most effective part of the local Resistance setup, men from the Eaux et Forêts Service[101] like Albert Freine.

Eventually the chaos on the drop zone was cleared, containers gathered, fires put out and all traces of the drop concealed. The long column of men led by Albert Freine, stretching for over half a mile, eventually moved off for the long climb to the Maquis camp. Progress was very slow but eventually they reached the Col des Herrins camp just before noon.

After some sleep, Druce and GOODFELLOW had a planning meeting with Gough and the local Maquis commanders to discuss next steps. Druce was hardly in a position to argue about the containers of weapons, but it was agreed that in return the Maquis would provide food, shelter, security, intelligence and local guides. In addition MAXIMUM and PLANETE would come the following day to plan the establishment of a base and further offensive action. It was also clear that team JACOB was virtually ineffective. They had lost all their radios, Sergeant Seymour was out of action, and Victor Gough couldn't speak French.

100 GMA Vosges Groupement Mobile d'Alsace, a Resistance combat unit recruited in the Rabodeau and Celles valleys.

101 Eaux et Forêts Service – literally waters and forest service – a cross between gamekeepers, water bailiffs and forest rangers. They would prove invaluable.

The Germans had observed the drop from their positions on the Col du Hantz and also had information from their networks of informers in the surrounding villages. The day before the drop, on the 11th of August, they had begun a counter-resistance operation codenamed WALDFEST,[102] designed to completely eradicate resistance in the area, and create a secure zone for the preparation of their defence lines. Also, unbeknownst to anyone at the time, one of the Maquis commanders on the ANATOMY drop zone had made a list of all the villagers from Moussey and elsewhere who had helped in the operation. This was a very serious breach of operational security and clandestine tradecraft, which in a few days' time would have massive repercussions.

Brian, monitoring events in his operations centre in Britain, was faced with a less than ideal situation: an ineffective Jedburgh team, unable to take on the burden of working with the Maquis command structure, an unco-operative Maquis commander, only one working wireless set, and the initiation of the German counter-resistance operation WALDFEST. Brian felt it was probably time to join LOYTON and take direct command of the operation.

*

The task of establishing the defensive lines in the Vosges was given to Robert Wagner, the Nazi Gauleiter of Alsace, to the west of the Rhine, and Baden on the east. Wagner wanted to ensure that his construction sites were free from Maquis interference. He overestimated the strength and capability of the local Maquis, but nevertheless was determined to destroy them. Wagner ordered the Commander of BDS[103] Alsace, Doctor Erich Isselhorst, to begin the operation. On the 11th of August, Isselhorst was unexpectedly summoned to Berlin to brief Himmler on the situation, so delegated command of the operation to SS Obersturmbannführer Wilhelm Schneider, who set up his headquarters in the Château de Belval.

102 WALDFEST – 'Party in the woods'.
103 BDS: Befehlshaber der Sicherheitspolizei und des Sicherheitsdienstes (Commander of the Gestapo and Internal Security Services).

Château de Belval

Moussey

Schneider gathered a mixed force of his own Einsatzkommandos,[104] Feldgendarmerie (military police) and Wehrmacht regular army units, altogether over a thousand men. Initially the Germans were not aware of the SAS presence although they were busily working all their intelligence assets to ascertain the details of the drop they had observed on the 12th/13th of August. By the 15th Schneider had read an agent report, which came from the wife of someone in the Resistance, confirming the presence of the SAS and giving away the location of the Maquis camp near Moussey. This information was immediately transmitted to Berlin. Himmler ordered Isselhorst to exterminate the Resistance in the Vosges, and the SAS, invoking Hitler's Commando Order[105] – in other words kill everyone.

On the evening of the 16th of August the Germans began their operation by flooding the area with troops. Their first target was the Maquis camp where Druce and his team were based.

*

Henry Druce was becoming frustrated. He wanted an urgent meeting with PLANETE to start planning offensive action and the training of his Maquisards, who contrary to his briefing from SOE, were in a pretty shambolic state. For two days he waited for the promised meeting. Finally, on the morning of the 16th PLANETE appeared, and spent a very short time at the camp demanding more drops of weapons and other supplies for his Maquisards. Druce had no choice but to agree as he needed to use PLANETE's radio post to maintain

104 Einsatzkommando: mobile killing squad.
105 See Annex D.

Jean Granjon

contact with SAS headquarters, and arrange for the planned arrival of reinforcements, in addition to resupply drops.

Early on the morning of the 17th Albert Freine arrived at the camp to warn them that the Germans had arrived in large numbers at Moussey and La Petite-Raon, and that the location of the camp had been identified by a traitor. Captain JOUBERT (Jean Granjon) the local Maquis commander, and Druce made a hasty plan to exfiltrate and rendezvous at the Bois du Mi-Mont. Druce gave out a quick set of orders and the SAS team set off for the new camp, leaving GOODFELLOW and a small group as a rearguard. JOUBERT and Druce were quick to move out, but some of the Maquis dithered, eventually being chased out by the advancing Germans. In the chaos they abandoned a lot of personal equipment including a valise in which the Germans found the list of those who had helped with the initial drop, and the full order of battle of GMA Vosges.

While the Germans were digesting this information and getting it to their headquarters at Château de Belval, Druce's group bumped into a party of Germans and a heavy firefight ensued. GOODFELLOW's rearguard were attacked and had to conduct a fighting withdrawal, during which Sergeant Lodge and Trooper Hall were captured.[106] Druce's group got away but had to leave Sergeant Seymour behind.

106 Sergeant Robert Lodge, real name Friedlander, a German Jew, was executed and his body delivered to the parish priest of Moussey, Abbé Gassman. Hall was kept alive but eventually executed at Natzweiler. His body was identified by Brian Stonehouse, an SOE agent imprisoned at Natzweiler.

He put up a fierce fight but was eventually also taken prisoner. Of all those captured during Operation LOYTON he would be the only one to survive. Sergeant Davis of Phantom became separated. He evaded capture for three days but on the 20th he approached the priest at St-Jean-le-Sauley, Abbé Clément Colin, who promptly betrayed him to the Gestapo.

During the morning of the 18th the SS took over the village of Moussey and took ten hostages including the mayor, eight village councillors and Abbé Achille Gassman, the village priest. All the men aged between 17 and 60 were rounded up and their names checked against the captured documents. Gassman, the mayor and councillors were released; 54 men were taken to Château de Belval, where they were interrogated and tortured; 44 of them were deported to concentration camps. Only eight would return.[107]

By nightfall the situation was looking grim. Druce's team was split into three groups and he had lost three of his men, most of the Maquis were proving ineffective and the area was flooded with Germans intent on killing all of them.

*

While Druce and GOODFELLOW were not impressed with the unco-operative and ineffective structure of the GMA commanded by Colonel MAXIMUM, there was another side to the Resistance, and a parallel structure which was much more low-key and much more effective. It was headed by the Moussey parish priest, Abbé Achille Gassman and his assistant Abbé Mollier. Gassman had been an army padre, evacuated at Dunkirk, but chose to return to his village and set up a Resistance group. '*It was he who had first organised a Maquis here at the beginning of resistance. Without him things might have been very different here.*' Christopher Sykes, Brian's intelligence officer, had never heard of him in all the SOE briefings, because Gassman kept away from both SOE and the GMA.

107 Seventeen of them were shot at Natzweiler on the 1st of September.

Abbé Gassman

Étienne Mallens

> *As the Germans kept so close a watch on him, more close than on any other man, his least abnormal movement was likely to be discovered. He posed as a neutral, and maintained contact with the Resistance only through a very few people and at well-disguised meetings. In the midst of the many secrets of the town his was the most thoroughly guarded.*

Gassman operated a very effective cut-out system. He used young girls from the villages as couriers and worked closely with the other stalwarts of the Resistance, the gamekeepers and foresters who would provide the most effective support for the SAS, providing intelligence, targeting information, food and shelter, as well as acting as guides. Key among them were Albert Freine, Gaston Ploussard, Alcide Charrier, René Folcher, René Lequeux, André Tisserant, and Étienne Mallens.[108]

Christopher Sykes would highlight Mallens and his unique band of operators:

> *Mallens was one of the most villainous-looking men I ever saw. Cruikshank's drawing of Bill Sikes in his night-cap bears a curiously close resemblance to him ... In addition to his terrible appearance, like a good Alsatian he spoke French with hideous*

108 See Annex F.

Germanic guttural consonants, interspersed with little flat vowels ... Add to this a black cap pulled over his brows and a simian gait, and you have some notion of what this ragamuffinly and courageous man looked like. He led a band as singular as himself and much in the same style. They were all elderly men for the job, the youngest not less than fifty, the oldest well over sixty. They came from heaven knows where, they seemed to be a band of old tramps and beachcombers ... They were not a melancholy band, however. They shared a weakness for the bottle with their leader, and on the many occasions when we met they were all alurch in the highest of festal moods.[109] *They ranged over these vast forests, killing Germans on lonely by-roads or surprising them horribly in houses where they were sheltering.*

Henry Druce had from the outset a poor opinion of the motivation and effectiveness of MAXIMUM and his Maquis, with one exception, Jean Granjon (JOUBERT), who ran a very effective group and eventually would place himself and his group under the direct command of Brian Franks.

*

By the 23rd of August the advance party had succeeded in regrouping, helped by Jean Granjon and the forest wardens. They had been joined by a Canadian airman, Lou Fiddick, who had been in hiding with Abbé Gassman.[110] Druce invited him to join the SAS team. Still without direct communications with the SAS brigade HQ, Druce sent a message via MAXIMUM to SOE that the advance party was OK but had no radios, and urgently needed resupply and reinforcements. He received a reply from Brian via the BBC on the 26th of August to JOJO 31 (Druce's call sign): '*Reference signal dated 23 Aug. Still awaiting DZ to send Peter and 75 men. Do not wish send such large party without your further confirmation.*'

109 Sadly Mallens was found dead of natural causes on the 22nd of September in the forest of Moussey La Charbonnière.

110 In addition to his local Resistance work in Moussey, Gassman also ran an escape line for downed airmen.

Brian, monitoring the progress of all his sub-units in north-eastern France, was becoming increasingly concerned. He signalled Roy Farran on Operation WALLACE: '*From FRANKS for FARRAN. LOYTON very sticky with no information of enemy in that area. I am determined to make LOYTON a main base unless impossible not. I am exploring all possibilities. Do you consider it feasible to move east for recce with four Jeeps. If so, I would accompany. More Jeeps available at short notice if required.*'

Druce sent a message via the Resistance wireless link, giving the DZ co-ordinates for the next drop. The Resistance radio operator sent two sets of co-ordinates, which caused confusion in London. In the event on the night of the 27th/28th of August Peter le Poer Power and nine men were dropped in the wrong place, 15 miles west of the intended DZ. Brian initially told him to operate in the area where he was dropped and then to make his way east to join up with Druce. This was a very difficult and tense period for Brian. On the 30th he sent signals to all his deployed detachments:

> *RUPERT 503A (Commanded by Major Oswald 'Micky' ROONEY) received at 17:45: From FRANKS for ROONEY. In view proximity Yanks with intentions VERDUN-METZ, regret cannot send you reinforcements or resupply as men urgently required further east ... Leave you to decide whether worth joining LOYTON or Yanks.*

> *LOYTON 603, POWER at 17:55: From FRANKS for POWER. Regret error in DZ. Your present area very important. Would like reinforce you earliest if you agree. FRANKS going LOYTON night 31/01 with MARX. Hope you will join this party later. ROONEY almost overrun by Yanks ... Can send you Jeeps if required.*

> *HARDY/WALLACE 303 at 18:25: From FRANKS. FARRAN action splendid. Main Yank advance VERDUN-METZ. Your area should remain busy for present. POWER at sheet 15 G 085105. Hope to reinforce him but will keep you informed. FRANKS goes for LOYTON night 31/01. Will give location when established.*

RUPERT 503 at 18:40: From FRANKS. On 29 Aug Yanks at VITRY. Presume you will be overrun shortly ... FRANKS going LOYTON night 31/01, will give location later. You must decide yourself what action to take according to existing conditions your area.

Druce was concerned that due to poor communications Brian was not fully briefed on the situation, and decided to send GOODFELLOW through the lines to get a report to him:

When we were unable to contact London through our radio setup, we thought it best to let GOODFELLOW go back through the lines and describe the picture to Franks so he'd know what he was coming into. What he was expecting to come to and what he did come to were two quite different things. He was expecting to come to an organised HQ, somewhere in the hills, away from any Germans, which he could use as a large HQ that could be resupplied and which he could operate out of. In fact, we'd already realised long before that, that we had to be on the move all the time so you couldn't make caches of arms etc. If you had a dropping of arms in the valley, to get it up the hill was a major operation in itself. To have to move it again would have been absolutely impossible.

Brian and his party of 23 left RAF Fairford just after midnight on the 1st of September. Containers of weapons were dropped first. When Brian landed the first person he met was Dusty Crossfield. '*Hello Dusty, where are the porters?*' '*It's not fucking Victoria Station, Colonel.*' He then saw Lou Fiddick dressed in SAS uniform. '*Who the hell are you?*' he asked. Fiddick explained how he came to be there, and that he would be happy to stay and get stuck in. Brian was delighted, and welcomed him as a member of 2 SAS. All round them the DZ was disintegrating into chaos. Fiddick looked a bit bewildered. Brian reassured him, '*Don't worry, you'll get used to it.*'

Brian was one of those people whose calm and courage were infectious: '*his courage made it easier for us to be brave*'. The Maquis, totally ill-disciplined, were breaking open containers, grabbing weapons, ammunition and food. One Russian member of the Maquis mistook a block of plastic explosive for cheese, ate it and died in agony from renal and respiratory failure.

Earlier in the day the Maquis had captured a prisoner, a Frenchman called Willy Fuchs who they believed was scouting the DZ, intending to lead the Germans there later. Suddenly he grabbed a sten gun, and tried to escape. His guards shouted a warning in German, '*Achtung*'. The other Resistance men thought the Germans were attacking and started shooting wildly in all directions. Brian and his group took cover while Druce tried to sort things out. The prisoner was recaptured and Druce ordered him to be shot. In the confusion Brian, Lieutenant Dill and Victor Gough, thinking the Germans had attacked, hid in a wood at the southern end of the DZ, where they spent the next day, separated from the rest. Towards last light, Brian sent Dill to try and contact Henry Druce.

Brian's arrival did a lot to calm the situation and dispel the aspect of doom that was beginning to settle on LOYTON. His striking presence, tall and imposing, combined with his natural cheerfulness, instinctive and immediate understanding of the difficulties in which LOYTON was operating, all had a massive morale-boosting effect on his men.

*

Brian's deployment to LOYTON on the 1st of September coincided with the day Patton's 3rd Army's advance ground to a halt on the line of the River Moselle 30 miles short of the Vosges. The 3rd Army consisted at various times of between nine and 41 armoured divisions. A typical US armoured division petrol burn rate was 600,000 gallons per day. The logistics plan post D-DAY was based on the delivery of fuel by tankers to port facilities but also by Operation PLUTO (Pipe Line Under The Ocean).[111] Due to technical difficulties and bad weather PLUTO did not come on stream until the 27th of September but on the 3rd of October both of its pipelines BAMBI and DUMBO

111 PLUTO was described as 'strategically important, tactically adventurous and from an industrial point of view, strenuous. Unfortunately too little, too late.'

Red Ball Express

failed. Patton had to continue to rely on 'The Red Ball Express'.[112] This did not bode well for LOYTON as the plan depended on a quick linkup with Patton. The concept for LOYTON was based on offensive action in the enemy's rear to keep him off balance, with the Groupe Mobile Alsace-Vosges (GMA). Resistance groups were to interdict the logistics routes and mountain passes of the Vosges. Timing and synchronisation were critical and for Brian's men to be able to operate and survive a rapid linkup was needed. The initial timeframe for LOYTON envisaged it lasting two weeks.

On his return Dill reported that Druce and his Maquis leaders' party were at a safe house, La Baraque farm, and they wanted Brian to join them. On the morning of the 2nd of September Brian held a council of war with Colonel MAXIMUM. The meeting was fractious: '*Col. Maximum was not particularly pleased to see me as he considered that his DZ was now compromised and he still had 400 unarmed men in the immediate area for whom he had expected weapons on the night before. I promised that I would do my best to obtain arms for him as soon as possible.*' The next day they were joined by Druce and most of Brian's party. The priority was to develop a plan for future operations and to establish a new secure base. Druce went off to find

112 The 'Red Ball Express' was a continuous rolling convoy system on cleared routes, one out, one back, kept clear by Military Police, and closed to all other traffic. Each vehicle had two crews to enable continuous movement. The system worked well but still could not deliver enough to keep Patton moving. Patton's fuel problem was compounded by Eisenhower giving priority for fuel to Montgomery for Operation MARKET GARDEN (17th–25th of September).

a suitable site for the base, returning on the evening of the 4th of September. He had found a place near Pierre-Percée, but also brought bad news about the Maquis. That morning a large group of Maquis shot up a German signals team repairing telegraph wires, very close to the farm where they were lying up. The Germans reacted quickly, surrounding the farm, and in the ensuing gun battle killed 250 of the Maquis, including Captain Baraud from Team JACOB. What became known as the Battle of Villembois was the end of the GMA in that region, although Abbés Gassman, Mollier, and the forest wardens would continue to provide invaluable support to the SAS.

Soon after Druce arrived, the Germans were seen advancing on the farm. The whole party bolted out of the farm into the woods. The farm was surrounded, searched and burnt. They marched all night and arrived at the new base at about 1100hrs the next morning. All was quiet and they received their first resupply drop that night on a DZ near the camp. The following night two planes were due to drop reinforcements, but ground mist rolled in halfway through the drop and only one plane dropped its men.

Brian had decided that the remnants of the GMA were unreliable and riddled with informers so from now on the SAS would keep their base locations secret, always meeting the Maquis at prearranged RVs. The next priority was to start offensive action. Brian sent out two parties, one under Lieutenant Marx, the other under Lieutenant Black to look for suitable targets. Major Reynolds and Captain Whately-Smith were sent to recce a new base as by now it was clear that there were so many German troops in the area carrying out Operation WALDFEST, and so many informers, that a large static base of operations was out of the question. Brian and his men would need to keep on the move.

While the recce parties were out,[113] a company-sized group of Germans appeared and was preparing to attack. Brian gave the order to leave in a hurry, abandoning most of their supplies, and they managed to find a way out before being surrounded.

Making their way across the Celles Valley, they found a new base which was easily defendable. A small gully led up to the base which

113 It is standard operating procedure to always have a prearranged emergency RV to go to.

would easily be commanded by a Bren gun position at the top of the gully. Brian gave clear instructions that they should not open fire at more than 30 yards' range.

At 0930hrs the next morning an enemy platoon started to move up the gully towards the base. Brian waited to hear the Bren gun open up: nothing, the French manning the Bren gun had deserted their post without firing a shot. They were now under serious threat and Brian gave the order to withdraw to the prearranged RV at Lac de la Maix. During the mêlée Lieutenant Black and his patrol became separated. The emergency RV was not defendable so they moved yet again to a new site north east of Moussey. By this time Major Reynolds, Captain Whately-Smith and both Lieutenant Marx and Lieutenant Black's patrols were all missing. Brian sent Sergeant Major White to man another emergency RV. A message was also sent asking for resupply on the 12th. No resupply arrived on the 12th or 13th, but eventually appeared on the 15th. They were helped on the DZ by Étienne Mallens and his band of cutthroats, who Brian thought were '*first-class*'.

Lieutenant Marx had had some success ambushing German transport and had also joined up with Peter Power. They returned to the new base, which Brian had set up on the high ground above Moussey. Power had left Lieutenant MacGregor on the far side of the River Meurthe to attack the main railway line. Brian had another meeting with MAXIMUM, who confirmed that the remains of his Maquis were now in hiding and ineffective. Brian was on his own except for the support provided by the Étienne Mallens group, the JOUBERT group, and the forest rangers.

On the 18th of September Henry Druce returned to camp and told Brian he had captured two Milice agents who had been working undercover and shot them both. Brian continued to try and carry out attacks on the enemy with varying results. Things started to look up on the night of the 19th/20th of September when the Jeeps and six more men were dropped. The Jeeps were put to immediate use with Brian leading a patrol of two Jeeps on the 20th, laying several ambushes – but no targets appeared. Captain Miller also carried out a successful attack on the railway line near Celles, derailing a train and knocking out a German staff car.

On the 21st of September there was a further drop of another three Jeeps and 14 men. On the 22nd Brian went on the offensive with six Jeeps all commanded by officers – himself, Lieutenant Dill, Major Power, Captain McGibbon-Lewis, Captain Druce and Lieutenant Manners. Captain Christopher Sykes joined Brian as his rear gunner. They left at last light for a harbour position in the woods above Celles. Druce and Manners left at first light with their two Jeeps to ambush a main junction on the Senones–Moyenmoutier road. They had just moved into position when they heard a vehicle approaching. On the basis that all vehicles were likely to be German, they opened fire with their eight machine guns. Unknown to them the Germans had allowed the mayor of Moussey, Jules Py, to keep an ancient electric brougham, and it was this that came around the corner. The car was shot to bits. The mayor rolled into the ditch unhurt. He then waved a handkerchief, which attracted another burst. The mayor crawled away down a ditch and escaped. Later that day Albert Freine came to see Brian with a worried look on his face and explained what had happened. As the story was being told a messenger arrived with two bottles of champagne and a note from the mayor saying: '*Merci pour le salut tiré en mon honneur cette après midi.*' ('Thank you for the salute fired in my honour this afternoon')!

The four Jeeps under Brian set off at 0830hrs to recce the Celles Valley with the idea of operating on the main Celles–Raon l'Étape road. On the way they stopped at a friendly farm to pick up information. Brian sent Major Power and Captain McGibbon-Lewis ahead with their Jeeps to ambush the main road, where he would join them later.

Whilst in the farm I heard the Vickers K firing and went outside to see Major Power and his two Jeeps come past shortly afterwards. I covered his withdrawal and followed him to a temporary base. He had found a large convoy and had accounted for three staff cars and one troop-carrying truck.

This early ambush meant that I could not cross the road, as planned, to operate in the Fôret de Reclos. Therefore I decided to go with Lieutenant Dill in his Jeep across country to Allarmont and ambush the road at V 465875 from there. After a very difficult journey I arrived there with Lieutenant Dill, only to find the track down which we had come was too steep to return by; the village of Allarmont was strongly occupied by the enemy and my track led out on to the main road only about 3 kms from where Major Power had effected his ambush.

After reconnaissance I decided to drive down the main road, hoping to find a suitable position from which to ambush transport. According to the map there was a good escape route down the track at V 4586.

We got on to the main road and I reconnoitred this track for a distance of about 600 yards; I found it satisfactory so returned to the main road to join Lieutenant Dill. We were probably seen by a patrol. However, we found a grassy bank on which we waited with both Jeeps. Shortly after getting into position, a German on a bicycle came slowly towards us and we heard men debussing from transport round both corners. We had been unable to test our guns so I decided to fire at the cyclist, who presumably was killed. We were then fired on from a house on the opposite side of the road which was occupied by Germans. Both Jeeps gave the house several bursts and then started to make towards the track; in doing so the rear wheels of my Jeep slipped and the Jeep overturned. I had to abandon it and went up the track on the bonnet of Lieutenant Dill's Jeep. After about 800 yards the track was blocked by some tree trunks. As infantry were now deployed on both sides of the track and coming towards us, we were obliged to abandon the second Jeep and eventually made good our escape.

This action stirred up the Germans who flooded the Moussey Valley. The weather was appalling so Brian dispersed his men and told them to lie low. Power and Druce returned with tales of shooting up lots of Germans in La Petite-Raon, Le Puid, Le Vermont, and Moussey, where Druce excelled himself. Before getting to Moussey he had bartered a massive Marcaire des Vosges cheese from a local farmer. The cheese was so big it had to be strapped to the bonnet of his Jeep. Druce was told there were Germans in Moussey, so decided it was worth a look. He drove into the village followed by Lord John Manners. The pair of Jeeps roared up the road into the main square by the town hall where an SS detachment was forming up. Again the eight machine guns wreaked havoc. At the eastern end of the village they turned and came back for a second shoot. Between them they killed more than 20 Germans. Both Druce and 'Machine Gun' Manners escaped unscathed. Unfortunately the cheese did not.

On the 24th of September an event took place which, together with the subsequent discovery of the murder of his men, would haunt Brian for the rest of his life. At dawn the Germans led by both the Einsatzkommandos, Ernst and Wenger, surrounded Moussey and the six other villages in the upper Rabodeau Valley. The male population was rounded up and held in the main square in Moussey. It was only through the intervention of Mayor Jules Py and Abbé Gassman that this involved only the male population and not everyone. A night of interrogation and beatings followed. In the morning 144 men from Moussey and 309 from the other villages were marched to the Château de Belval, and then sent to Dachau and other concentration camps; 317 out of 453 men did not return.

Over four days from the 26th to the 30th Brian's men regrouped, and moved to yet another new camp. On the 29th Brian decided to send Druce through the lines to the Americans with the Order of Battle of 21st Panzer Division and other valuable intelligence which the Maquis had acquired. Lou Fiddick, the Canadian airman, would go with him. They arrived with the Americans on the 1st of October.

In the meantime MAXIMUM told Brian that he would not conduct any further operations until the Americans arrived. Between the 2nd and 5th of October more successful offensive action took place. The Operation PISTOL team under the command of Lieutenant Castellain joined Brian's group after successfully blowing up the railway line near Sarreguemines.

On the 6th intense German activity found all the Jeeps and cached supplies, forcing Brian to move again. The enemy were all round them and the locals very frightened. The Germans were raiding all possible safe houses and burning them down. There was little food available and the men were down to one 24-hour ration pack each. They were out of explosives and ammunition was low with little chance of resupply. To cap it off the weather was atrocious. They were all permanently soaked. Winter had arrived early with a vengeance, and the American advance had stalled. Brian was also beginning to get reports that some of his men, who had been captured, had been summarily executed.

CHAPTER 10 – ON THE RUN

> 'No plan of operations can look with any certainty beyond the first meeting with the major forces of the enemy. The commander is compelled ... to reach decisions on the basis of situations which cannot be predicted.'
>
> Helmuth von Moltke

Operation LOYTON had originally been planned to last two to three weeks, causing enough damage and confusion behind the German lines to enable Patton's 3rd Army to cross the River Meurthe and advance through the Vosges and into Germany. LOYTON was now in its second month, the Maquis that was due to help the SAS was largely destroyed or ineffective, with the exception of the foresters, the Étienne Mallens band, and the Joubert group, and to cap it all, the American advance had stalled. The Germans, not having to fight a defensive battle for the moment, could turn their full attention to destroying the remnants of the Resistance, intimidating the local population and hunting down Brian's men.

On top of this they had been forced to split into small groups, always on the move. They had lost their Jeeps, and were very short of food and ammunition. The weather had become extremely wet and cold, with mist and fog preventing air resupply. Many of his men were dead or captured. He was increasingly concerned that as the American advance had stopped there was no pressure on the Germans in the Vosges, enabling them to turn all their attention on to LOYTON. From the 17th of September the signals traffic between Brian, SAS HQ and the SAS liaison cell manned by Potter Miller-Mundy at the US 3rd Army HQ highlights Brian's dilemma.

On the 18th of September Brian received a signal: '*15th US Corps expects to be with LOYTON in two days.*' The same day John Hislop sent a message to Jakie Astor commanding F Squadron Phantom at SAS HQ: '*Franks urgently needs to know US intentions ... to know if he should wait for the Jeeps or start operations now with his own scarce resources. Can you find this out via Phantom or any other reliable course as soon as possible.'*

On the 19th Brian received: '*US in your sector intend to push towards the Rhine. GOODFELLOW with 15th US Corps. Confident will join you soon.*' Still nothing happened. Brian continued to operate with what he had in spite of increasing enemy pressure. At 1800hrs on the 24th he signalled: '*Pass info to US ASAP. MOUSSEY MAP 15G 4781 filled with HUNS.*'[114] At 1845hrs he received the response: '*What a mess you are in! How can we help you. Your previous passed to US.*' Simultaneously to Miller-Mundy: '*Urgent. Ask GOODFELLOW when the US will reach LOYTON. Brian situation not good.*' On the 25th SAS HQ requested air strikes in support of LOYTON: '*... situation delicate because of weather and numerous enemy troops on all potential drop zones*'. Brian signalled: '*Food situation catastrophic ... are on our last reserves. The best way to help is to ask the US to come to us as soon as possible.*' Miller-Mundy replied: '*Situation regarding LOYTON is difficult ... They are held up by the enemy and will advance when possible. They will not commit any further.*'

On the 26th Miller-Mundy reported that an attack on the Belfort Gap had been postponed. Brian had sent a long list of targets to bomb, which was passed to the 3rd and 7th Armies but all aircraft were grounded due to bad weather. Brian continued to do what he could to maintain offensive operations. He ordered Lieutenant McGregor's group to move east to join him, and continued to use his Jeeps and foot patrols to attack the Germans.

Henry Druce had been backwards and forwards through enemy lines twice already to deliver important intelligence to the Americans, who were largely unreceptive. On the 5th of October Miller-Mundy signalled: '*Druce leaves for LOYTON tonight. In light of American attitude proposes to advise LOYTON to prepare to return ...*' Later Miller-Mundy received: '*Your suggestion for a return of LOYTON endorsed.*' Brian had already received a signal from Brigade headquarters on the 3rd of October: '*Continue to operate as long as possible but avoid at all costs getting shut in ... it might be advisable to exfiltrate your party.*'

114 HUN: pejorative term used to describe Germans. Brian called them 'grey lice' and the locals in the Vosges 'doryphore' (potato bugs).

Coichot sawmill

Brian took the only decision possible, signalling Brigade headquarters requesting permission to end the operation. This was agreed and on the 9th of October he gave the order to exfiltrate in small groups to reach the American frontline on the western side of the River Meurthe.

I decided to end the operation and instruct parties to make their way to the American lines as best they could. I gave out an emergency RV near the Celles valley, where I would be for the next 48 hours. I moved to the RV and spent the night 10th/11th in a deserted house there. I had with me Major Power, Captain Sykes, SSM White, Captain Hislop and Corporal Owens. On the 11th having received a message from Brigadier McLeod saying that he agreed with my arrangements, my party left for the American lines.

On the 5th Brian told his remaining teams to RV in the woods adjacent to the sawmill at Coichot. The RV would be open from 1800hrs on the 7th. Brian had a number of loose ends to tie up. Henry Druce was making his way back through the frontlines for the third time, so Brian instructed Lieutenant Dill with five men to wait for 24 hours for his return and then exfiltrate. He had still not been able to link up with Reynolds and Whately-Smith (his Second-in-Command and adjutant) so sent a message with Alcide Cherrier to tell him not to try and exfiltrate but to lie low and wait for the Americans. A coded message was sent via the BBC to all patrols telling them if they couldn't make it to the RV to exfiltrate to the American lines from where they were.

Arriving in the area of the sawmill the teams were to witness one last tragedy.

> *The family in the house had helped us in the past and the Gestapo, having discovered this, arrived to take away the husband. Not finding him, they departed after saying they would return and, if he was not at home when they came back they would burn the place down. In the afternoon the Gestapo appeared, five of them. From our hiding place we watched the scene, as from the dress circle of a theatre. The Germans called out the family, an old woman, a younger woman and a child, and started to cross-examine them. The rain was teeming down and they stood in the open while the inquisition dragged on, the victims in a state of terror and distress. It was as much as we could do to resist killing the five Germans, which would have been only too easy, but we dared not to do so for fear of the appalling reprisals on the district, which would have resulted in due course. Besides, we could not have taken the old woman and the child with us, and had they been left behind the probability was that they would have been caught and shot. In helpless mortification we were compelled to see out the tragedy. When they had finished their enquiries, the Germans turned the woman and child into the road, set fire to the buildings and having collected all the chickens and put them into one of their cars, drove away. We went down to offer what comfort we could and to express our gratitude for their loyalty in not betraying us. They had been questioned persistently about our whereabouts and by giving us away could have saved their belongings, but they remained staunch in face of the destruction of all they possessed. Sadly we watched the closing scene. They were last seen walking down the road towards the northern valley, in the pouring rain, weeping bitterly.*[115]

115 Christopher Sykes, *Four Studies in Loyalty*.

Each group were told to destroy their radios, burn the code books, and bury all other kit. They were leaving in the clothes they were wearing, with their weapons and anything they could carry in their pockets. Having done all he could to collect and brief his teams Brian's group of six – Major Peter Power, Captain Christopher Sykes, Captain John Hislop, Sergeant Major White and Corporal Owens – set off. Their plan was to cross the river in the area of Sainte Blaise, head into the Fôret de Sainte Barbe, then via the Grand Bois de Glonville to Domptail which was occupied by the Americans.

They set out in a south-westerly direction, planning to cross the triple obstacle of the main road, railway line and River Meurthe. They moved stealthily through the woods just below the ridge line and reached a position overlooking the river at 1800hrs. Brian and Peter Power moved forward on a recce. They decided to bring the rest of the party forward to lie up in a ditch until midnight and then cross the road, railway and river. At midnight they set off, reaching the river an hour later. Peter Power had crossed the river on his way in to join LOYTON using some lock gates. They spent some time searching for them but could only find a bridge.

By this time it was 0500hrs and would soon be light. To complicate matters they were seen by a sentry who rushed to his guard hut to get a grenade to throw at them, but by the time he returned they were long gone. They had no choice but to swim across. Sergeant Major White couldn't swim but Brian was adamant he would get him across.

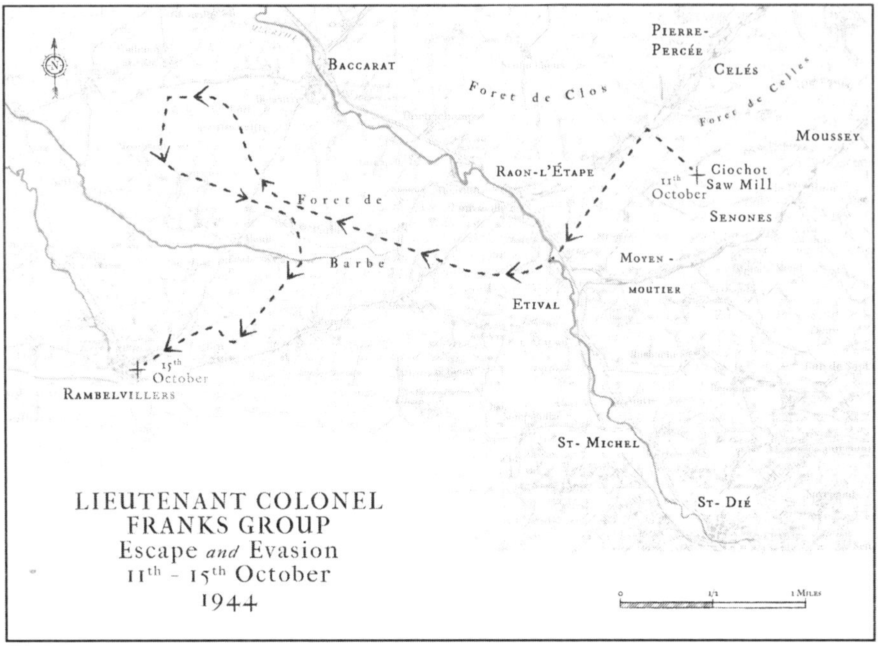

They waded out and luckily the river was shallower than they had assumed, only about chest height, and they were all able to wade across. As they were about to emerge they saw another sentry on the bank, so quickly moved up to the edge of the river until it was safe to get out.

By first light they were well into the forest. They made good time, reaching the Baccarat – Rambelvillers Road at 1600hrs. They crossed the road into the Grande Bois de Glonville hoping to find the American lines. Instead they found themselves in the middle of a well-prepared defensive position: *'It was raining hard and Major Power and I discussed whether they might be friendly or enemy. While this discussion was going on, two Germans came out of their burrows and we took to our heels with several of them firing at us. We ran into a further position, skirted that and lay up for a short amount of time.'* They then headed towards the edge of the woods to try and orientate themselves and work out where the Americans were. As they were studying the map, a hand came out of the darkness and a voice said in German '*Du bist heir*' (You are here). A German patrol had crept up on them but thought they were another German patrol. They ran for it, being chased by some quite accurate fire. Luckily no one was hit and once away they took cover in a potato field immediately behind what they thought was the German frontline.

Brian didn't think they could get through, particularly as the Germans were alert to their presence, so they circled back to try further south near Rambelvillers. They slowly worked their way out of the open ground and back into their cover of the Fôret de Sainte Barbe, where they lay up for three or four hours until dawn. Brian decided to use the cover of the woods all the way to Rambelvillers. They continued all day with little rest reaching a clearing due north of Brû at 1700hrs. They had started skirting the clearing when they were spotted by some Germans. The party split into two, Power, Hislop and Owens, and Brian, Sykes and Sergeant Major White. The Germans chased them into the woods, where both groups went to ground in dense bushes. There followed a very tense hour or so with the Germans (who Brian described as having excellent fieldcraft) moving silently through the forest and jabbing their bayonets into likely cover. Luckily as the Germans were getting too close for comfort, the Americans put in an attack close enough to get the Germans' attention and they moved off in a hurry.

Under cover of the attack the two parties joined up again and moved off south and stopped just short of Brû. Brian took the decision not to approach the American positions at night. At first light they moved off, out of the cover of the woods and into some open ground. While crossing this a machine gun opened fire at them. Brian was hit in the upper left thigh, luckily only a flesh wound which he later described as a '*rather gentlemanly wound*'. They took cover and remained there all day during which they were mortared for two hours. After last light they moved off following a stream towards Rambelvillers, at about 2200hrs reaching some outlying houses which were occupied by the Americans of the 45th Division.

After some food and a night's sleep, they gave the Americans all the intelligence they had on German dispositions and were then taken to Épinal, where the SAS brigade had set up a rallying point

LOYTON escapees: (l–r) Ssm Taylor, Cpl Redhead, Capt Miller, Cpl Sparrow, Cpl Webb

Robert de Lesseps (GOODFELLOW) glad to be out

manned by Potter Miller-Mundy to collect all the LOYTON survivors. All nine exfiltration parties got through to allied lines. The only casualties were in the Phantom group commanded by Lieutenant Johnsen. They were ambushed; Johnsen was wounded but survived. Privates Johnston and Bannerman were killed. Miller-Mundy arranged for all the escapees to be evacuated by air back to Britain, where they reported to Moor Park and were extensively debriefed by Eric Barkworth.

*

After LOYTON there was the inevitable debrief, and as is the SAS way, a full and frank exchange of views. The official LOYTON report was written immediately on return to Wivenhoe. It runs to over 100 pages and is very detailed, with a large amount of comment by Brian. In Brian's absence Sandy Scratchley, his Second-in-Command, and Tom Burt the quartermaster had done sterling work in supporting LOYTON.

Tom Burt in particular had overcome a badly organised, convoluted and cumbersome resupply system. There was much to criticise: carbines that arrived solid with rust, bent Vickers ammunition which would have caused jams if not sorted by hand, training bombs sent with bazookas, Jeeps with no oil, and Thompsons with no magazines. '*Four out of six jeep mountings were useless owing to the welding*

Attack on SS Barracks at Vincey School, arrow indicating SS men caught on parade

going before the guns were even fired.' There was quite a list and a severe inquest was held at Station 1090, the SOE equipment packing depot, on Brian's return. It was staggering that such laxness had been allowed to creep into the organisation. In a subsequent report to Airborne Corps HQ, it was stated that on investigation it '*was found that the defective arms came from pre-packed Special Forces (SOE) containers*'.

There was some criticism of the operation in general and of Brian's decision to parachute in to join Druce's advance party. In particular, some believed the whole operation was unnecessary and too dangerous given the German deployments, and should have been called off as soon as the American advance stalled. These criticisms were based on retrospective intelligence reports not available at the time of planning and a lack of understanding of the overall HARDY/WALLACE/RUPERT/PISTOL/LOYTON concept. In fact one of the key intelligence reports was hand-carried through the lines by Robert de Lesseps (GOODFELLOW) as Druce believed it to be critical, not only for LOYTON but also the advance of Patton's 3rd Army. However the report did not arrive until after Brian's party had left.

Some, including Bill Barkworth, believed the whole operation would have been more effective if small teams equipped with foolproof communication had gone in and remained covert while radioing back target information for RAF strikes on high-value targets. However, of the 16 target messages sent back from LOYTON only two were acted on: the successful attack on the SS barracks at Vincey School which killed 200 SS troops and the fuel dump at Nomexy which destroyed eight million litres of fuel.

Brian's decision to join the operation was based on the fact that by the 30th of August most of his regiment was deployed in the large north-east quarter of France, and had been since the 9th of July, on operations RUPERT, HARDY/WALLACE and PISTOL in addition to the unnamed operation to the north of the LOYTON area. At the time he joined LOYTON, it looked as though there could well be a linkup with Roy Farran's WALLACE team. This would enable 2 SAS to fulfil the original strategic concept, with Patton's 3rd Army punching through the Vosges defence line while the SAS and Maquis caused havoc in the enemy's rear and secured the passes through the Vosges. Therefore he would have had most of 2 SAS on the ground under his direct command. Nobody foresaw the stalling of the American advance due to lack of fuel and ammunition and the poor state of the Maquis.

Also one must put oneself in Brian's shoes. The role of a Commanding Officer, whether he be an infantry battalion, armoured regiment, or SAS regiment Commanding Officer, is to be where he can exercise both command and leadership. The post of Commanding Officer – a lieutenant colonel – is a hard one, requiring a balance between leadership by example, and effective command and control. After command, an officer is either on the staff, or a formation commander, which requires a different balance and skill set with little or no need to lead from the front. Soldiers in action like to have their Commanding Officer among them. Leadership in a dangerous and rapidly changing situation is vital, particularly when things are falling apart. It is exactly at that time that soldiers need their Commanding Officer to lead them. Brian provided that leadership.

However, one cannot help thinking that he may have had three other things at the back of his mind: the fact that Paddy Mayne had already deployed to France with 1 SAS, that before he took command of 2 SAS there had been much criticism of Bill Stirling by some of his officers that he did not go on operations, and of course that his own father had died leading his regiment from the front. It is unlikely, though, that any of these thoughts would have unduly coloured his judgement.

Criticism of Brian's decision was clearly made by those who have never commanded soldiers in battle. His decision was quite straightforward. A Commanding Officer is either among his men or a matter of a few hundred metres behind them, not 450 miles away in Britain, commanding from a safe headquarters, at the end of a tenuous communication link.

While LOYTON was tragic for those SAS soldiers captured, tortured and murdered, and for the people of Moussey and the other villages of the Rabodeau who were deported or shot, on balance the operation should be considered a success. It unbalanced the German command in the area, by constant attacks, tying down two divisions of troops, deflecting capability from completing Hitler's last-ditch defence lines in the Vosges and preventing them blocking the Vosges passes through which Patton was to advance into Germany a month later.

John Hislop summed it up:

> *At the time, it added up to an expensive failure – expensive in lives, materiel and effort, with little to show for it in damage to the enemy. In all 92 men took part and 31 were killed, all but three after capture. It was not until later that the discovery was made of the disruption and alarm to which our presence gave rise among the Germans. The troops in the area were kept in a state of permanent tension, never knowing when they were likely to be ambushed, or blown up by a mine laid on a road, or the strength of our force and how to pin it down. Instead of being able to contain the district with a few sparsely scattered units of mediocre calibre, they had to divert an increasing number of first-class fighting troops from the American front until, finally, an entire SS division was withdrawn for the sole purpose of destroying us. This threw a very different light on the operation, for it showed that the comparatively little material damage we inflicted was more than counterbalanced by the number and quality of the German troops which our presence tied down.*

Abbé Mollier

Abbé Gassman and Padre Kent

LOYTON was a defining moment in Brian's life. As well as by the loss of his soldiers, he remained plagued by guilt throughout the rest of the war about the mass deportation of 943 people from the Rabodeau Valley, of whom 661 died in concentration camps and 64 were executed. He was concerned that he and the SAS would be vilified by the people of Moussey and the surrounding villages.

2 SAS would end the war in Norway, and in August 1945 a flurry of signals from Christopher Sykes indicated that the first memorial service for the missing deportees and SAS would take place in Moussey on the 19th of August, and that the French would very much like Brian and a guard of honour of SAS men who had been on LOYTON to attend. Brian was also making preparations to present an SAS guidon to the village.[116] For a while it looked as though Brian and the LOYTON men would not be able to make it, due to the regimental move back to Britain taking place at the same time. Brian did everything he could to attend, arriving there on the 18th with Christopher Sykes, Eric Barkworth, the padre John Kent and Squadron Sergeant Major White.

He needn't have worried. They were welcomed as heroes, and the SAS has returned to Moussey every year since. It had been the suggestion of Abbé Gassman that the remains of the murdered SAS soldiers be buried in a special plot in the village cemetery. Of the

116 It still hangs in the church in Moussey today.

First memorial service

31 SAS casualties, ten had been murdered in the immediate vicinity of Moussey. The entire population of Moussey and the surrounding villages attended the service.

Since those to be buried were of different religions, the service was bi-denominational. A Requiem Mass was said in the church by Abbé Gassman, followed by the Anglican service for the dead conducted in the church by the regimental chaplain, John Kent. At the gravesides the same order was followed: Abbé Gassman performed the Catholic rites, Captain Kent the Anglican ones. Brian read out a letter from Brigadier Mike Calvert:

> *To the citizens of Moussey: I wish to express to you something of the gratitude which all the officers and men of the Special Air Service Brigade ... feel towards you for the selfless devotion and memorable courage with which you aided them in the accomplishment of their tasks. The help you gave contributed in a large measure to any success we achieved, and we are full of admiration for the disregard of danger and generosity of spirit with which that help was given.*

Brian's guilt was somewhat assuaged but some part of it, both for his own men and for the Frenchmen, never left him. He would later say of Abbé Gassman: '*He quietly and inconspicuously organised civilian help, and he gave most valuable information to us. He showed a cool,*

SAS graves in Moussey churchyard, 1945

calm gallantry which I have never ceased to admire. We owe him a great deal of gratitude.'

The struggles of Operation LOYTON are best summarised by Theodore Roosevelt:

> *It is not the critic who counts; not the man who points out how the strong man stumbles, or where the doer of deeds could have done them better. The credit belongs to the man who is actually in the arena, whose face is marred by dust and sweat and blood; who strives valiantly; who errs, who comes short again and again, because there is no effort without error and shortcoming; but who does actually strive to do the deeds; who knows great enthusiasms, the great devotions; who spends himself in a worthy cause; who at the best knows in the end the triumph of high achievement, and who at the worst, if he fails, at least fails while daring greatly, so that his place shall never be with those cold and timid souls who neither know victory nor defeat.*

Brian and his soldiers of 2 SAS were very much in the arena.

For his bravery and leadership Brian was awarded a DSO, Croix de Guerre and Légion d'Honneur, as was Henry Druce. There were also a number of other DSOs, MCs, DCMs and MMs awarded. Jean Granjon was awarded the MBE. The King's Medal for Courage was awarded to seven members of the Resistance including Albert Freine and Alcide Cherrier.[117] In addition many French decorations were awarded to both British and French recipients.

The village of Moussey would be awarded the Croix de Guerre by the French Government on the 11th of November 1948, in recognition of its resilience and bravery.

117 The seven were: Alcide Cherrier, Albert Freine, Rose Colmant, Henri Dory, Lucien Gander, René Le Queuix, Roger Souchet. The awards were presented at the Épinal Chamber of Commerce on the 6th of February 1949. Brian Franks and Christopher Sykes were in attendance. For a full summary of the support given to Operation LOYTON, see Annex F.

CHAPTER 11 – A SPECIES OF BANDITTI

> 'All the time I served with the SAS, I never overcame the impression that I belonged to a Species of Banditti.'
>
> John Hislop, F Squadron Phantom

Brian's leg wound was treated by the Americans. It was described as '*superficial lacerations of the left leg*'. He was well enough to avoid a direct repatriation flight back to Britain, and joined John Hislop and Christopher Sykes for a few days' 'R and R'[118] in Paris, where the atmosphere had not changed much in the two months since liberation. The city had made a remarkable recovery. As well as enjoying the party atmosphere, good food and excellent wine, they went to the races at Longchamp to watch the Prix de l'Arc de Triomphe. At a second day's racing they bet all the remaining operational funds on a 'dead cert'. Unfortunately the horse, Fair Copy, was beaten in a very close finish. On return to Colchester Brian came clean and the accounting team showed '*considerable tolerance*' about the missing funds!

After a short spell in a military hospital checking on his leg wound, Brian took some leave in London with Zoe and Valerie before returning to his regimental headquarters, which was still at Shipton Bellinger. The SAS brigade was spread across southern England with tactical HQ still at Moor Park with the rear HQ at Sloe House, Halstead in Essex. 1 SAS had moved from RAF Fairford to Nettlebed in Hampshire. At the end of October there was a consolidation of the brigade into south Essex to be closer to future operating areas in Holland, Belgium and Germany. 1 SAS moved to Chelmsford and 2 SAS to Wivenhoe Park.

Brian and those deployed on LOYTON immersed themselves in writing the operational report, citing lessons learnt, not only from LOYTON but the other operations in eastern France, with a view to

118 'R and R' – Rest and Recuperation.

Wivenhoe Park

planning future involvement of the SAS in the final stages of the war in Europe. What emerged from all the post-operational reports were three key factors for the future deployment of the SAS, still valid today: working with Phantom had proved the need for first-class soldiers who can communicate from extremely difficult places far behind enemy lines; mutual trust and very close liaison with national intelligence agencies and the ability to work with indigenous forces and among the local population.

There was still both scepticism and lack of understanding of Special Forces among some, not all, senior military commanders and it was in this climate together with the misapprehension that the Germans would give up soon and that the war would be over by the New Year, that SAS brigade started looking for new opportunities for deployment. Brigadier McLeod wrote several papers with suggestions for future operations. He also visited SHAEF headquarters and both 21st and 12th Army groups looking for business. Meanwhile the two regiments consolidated, re-equipped and carried out winter warfare training at Banchory in the Scottish Highlands.

The first breakthrough came on 8 December when a signal arrived from Allied Forces HQ in Italy asking for an SAS squadron to be deployed to northern Italy to work with partisans behind enemy lines. Roy Farran, having returned from WALLACE in early October, and desperate to get back into action, had taken himself off to Greece to advise the embryonic Greek government on operations against communist guerrillas. After a heated row on the telephone with John Bingham, who was temporarily in command of 2 SAS while Brian was away, who had tried to stop him going, he just left. Farran later said that he felt bad that he had not sought his Commanding Officer's agreement but Brian was somewhat preoccupied in the Vosges. When Brian returned from France all was soon smoothed over, and Farran quickly forgiven.

*

Although Farran was detached to Special Forces headquarters in Florence, Brian monitored events closely and kept in touch by signal. Roy Farran and his advance party arrived in Naples on the 15th of December. From the outset Roy was told that he was to be the force commander and not deploy on operations. The first operation, GALIA, took place 12 days later on the 27th of December, in conjunction with the SOE BLUNDEL mission and Ligurian partisans. It was to support a US ground operation in the Italian Riviera between Genoa and La Spezia, and persuade the Germans that a British airborne battalion was operating in the area. The operation was commanded by Captain Bob Walker-Brown.

The drop was successful and on the 3rd of January 1945 they attacked the Genoa–La Spezia road, calling in airstrikes on enemy convoys. A band of about 50 partisans were recruited and armed. An enemy headquarters was attacked with Brens and a three-inch mortar. The following day it was reported that a German prisoner had told them that the German offensive in the Serchio Valley had not been followed up because of '*uneasiness caused by the Allied raid on the coast*'. Farran felt that this was excellent proof of the value of such raids by SAS troops.

Walker-Brown and his men operated in very harsh weather conditions and extremely difficult mountainous terrain for nearly two months. They were hunted by up to 6,000 German troops. Resupply was difficult owing to the weather and the lack of suitable DZs, and many of the SAS men suffered from exposure and frostbite. In spite of the tough conditions, they kept up the pressure, mining roads, setting ambushes and killing a large number of Germans in the process.

Operation GALIA team. Walker-Brown, extreme right

It was a remarkable example of how things should work: SAS, SOE and local resistance forces, all operating together and having a strategic effect out of all proportion to the numbers involved. By the 15th of February, Walker-Brown decided that the area was too hot and it was time to exfiltrate. In his operational report he stated: '*German intelligence by that time had established that we were really fewer in number than at first reported, and I think we had exhausted the potential of surprise and exaggerated rumours. I thought it was time to withdraw from that particular operation with a view to being deployed in another area, where once again we could exploit surprise and rumour.*' Bob Walker-Brown was awarded the DSO for his courage and exemplary leadership.

A second operation, Operation CANUCK, also started in January 1943 in harsh winter conditions. Captain Robert 'Buck' McDonald, a Canadian, led a 34-man team from Roy Farran's squadron parachuting into the mountains of Piedmont near the town of Alba. Their mission was to link up with partisans and attack German supply lines, communication centres, carry out ambushes, destroy rail lines and generally cause mayhem. The operation was a complete success, lasting until April and culminating with the attack and capture of Alba and the surrender of its garrison. McDonald was awarded the MC.

Farran's main body had arrived by sea, and was to come under the command of an American, Colonel John Riepe, who was responsible for all clandestine activity in Italy. SOE was to handle their

2 SAS Vickers machine gun team

Operation CANUCK. 'Buck' McDonald standing on car

administration. This really didn't suit Roy Farran, who was only too aware of the friction between SOE and SAS that had dogged operations in France, so when Walker-Brown returned from GALIA he put him in charge of all resupply in the field, in which capacity he was extremely effective, ably assisted by the officer in charge of air operation, Lieutenant Colonel Jack Profumo.[119]

A number of small operations were mounted, including COLD COMFORT – a 12-man team under Captain Ross Littlejohn, to blow up the main railway line in the Brenner Pass. The weather and intensive enemy activity prevented them from succeeding. Littlejohn and Corporal Crowley were captured and – like those on LOYTON – immediately executed.

The main squadron operation was codenamed TOMBOLA, and Roy Farran was determined to lead it in spite of orders to the contrary. What was in his mind was a large-scale operation involving his squadron training and leading parties of partisans on operations. SOE headquarters were nervous about German reprisals, but their regional liaison officer with the partisans, Michael Lees, had no such qualms and was keen to receive SAS support.

An advance party under the command of Captain Jock Easton dropped in daylight on to the northern slopes of the Apennine

119 John Profumo, known as 'Jack'. After the war Conservative MP. Secretary of State for War 1960. In 1965 he resigned over his affair with Christine Keeler. He was a supporter of the Yemen operation – see Chapter 16.

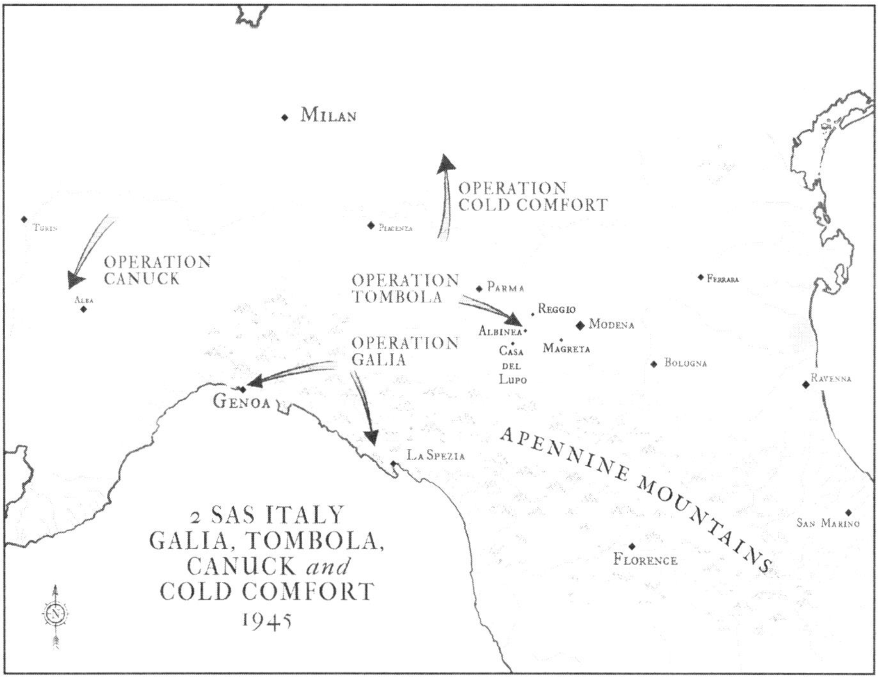

Mountains on 4 March, accompanied by Farran, who was supposed to have acted as dispatcher. Of course Farran had worn a parachute '*in case the aircraft got into difficulties*', and of course he used it, with typical Nelsonian blindness towards his direct orders, feeling that Brian would fully understand and endorse his decision to lead his men on operations. The area where they were to work was in the mountains south of Parma, which overlooked the wide plain that runs east–west across northern Italy.

Farran's party was received by Lees on the DZ and an agreement was reached to form the Partisan 'Battaglione Alleato' under SAS command, absorbing various partisan units but remaining separate from the local command structure. The new formation eventually consisted of 42 SAS officers and men, and a company of 100 Russians, who had escaped from German forced service in the army, led by a former Red Army lieutenant, Viktor Pirogov, known as 'Modena'. They were well armed and efficiently led. The remainder

Training the couriers

Partisan

of the force of 100 Italians was a hotch-potch of Garibaldini,[120] royalists and communists.

Farran had been ordered not to begin offensive operations before the 23rd of March, but to concentrate on training his force, and welding them into a cohesive fighting unit. With his inspired leadership and understanding of human nature, he asked Walker-Brown to provide green and yellow feather hackles for the Italians to wear in their khaki berets and woven badges with the motto 'Who Dares Wins' on their pockets. There was also a group of very attractive women who acted as couriers. They had 'McGinty'[121] embroidered on their pockets and a badge consisting of a bow and arrow. Farran understood the need to give them an identity to be proud of. The final touch of military panache was the arrival of Piper Kirkpatrick, dressed in his kilt, which caused great excitement among the lady partisans. He had been recruited by Walker-Brown while lurking in Florence, and in spite of no parachute training, he agreed to jump. Nothing was too difficult for Walker-Brown. Ordinary staff officers would have found Farran's requests impossible. Farran also knew that Jack Profumo would get him the aircraft: '*There is nothing like a co-operative politician for cutting through red tape.*'

120 The Garibaldini (formerly Brigate Garibaldi) were the principal communist-led partisan formations in Italy during the Second World War. Named after the nineteenth-century nationalist hero Giuseppe Garibaldi, they operated following the Italian armistice of September 1943. They became the largest and most organised guerrilla force fighting German forces in Italy, politically communist in leadership but militarily part of the wider national resistance.
121 Farran's *nom-de-guerre*.

Villa Rossi

Once the partisans were trained and equipped, Roy and Michael Lee planned to attack the German corps headquarters at Albinea in the Po Valley. Initially the plan was approved but at the last minute, when Farran's force was already on the move, the decision was revoked. Again Farran, gambling on a court martial, chose to ignore orders and carried out the attack. A fierce battle developed; six SAS and 11 partisans were killed. Michael Lees was wounded. They killed 30 Germans and blew up the headquarters. Inevitably there was an ensuing row and a move to court martial Roy Farran for disobeying orders. He was well protected by Brian and Mike Calvert, who had replaced McLeod as commander of the SAS brigade on the 3rd of March 1945. In the end the matter was quietly dropped and Farran awarded the US Legion of Merit by Colonel Riepe. Michael Lees was not so lucky. He was fired by SOE and given no decoration of any sort. He was made, entirely unfairly, the scapegoat.[122]

*

Back in Britain plans were developing for the use of the brigade in operations in Holland and Germany. By the beginning of March, Montgomery's 21st Army Group had closed up to the Rhine, and were planning to use the whole SAS brigade (less Roy Farran's squadron)

122 For the most comprehensive account of TOMBOLA, see *SAS Italian Job* by Damien Lewis.

as a reconnaissance and penetration screen in front of the advancing armoured divisions. Yet again this was a total misuse of SAS troops, for a job that could and should have been done by armoured reconnaissance regiments in armoured cars not soft-skinned Jeeps. However the feeling in 1 and 2 SAS was that they would take any opportunity to be in on the last act of defeating Germany, and as ever could adapt their mission to suit themselves as they saw fit, once launched.

Brian would command a composite force of two squadrons, one each from 1 SAS and 2 SAS. It would be called FRANKFORCE. Their operation would be codenamed Operation ARCHWAY. Paddy Mayne would command a second force of two squadrons of 1 SAS, codename Operation HOWARD. Henry Druce, as irrepressible as ever, would command a squadron group in a separate operation, Operation KEYTONE, initially operating in Holland, then catching up and joining FRANKFORCE in Germany.

On the 5th of March 1945 Brigadier McLeod was replaced by 'Mad' Mike Calvert, who brought with him a fearsome reputation for daring and courage while fighting with the Chindits in Burma. Calvert was anything but mad and an ideal commander for the SAS. He understood David Stirling's original principles only too well, and had extensive experience working behind enemy lines. However his hands were tied by the need to find a role for his regiments in the final phase of the war – or face disbandment, a move that was already being mooted in the upper echelons of the War Office. Calvert wasted no time and set up a tactical headquarters at Nijmegen in Holland to command all the operations of his brigade. He made his views quite clear: '*You are special troops and I expect you to do special things in this last heave against the Hun. There will be plenty of worthwhile jobs to do.*'

Brian organised FRANKFORCE as follows: two squadrons of 1 SAS commanded by Major Harry Poat, subdivided into three groups, commanded by Majors John Tonkin, Bill Fraser and Alex Muirhead. The 2 SAS squadron commanded by Peter Power was divided into two groups under Captains Mackie and Miller. They were to be joined on the ground by Grant Hibbert's squadron and Henry Druce. Major Hugh Verney, who had recently returned from his escape from

Jeeps modified for ARCHWAY with armoured glass windshields

an Italian POW camp, would act as Chief of Staff, running the force headquarters.

Before leaving Britain Brian got the whole force together to give them a briefing on the plan and concept of operations. Part of the briefing was given by Eric Barkworth, in which he revealed the existence of the Hitler Commando Order and that many of those missing after LOYTON, and other 1 SAS operations in France, may have been murdered as a result. Barkworth began, '*We must face the situation, which is that any SAS personnel captured by the Germans run a very great risk of being executed and that the fact that they may be wearing British uniform and carrying out a military task is absolutely no safeguard at all.*' There was a heavy silence. Brian then said, '*Any man who wishes to withdraw from this operation and the regiment may do so now with no stain on his record.*' No one moved. They were also given the opportunity to exchange their red berets and winged dagger insignia for black Tank Regiment berets. Again no takers.

FRANKFORCE left Wivenhoe in Essex for Tilbury Docks, where they embarked on landing craft for Ostend, arriving on the 20th of March. Brian had 430 men under his command mounted in 75 Jeeps, and a number of 15 CWT trucks to support their operations and resupply the Jeeps, which had all been modified following the lessons learnt from operations in France. They each now had an armoured glass windshield for the driver and commander, additional weapon systems, notably three-inch mortars, and reinforced suspension.

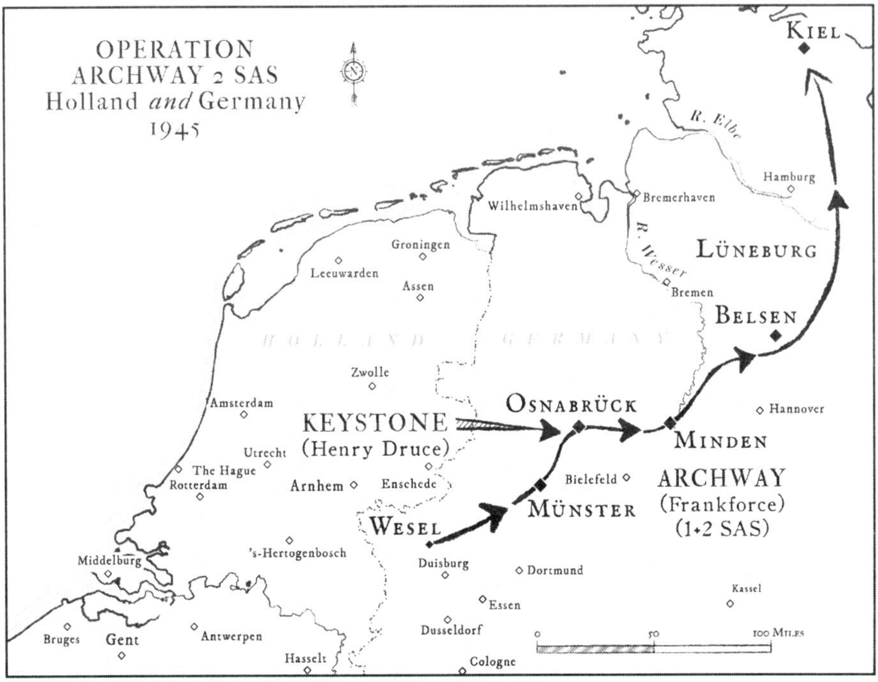

Calvert had issued his Operational Order Number 2 on the 15th of March outlining the two-phase operation: first, operations ahead of the parachute landing supporting the Rhine crossing, Operation VARSITY, followed by the second phase, penetration into Germany ahead of armoured forces with the ultimate destination of Kiel on the Baltic coast.

Brian's outline concept was to attach Hugh Verney and force headquarters to whichever armoured formation they were working with, while Brian would be further forward with a small mobile tactical headquarters mounted in Jeeps to control and direct his Jeep squadrons. Their job would be to reconnoitre the terrain ahead of the advancing infantry and armour, identifying enemy positions, gaps in defences and where possible penetrate enemy lines causing mayhem, by attacking logistics units and headquarters.

FRANKFORCE crossed the Rhine at 1130hrs on the 25th of March 1945, in Buffalo amphibious vehicles, landing on the northern bank

Jeeps loaded on to Weasel amphibious vehicles

FRANKFORCE prior to crossing the Elbe

at Bislich. From then on they followed what would now be called 'mission command' – in other words the senior commander sets out the overall mission, but how it is achieved is up to his subordinate commanders. This suited Brian very well and he passed this on to his squadron commanders, enabling them to carry out the mission as they saw fit. Brian was never far behind the leading squadron, leaving Hugh Verney to co-ordinate with brigade or divisional headquarters and to liaise with Mike Calvert's headquarters or their own regimental headquarters back in Essex.

Whilst the advance was rapid, the Germans proved not to be the pushover that some had expected, resulting in some fierce local actions between the 26th of March and the 19th of April. There were several casualties, including Bill Fraser, who was wounded in the hand. On the 8th of April the lead troop under Ian Wellstead were ambushed driving through a large wood. The troop suffered three killed and five wounded, including Wellstead. On the 14th/15th of April they were the first British troops to enter the Belsen concentration camp just outside the town of Hohne, but realising there was little they could do given the appalling conditions, they withdrew leaving the management of the camp to the 63rd Anti-Tank Regiment RA and the Army Medical Services.

By the 19th of April they had reached the River Elbe, where they paused to rearm and refit. Brian returned to his headquarters and dealt with administration matters such as honours and awards,

Henry Druce: combat sartorial elegance

Checking a road block for booby traps

including those for the French in the Vosges, promotions, replacements and the ever-present question 'what's next?' Grant Hibbert and Henry Druce joined them at the Elbe, which was crossed on the 30th of April/1st of May.

On the 1st of May an incident took place which enabled Brian to at last write a citation for Eric Barkworth:

On 1st May 1945, Major Barkworth as intelligence officer was ordered to interrogate an SS officer who was captured in Schwarzenbek shortly after the crossing of the River Elbe. Finding that this officer considered that there was a possibility that the SS commander who was holding up the advance would surrender his force Major Barkworth went alone with the German officer to the SS HQ to attempt to negotiate a surrender. Final negotiations broke down and Major Barkworth found himself disarmed and a prisoner. Nevertheless he escaped and returned to our own lines bringing with him 70 SS troops whom he had persuaded to surrender. This officer had been intelligence officer of this regt since its formation in Apr. 1943. As such this officer has been responsible for much of the detailed planning of the very large number of small operations which have taken place in North Africa, Italy, France and Germany. The success of many of these operations has been largely due to the extremely careful briefing of the troops taking part. This care in briefing has entailed an immense amount

Lord John Manners and 'spoils of war'

Sergeant Daniels with Bebe

of work and sorting of information at which Major Barkworth has shown the utmost efficiency at all times.

The citation was endorsed by Mike Calvert and Barkworth was awarded an MBE.[123]

By the 3rd of May FRANKFORCE had pushed on to join up with Ian Fleming's 30 Assault Unit helping gather technical intelligence. Hitler had committed suicide on the 30th of April, and on the 4th of May German forces in north-west Germany, Holland and Denmark surrendered.

In spite of some hard fighting and casualties when the end of the war was in sight, the indomitable SAS humour prevailed. John Tonkin sent the following signal: 'T*he 12th of April will go down as being the greatest in the squadron's history. At 1500 hours, alone, and with no supporting arms, it captured, at great risk to the personnel involved, a German baggage. This was an attractive female Luftwaffe corporal. Sergeant Valentine showed great bravery in searching her kit. She was removed as quickly as possible to a POW camp by the squadron commander. There were no casualties.*'

By way of reply Brian passed on a signal warning all personnel

123 Brian later tried to amend the citation to an OBE for Barkworth's war crimes work, writing; '*I am very much hoping that the award may be advanced to an OBE.*' In spite of Brian's strong recommendations, the reward remained an MBE due to '*severe competition and in view of his rank*'.

The Manneken Piss
Brussels, in SAS uniform

to be on the alert for fanatical Nazi stay-behind groups known as 'Werewolves'. The signal concerned the issue of special ammunition: '*Silver bullets werewolves for the destruction of.*' It continued: '*There is ample evidence, both historical, and mythological, that werewolves are only susceptible to penetration by a silver bullet. The lethal effect of such a bullet is believed to be enhanced by the following aids:*

a) The bullet should be blessed by a priest. It is not known whether any particular denomination is more effective in this connection.
b) The firer must be a person of blameless morals.'

After the German surrender FRANKFORCE was ordered to join Paddy Mayne's 1 SAS group at a concentration area outside Brussels prior to embarking for Britain. Much celebration took place in Brussels involving gallons of champagne and horizontal fraternisation before the SAS were ordered home.

On their way across north-west Germany many war souvenirs had been picked up which were traded with rear echelon troops for hard cash. In addition they had come across an abandoned train which happened to belong to Frau Goering. It contained considerable treasure to which they helped themselves: jewellery, furs, rugs and paintings. Jeeps were well loaded. Brian took a large oriental rug which later he had in his office in the Hyde Park Hotel.

John Bingham, back in Wivenhoe, had signalled Brian: '... *best of luck for the rest of this "Do" and the return of 2 SAS in a convoy of Mercedes Benz Cabriolet de Villiers should be an inspiring sight. You might find me a nice telephoto lens for a Contax 3 Camera.*' Little did he know.

FRANKFORCE was ordered to embark for Britain on the 9th of May. Waiting for them at Harwich on the following morning were a combined force of customs and military police. This had been anticipated and Brian gave the orders for all the Jeeps to be revving their engines and all weapons manned. As soon as the ramps went down, the Jeeps drove off at full speed through the docks and away, customs being disinclined to interfere. 'Machine Gun' Manners drove straight to Arlington Street in London, behind the Ritz. En route he stopped to telephone the general manager: '*George, this is Lord Manners. I will arrive in Arlington Street in one hour. Please have the cargo lift entrance open. I will drive in and be taken to the top floor where I would like as many of the staff assembled as possible.*'

'*Certainly your lordship.*'

Within the hour Manners drove his Jeep into the lift, was taken to the top floor where he distributed a considerable amount of 'prizes of war' in the shape of jewellery, fur coats and other assorted 'goodies' to the staff.

ARCHWAY marked the end of the war in Europe for 2 SAS, and had cost seven killed and 22 wounded.

*

On VE Day both regiments received a warning order that as soon as they returned to Britain they should refit and exchange their battle-damaged equipment and shabby clothing, followed by short-notice redeployment to Norway, Operation APOSTLE, to disarm and remove the 300,000-man German occupation force to Germany. In addition, they would guard key installations and assist the Norwegians to hunt down collaborators and war criminals.

Brian's regimental headquarters was a flurry of activity. Under the expert hand of the quartermaster, Tom Burt, sixty new Jeeps were issued, clothing exchanged, weapons checked and accounted for. Brian attended numerous briefings at brigade headquarters and in turn gave out orders for the move. He managed to snatch 24 hours

Brian Franks briefing 2 SAS for operation APOSTLE

in London with Zoe and Valerie, as well as having dinner in White's with David and Bill Stirling, David having just returned from his stay in Colditz.[124] Roy Farran, just back from Italy, joined them for a drink, and they all had a good laugh about his 'accidental' participation in TOMBOLA.

The advance party flew to Stavanger on the 12th of May, with the main body leaving on the 15th. After an initial deployment to Kristiansand, the brigade moved to Bergen, where they were to remain for the duration of the deployment. Brian had mixed feelings about the deployment.

On the one hand he was disappointed that his men had no leave and a very quick turnaround after their three months on ARCHWAY. On the other, he could see the value of a less than onerous deployment to a friendly country, with little or no threat of enemy action, and what would be called in modern parlance a period of post-operational decompression. He wondered how his battle-hardened veterans would react, and knew that he and Paddy Mayne would have to manage things carefully, ensuring there was plenty for their men to do, while keeping a light hand on the disciplinary tiller.

The day-to-day work was not onerous, consisting of disarming the

124 Stirling had returned on the 18th of April to an absurd welcome. All the newly released inmates of Colditz were deemed to be in need of psychological evaluation before returning to normal society. They were placed in a sealed camp with a barbed-wire perimeter. By the end of the first day there was no one left in camp, all having rendezvous in London or heading home.

Germans and stockpiling their weapons – another great opportunity for souvenirs – and assisting intelligence and scientific staff with the examination and dismantling of advanced submarines and other weapons systems. Brian's men were also enthusiastic in hunting down SS and Gestapo war criminals among those being repatriated, in addition to Norwegian Nazis and collaborators. Their biggest catch was the head of the Gestapo in Norway, SS Obersturmbannführer, Ernst Weimann.[125] The memories of LOYTON and the discovery of Belsen were fresh in their memories. They also released 4,500 Russian prisoners and on the 20th of June Brian organised a dinner in his officers' mess for the Russian officers.

The fate of the 31 missing from LOYTON was uppermost in Brian's mind. He had set Christopher Sykes and Eric Barkworth to begin a detailed investigation in France and Germany. With the end of the war in Europe and the return of POWs with no trace of his men, it was becoming increasingly apparent that they had disappeared under the Nacht und Nebel directive.[126]

The other matter that preoccupied him was what would become of the SAS, and what his own future would look like. Mike Calvert returned to Britain in June to lobby for the continued use of the SAS in the Far East, and for their ultimate survival in the order of battle. Calvert was helped in this by David Stirling and Fitzroy Maclean. They lobbied Winston Churchill to deploy the SAS to the Far East. Churchill was supportive and knew the value of retaining the SAS in the order of battle, but he was also one of the very few who knew of the impending use of the atomic bomb on Japan. When it was dropped on the 15th of August it put paid to any SAS deployment to the Far East.

125 He arrived in Bergen in July 1944 as head of the German Sicherheitspolizei. He held the rank of Obersturmbannführer and the title Oberregierungsrat. Sentenced to death by the Gulating Court of Appeal on the 13th of September 1946 as responsible for torture and murder. The judgment stated that he had not personally carried out the ill-treatment. On appeal to the Supreme Court his sentence was commuted to life forced labour. Pardoned by royal decree in 1953 and expelled from Norway the same year. Later associated with the Gehlen Organization, which was financed by the CIA until 1956, and subsequently became an important component of the West German intelligence service.

126 Literally 'Night and Fog', the phrase used by the Nazis to 'disappear' prisoners under the Commando Order. See next chapter.

'Tanky' Challenor and Norwegians – the caption on the back reads 'locals who wanted our bodies – and got them!'

Brian and Potter Miller-Mundy

For the SAS regiment Norway was most enjoyable and both officers and men found themselves very attractive to the Norwegian ladies. This was helped by an endless supply of British and American cigarettes, the use of which in furtherance of pleasurable activities became known as 'fishing for Norwegians'.

Brian, a fanatical fisherman of a different kind, was able to indulge his passion most days. John Hislop became involved with the Norwegian racing fraternity, including riding in several races, one of which he won. Soldiers were kept as busy as possible with sports competitions and the like, but inevitably towards the end of their tour, Norwegian men folk were getting very fed up with the attentions paid to the women of Bergen. Finally things came to a head with 'The Battle of Bergen', when an extensive brawl broke out involving SAS soldiers, the Norwegian police and local males. 'Tanky' Challenor describes what happened: '*The local girls took a fancy to the lads of the SAS whose exploits were for the first time being made public, and naturally enough this caused a great deal of resentment among the Norwegian boys. Three of our lads were beaten up, and this sparked off a mammoth punch-up with the police being called out.*' Although '*a full-on punch up*', no one was seriously hurt, and Brian and Paddy Mayne were able to calm the local authorities. It was certainly time to leave.

Both regiments were back in the Chelmsford area by the 25th of

Surrender parade Bergen. Paddy Mayne (right) Brian (third from right)

Regimental sports day

August. After the post-tour debrief and the handing in of weapons and equipment all ranks went on two weeks' leave. Brian had been getting regular updates on the fate of the 31 LOYTON missing and it was not looking good. He was glad to have attended the memorial service in Moussey but was determined to find out the fate of his men.

On return from leave in September 1945, the disbandment of the regiment was confirmed. The official War Office order for disbandment, Army Order 128, was issued at the beginning of October and the disbandment parade took place in Colchester on the 5th of October. Except for a skeleton staff disposing of stores, equipment and tidying up paperwork, it seemed to be the end of the SAS – or was it?

CHAPTER 12 – NACHT UND NEBEL

'Went the day well? We died and never knew.
But well or ill, freedom, we died for you.'

John Maxwell Evans

'To forget the dead would be akin to killing them a second time.'

Elie Wiesel, Auschwitz survivor

The term 'Nacht und Nebel' (Night and Fog) was the term used by the Nazis to describe those prisoners marked for killing who would disappear into the 'night and fog'. There was to be no trace of them left.

By the time Brian had returned to his headquarters at the beginning of November 1944 after having had his wound treated in the Royal Masonic Hospital, and taking some leave, the full extent of the losses on Operation LOYTON was known. Thirty-one officers and men of 2 SAS and Captain Victor Gough, the sole survivor of Jedburgh team JACOB, were missing, either killed or taken prisoner. Brian had witnessed first-hand how the Germans dealt with the local population of Moussey and the other villages of the Rabodeau Valley and the medieval brutality and ruthlessness of their Operation WALDFEST. He was determined to find out what had happened to his men. He had an intense loyalty to his soldiers, a feeling shared by all his officers but in particular, Eric 'Bill' Barkworth, his intelligence officer. They both had an unrelenting commitment to finding out the fate of the missing men. '*None could be more anxious than men of this regiment to see the murderers of their comrades brought to book.*' Brian felt responsible for keeping the next of kin of the missing men informed with as much information as he had available, which would be little until he dispatched Sykes and Barkworth to investigate.

While still in hospital on the 22nd of October 1944 he wrote to David Dill's step-father:

Nacht und Nebel clothing, Natzweiler concentration camp

I am writing to you about David who I'm afraid is not back yet and it is no good pretending that I am not very worried that he failed to arrive. I last saw him on the 7th October when I left him at our old base near the village of Moussey ... I had arranged a rendezvous with him but had to leave before I could keep it. He had a wireless receiver with him and I broadcast to him telling him to rejoin the American lines.

... David was absolutely first-class throughout the operation ... always cool, calm and collected under the most trying and difficult circumstances ... If you would like to come and see me to get any further details, I would love to see you at any time. I thought you would like to tell Mary as much of this as you feel you should.

By the end of November General Patton had finally got moving and punched through the valleys in the Vosges, as per the original LOYTON concept. Fighting was hard in the difficult terrain and freezing weather, but by the 21st of November Mulhouse had been captured followed by Strasbourg on the 25th. Accompanying the advancing Americans was a 21-year-old White Russian officer, Count Yuri 'Yurka' Galitzine, the son of a member of the Russian aristocracy and an English mother. He had been cleared to work with the Political Warfare Executive.[127] Two months earlier he had landed in the south

127 PWE: The information operations department of the government, charged with damaging enemy morale.

Yurka Galitzine

of France as part of Operation DRAGOON.[128] His first encounter with German atrocities came with the discovery of the Gestapo headquarters in Nice and evidence of extreme torture and the murder of French Resistance and SOE personnel. Arriving in the Vosges he was one of the first into the Natzweiler-Struthof concentration camp and its subcamp Schirmeck-Vorbrück. Galitzine wrote a detailed report[129] on Natzweiler and its associated atrocities, expecting it to be fully published as part of his work for PWE. The report was suppressed as part of a misguided attitude that revealing reports of war crimes would serve to make the Germans fight harder in the coming battle for Germany. This made Galitzine all the more resolved to find out the extent of war crimes, which was to prove fortuitous for Brian's determination to discover the fate of his men. Yurka Galitzine was also a friend of SAS officers Henry Druce, and two of the LOYTON missing, Reynolds and Whately-Smith.

Ominous evidence had been building for some time about the so-called *Nacht und Nebel* Hitler Commando Order. It had started in 1943 with John Tonkin being tipped off that he was to be murdered, and in early 1944 with the escape of Lieutenant Quentin Hughes in Italy after he had also been tipped off by a sympathetic German doctor that the Gestapo planned to kill him. Brian and Christopher Sykes

128 Operation DRAGOON, Allied landings in the south of France on the 15th of August 1944.
129 'Investigation Report on the Life in a German Extermination Camp (K2 Natzweiler) and the Atrocities Committed There 1941–44'.

Eric Barkworth and 'Dusty' Rhodes

had been told by Abbé Gassman in Moussey that he had examined the body of Sergeant Lodge[130] and believed he had been executed with a bullet in the back of the head.

As soon as Brian was out of hospital and back with his regiment he started working on his two priorities: first the future deployment of 2 SAS in what looked like the closing stages of war; second, and certainly uppermost in his and his regiment's mind, to find out what had happened to his missing men. In early December he sent his intelligence cell to the Vosges to start an investigation. Christopher Sykes, Eric Barkworth and 'Dusty' Rhodes were a formidable team. Sykes knew his way around the LOYTON area, and knew all the French men and women who had helped them. The question was how many of them had survived the further onslaught of WALDFEST once the SAS had exfiltrated.

Barkworth, although not deployed on LOYTON, knew every one of the missing men, and had briefed them all immediately before their insertion. He felt responsible for them in the same way as their commanding officer. Barkworth's daughter Amy would say, '*Both Brian Franks and my father had in common an intense loyalty to the men in the regiment and an unrelenting commitment to finding out what happened to the missing men.*'

Eric Barkworth's deployment in December 1944 would start a

130 Sergeant Lodge was the *nom-de-guerre* adopted by Rudolf Friedlander, a German Jew. He was awarded the DCM for his actions on Operation LOYTON.

four-year trail that would eventually lead to the discovery of the fate of all the missing, and to the capture and punishment of all but one of the perpetrators. Barkworth was a man of great education and intellect. Fluent in French and German, he was ruthlessly determined and single-minded, capable of much clever ingenuity in pursuit of his objectives but very fair in his treatment of those he pursued and captured, even though they had committed appalling atrocities against his SAS comrades and the people of the Rabodeau. He also had a healthy disregard for the incompetent or self-servers of whatever rank, and was definitely of the '*rules are for the observance of fools, and the guidance of wise men*' school of thought. The one man he did have a lot of respect for was his Commanding Officer, whom he would describe as '*first-class*' and '*a brave soldier and leader of men, and a thoroughly good person*'. The respect and friendship was mutual. 'Dusty' Rhodes would comment in a letter to Eric's widow in 1986: '*Colonel Franks told me many times when we spoke of Major Bill, that no other officer could have given him the loyalty and guidance during SAS operations.*'

Sykes was nervous as to what he would find and how people would react to him two months after LOYTON: '*I must confess that it was with a feeling of some trepidation that I returned to our town.*[131] *So much had been suffered, and so much of it for our unworthy sakes. But their loyalty was without stint. I was acclaimed as if I had saved the world. We had become a legend.*'

Very quickly the fate of six of the SAS would be discovered. Abbé Gassman and Albert Freine directed them to a farm called La Fosse where three of the SAS soldiers were murdered: Sergeant Fitzpatrick, and Troopers Conway and Elliot.[132] Then followed a visit to the small village of Le Harcholet, where Madame Gerard, the owner of the Maison Quirem, told them she had asked a German soldier what would happen to the two soldiers locked in her barn, Brown and Lewis. She was told that '*they will be shot*'. When she replied, '*Surely not, they are in uniform,*' she was told, '*that makes no difference*'.

Sykes and Barkworth returned to Britain at the end of December

131 Moussey.
132 A full list of those murdered is at Annex E.

1944 with proof that six of the missing had been summarily executed and that all prisoners taken in the Vosges had been handed over to the Gestapo. They submitted their report at the beginning of January. By this time further evidence about the treatment of SAS captives was arriving in Brian's headquarters. During December a letter had been forwarded to Brian from Henry Dunning of the American Red Cross in Paris. It concerned a report from a Mr G. Stell of Mulhouse which said: '*I am sending you a list of names of American and British prisoners of war held by the Gestapo at the concentration camp of Schirmeck-Vorbrück in Alsace*.' The list included Captain Whately-Smith, Major Denis Reynolds, Lieutenant David Dill and Captain Victor Gough. They were known to be alive on the 8th of November 1944. The arrival of the letter coincided with official confirmation that the Commando Order existed. Also in December, four copies were delivered to Brian from SAS headquarters. On the 15th of January 1945 Brian delivered the Sykes/Barkworth report to Brigadier McLeod, stating in his covering letter: '*The report proves beyond reasonable doubt that six men were murdered ...*' It goes on to say: '*Of the remainder ... all the evidence points to their safe arrival at Schirmeck camp ... the possibility of further atrocities cannot be entirely ruled out*.'

Eric Barkworth was so concerned about the implications of the Commando Order for future operations that he wrote a strongly worded letter to Brian on the 20th of December insisting that all troops deploying on future operations should be briefed accordingly before deploying. Brian agreed, hence the blunt warning delivered before Operation ARCHWAY.

*

By the end of January preparations for future operations were underway and both Sykes and Barkworth were needed to concentrate on the intelligence preparations for ARCHWAY. It would not be until 2 SAS returned to Britain on the 10th of May 1945 that the war crimes investigation would resume. During the five-day turnaround between ARCHWAY and the move to Norway, Brian briefed Eric Barkworth that he wouldn't be coming to Norway but would take a team back to France to find out what had happened to the remaining missing soldiers. Christopher Sykes would remain in Britain to liaise with the War Office about potential war crimes investigations and prosecutions. He would also keep an eye on returning POWs in case any of the SAS had survived captivity.

On the 15th of May, the same day as the move to Norway, Brian gave formal orders to Eric Barkworth to liaise with the War Office War Crimes Investigation Team, rather fortuitously commanded by Yurka Galitzine and based at 20 Eaton Square in London. His team would be formally designated the Special Air Service War Crimes Investigation Unit. The team would proceed to eastern France and continue their work. They would also liaise with military authorities on the ground.

The team left for France on the 10th of June and headed across France to Alsace. Not only did they have full backing from Brian, but

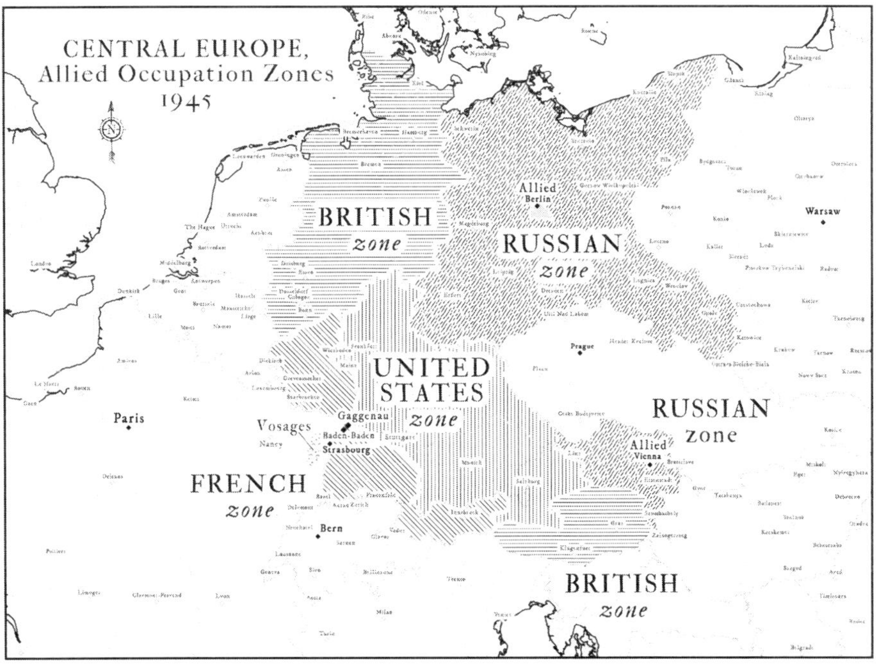

Brigadier Mike Calvert, now the SAS brigade commander, was adamant that '*every effort should be made to apprehend these criminals, to seek out the evidence and bring them to trial*'. Franks and Calvert were at pains to point out that this was not an operation of revenge, but an investigative and judicial process that would operate entirely within military law and the Law of Armed Conflict.

By now all the Germans in France were either dead, in captivity, withdrawn to Germany, or on the run. Germany had been divided into allied zones of occupation: American, French, British and Russian.

The French zone was closest to the LOYTON area and Barkworth chose to base himself in Gaggenau in the German state of Baden-Württemberg about 200 miles east of Moussey. He commandeered a villa, the property of a prominent Nazi, the Villa Degler.

Gaggenau was partly chosen because Brian had received a letter from the French military authority via the War Office, that some bodies had been found buried in the Erlich forest close to the Rotenfels concentration camp just north of Gaggenau, and that one of the bodies had been initially identified as one of the missing. Barkworth's team were the only British troops in the area. The authorities in the British zone were not particularly helpful, and had in general lost interest in anything that would delay their return to Britain. Although officially accredited to the War Crimes Commission, Barkworth's team was considered a nuisance and were not given much help. Barkworth was dependent on his communication with SAS headquarters for logistic

Villa Degler

Villa Degler team

support. The indifference of what was now the British Army of the Rhine (BAOR) suited Barkworth, enabling him to use his considerable guile and initiative to operate quite freely.

One organisation that did provide close and comprehensive support was a US Army War Crimes Investigation Team commanded by Colonel David Chavez which contained pathologists and other experts in the exhumation and identification of bodies. Having been marched into the forest and shot, the soldiers were buried in two bomb craters. Their bodies were identified as those matching the letter sent to Brian by the American Red Cross: Dill, Reynolds, Whately-Smith and Gough, as well as some American airmen. The list of missing now stood at 18.

At Brian's instigation the team was now increased to three officers, 'Dusty' Rhodes and nine men with four Jeeps. The work was relentless. The 'Barkworth system' was based on a diet of whisky, Benzedrine and little sleep, but there was a tremendous sense of camaraderie within the team, and an unshakable determination to find the remainder of the missing soldiers and to hunt down their killers.

In August Barkworth took his team back to Moussey to try and unravel the fate of the outstanding 18. Quite quickly he was able to discover that some had been murdered in the Forêt des Moitresses near Saint Dié-des-Vosges and a further eight at La Grande-Fosse. Private George Johnston, one of the Phantom signallers, was wounded on the 20th of October during his escape and evasion. He was taken to the bank of the River Meurthe, shot, his body weighted, and thrown into the river.

The winds of change were already blowing through the Special Forces world. Franks had visited the team in Gaggenau and saw them again at the first Moussey memorial. He warned Eric Barkworth that it was likely that before the end of the year, the SAS would be disbanded, but that he was working on a plan to allow the war crimes team to continue operating in order to fulfil its role of tracing all the missing personnel and bringing their killers to justice.

He wanted the team to continue to be known as the SAS War Crimes Investigation Team and continue to operate visually with their winged dagger insignia. This was part of his undeclared programme to keep the SAS alive and, after disbandment, rapidly bring them back into the Order of Battle. On the 29th of September Brian received a letter from the War Office referring to Barkworth and his team: '*We are anxious that no misunderstanding should exist in regard to your team. Will you please say in the case of Major Barkworth's team, what was the originating authority for dispatch and to what headquarters and unit they are accredited to*.' As a result Brian concocted a plan with Yurka Galitzine, that Brian would obtain high-level support from his extensive connections and that the team could continue to operate after disbandment, but would be under operational control of Galitzine's department of the Judge Advocate General's War Crime Investigation Staff based at Galitzine's office at 20 Eaton Square. The team would be designated AG3 (VW), standing for Adjutant General Branch 3 – violation of the law and usages of war.

Thus by a combination of influence and administrative legerdemain concerning pay and logistics the team was able to continue its work. BAOR was told to support them but Brian and Barkworth became increasingly frustrated at their apathy and incompetence, so continued to circumvent them and operate on their own. Confirmation of the disbandment came through to the Villa Degler by signal from Brian to Barkworth towards the end of September. Barkworth was summoned back to London to be briefed on the plan for the future of the team. After briefing at Colchester and Eaton Square he telephoned Gaggenau to tell the team that all was well and they could continue their work. Barkworth returned after three days and explained that it was due to Brian's efforts and Yurka Galitzine's support that things would continue as normal, and hinted to 'Dusty' Rhodes that Calvert, General Dill, Randolph Churchill, the Stirlings and Winston himself had all had a hand in it.

By the time Barkworth returned the SAS had been disbanded. Brian had returned to the Hyde Park Hotel where, in addition to his civilian work, he continued to oversee the team's progress and issue instructions and encouragement via signal from Eaton Square, and from a 'Phantom' out-station hidden away in the upper floor of the Hyde Park. Two signallers, Freddie Oakes and John Jumnall, lived in room 403 and operated the radio both at the hotel and 20 Eaton Square.

Life at Gaggenau continued at a frantic pace, flavoured with Eric Barkworth's unorthodoxy – even using a planchette or ouija board to contact the spirits of the missing, with some success. Yurka Galitzine witnessed one session and was somewhat surprised at how it appeared to identify the location of two of the missing men.

A welcome visitor to the villa, at Galitzine's suggestion, was Vera Atkins, who had worked in SOE French Section (SOE had also been disbanded). She was as determined as Eric Barkworth and Brian to find her missing agents. The combination of Barkworth, Atkins and Galitzine was formidable and they worked very effectively together. They were later joined by former SOE agent Brian Stonehouse, who had survived Mauthausen, Natzweiler and Dachau, and was now working for the Allied Control Commission. He was able to prove the fate of four of Vera's missing agents, having seen them at Natzweiler.[133] He also confirmed that Lance Corporal James Hall, one of the missing, had been murdered en route to Natzweiler and cremated there, having seen his body outside the crematorium.

133 Andrée Borrel, Vera Leigh, Sonya Olschanezky and Diana Rowden. Stonehouse saw them being taken to the crematorium where they were given a lethal injection and burnt in the crematorium ovens. In 1985 Brian painted them from memory walking through the camp, to the crematorium block. The painting now hangs in the Special Forces Club in London.

War crimes team on mission. 'Dusty' Rhodes, second right

'Dusty' Rhodes at Moussey, 1970s

There was little official recognition of the team's work. Even the SAS War Diary is suitably cryptic: '*In October 1945, the SAS was disbanded. Colonel Franks came to an unofficial arrangement with one individual from the War Office and the unit continued. It operated totally openly, as if it was official. The unit ended its hunt in 1948, three years after the SAS was disbanded.*'

Yurka Galitzine summed it up as follows: '*Bill found that his missing comrades had been killed after being taken prisoners of war. He found nearly all their bodies and went on to seek out their murderers. They have been traced or arrested in Germany, France, Italy and Austria, over 100 of the Germans involved, and at last brought the criminals to justice.*'[134]

As 'Dusty' Rhodes put it: '*We had a job to do and that was to bring these people to justice, and once we'd achieved that then we thought we'd done our work. But revenge, no, we didn't seek revenge.*'

If it hadn't been for Brian Franks's loyalty to his soldiers and his high-level connections, together with Barkworth's tenacity and determination, this would never have happened.

134 Eventually Barkworth would widen the net to include other crimes against the SAS. Operation BULBASKET when 31 men on 1 SAS were murdered and the SBS Operation FRANKTON, popularly known as the 'Cockleshell Heroes'.

CHAPTER 13 – PHOENIX

'The staff knew so much more of war than I did that they refused to learn from me of the strange conditions in which irregulars had to act: and I could not be bothered to set up a kindergarten of the imagination for their benefit.'

T. E. Lawrence, *Seven Pillars of Wisdom*, 1926

'The British soldier can stand up to anything except the British War Office.'

George Bernard Shaw

The formal order for disbandment of the SAS was received on the 4th of October, effective from the 5th with a completion date of the 16th of November. Officers and soldiers alike were given three choices: volunteer for the Parachute Regiment, return to their original regiment or return to civilian life.

The traditional parts of the Army establishment had not warmed to the idea of what they viewed as '*private armies*', and '*ill-disciplined mavericks*', in spite of Winston Churchill's enthusiastic support for the concept of irregular warfare and special operations. This prejudice was epitomised in an exchange in Parliament in 1943 with Simon Wingfield Digby, MP for West Dorset: '*Is it true, Prime Minister, that there is a body of men out in the Aegean Islands, fighting under the Union Flag, that are nothing short of being a band of murderous, renegade cutthroats?*' Wingfield Digby had clearly been put up to this by one of the opponents of Special Forces. Churchill's reply was entirely appropriate: '*If you don't take your seat and keep quiet, I will send you out to join them.*' Unfortunately Churchill had, unbelievably, lost the General Election held on the 5th of July 1945, and out of office, was no longer able directly to protect his '*species of banditti*'.

At Wivenhoe Park, much was still to be done to meet the target date of 16th of November. One of the first things the officers of 2 SAS did, after the formal disbandment parade, was to hold a ball for 200 guests. In spite of wartime austerity it was a grand affair. Brian and his officers were determined to go out in style. The main rooms in the

Yurka Galitzine enjoying the farewell ball

house were decked out in multi-coloured drapes and curtains made from parachutes. Tom Burt the quartermaster organised oysters and lobsters from Mersea; Basil Bennett and Brian mobilised their London contacts in the wine trade to ensure the party did not run dry. Roy Farran's squadron contributed several barrels of wine brought back from Italy disguised as 'G1098'[135] stores.

In spite of the 'end of term' atmosphere, soon many would experience the difficulty of returning either to peacetime soldiering or to civilian life. Men who had lived on the edge for the last four years with all the thrill and danger of operating behind enemy lines would naturally find it hard to settle into the routine of an army not at war and to a family which had evolved its own method of operating and its own routines without husband or father. John Hislop summed it up when he and his squadron sergeant-major went through the demob process: '*After emerging from the factory of a metamorphose, which received us as soldiers and dismissed us as civilians, we stood for a moment, faintly bemused by our changed state.*' Brian was fully aware of all this; not only was he deciding what to do himself, but with his usual concern for his soldiers wanted to make the process as easy as possible for them. Some would not cope with it and Brian would ensure that he was always there to help them.

135 'G1098' refers to an army unit table of stores, usually controlled stores such as binoculars or watches, which have serial numbers. When a unit moves they are packed in sealed containers and usually not subject to external scrutiny.

To that end he and Paddy Mayne quickly organised a regimental association to act as a support system for ex-members of the regiment and as a means of maintaining an SAS network and database for the future. The first meeting of the association took place at Wivenhoe Park on the 12th of October 1945. David Stirling was nominated President, Mike Calvert Vice-President, and Brian the Chairman, which he would remain for 30 years. Committee members included Paddy Mayne, Bill Stirling, the Reverend McLuskey,[136] John Astor the Phantom Squadron Commander, both sergeant majors of 1 and 2 SAS, SSM White who had escaped LOYTON with Brian, and four other ranks representing the soldiers of both regiments. The purpose of the association was '*to provide a means by which the regiment can keep in touch with one another and maintain the "esprit de corps" and to organise the reunions of members of the regiment in different districts of the country*'. Winton Churchill was invited to be the patron and wrote to David Stirling: '*I accept your invitation with pleasure and I shall be proud to be connected in this way with so many brave and patriotic men.*'

Brian, never really happy with the minutiae of administration, was always very good at delegation. The day-to-day details of disbandment were run by his truly outstanding quartermaster Tom Burt, who had worked wonders during the war and would continue to do so, ensuring that the demobilisation process, and the accounting for stores, went smoothly. Tom was always accompanied around the sprawling base of Wivenhoe Park by Rob, his faithful black and white collie/retriever cross. Rob had been allocated to 2 SAS as a war dog in May 1942, being 'posted' to 2 SAS at Philippeville where Tom employed him to stop pilfering from the stores. As Tom Burt described it, '*pilfering locals became honest men overnight*'. Rob stayed with the regiment and was demobbed on the 27th of November 1945.[137]

As well as planning his future, Brian had two things uppermost in his mind in October 1945: Eric Barkworth's ongoing war crimes

136 Reverend Fraser McLuskey MC, padre of 1 SAS.

137 Rob was later awarded the Dickens Medal, the animal VC, for his work with 2 SAS, parachuting on operations in Italy. There is some debate about the exact details of how many operations Rob took part in but nevertheless on 16 July 1947 he led a parade of 32 war dogs at Wembley in front of 100,000 spectators.

Rob the war dog with his Dickin Medal

operation, and what in Brian's and many other minds was the folly of disbanding the SAS and other wartime Special Forces. SOE was also being wound down and already in the secret world this was seen as very short-sighted.

In order to ease the complexities of disbandment, and to buy time to set up watertight arrangements for Barkworth's support, Brian wrote to the War Office on the 6th of November 1945 asking for an extension to the deadline for disbandment from the 16th to the 30th of November. His letter was suitably vague: '*Most of the men will have been posted to their new units, but there will inevitably be a few exceptional cases which will not be settled by the 17th. After the men have gone there are a number of outstanding questions of various sorts which will have to be sorted out in the Orderly Room …*' More telling and in line with Brian's future plans: '*The Director of Tactical Research at the War Office requires as much information as possible on SAS methods. Records are being compiled but they will not be compiled until after the 17th.*' A similar letter was sent by Paddy Mayne. The War Office Director of Organisation replied on the 12th of November, granting a reprieve until the 30th.

Brian had decided not to stay in the Army. The thought of peacetime soldiering didn't appeal. He planned to return to his old job at the Hyde Park Hotel, where in a reversal of roles he would be working for Basil Bennett. He also needed an anchor point for his dual plan of reviving the SAS and attaining closure on Operation LOYTON. Basil

Bennett fully supported his plan to come back and get the Hyde Park Hotel back on its feet, and at the same time make it an 'alternate headquarters' and rendezvous for the SAS and intelligence services.

*

Brian drove out of the gate of Wivenhoe Park with mixed feelings. He was now a 'civvie' again. On the other hand he had much to look forward to: reigniting his career at the Hyde Park Hotel and getting it shipshape for peacetime, managing the unfinished business of LOYTON, and lighting a fire under those who had misguidedly disbanded Britain's special operations capability. Mike Calvert had told him that the Director of Tactical Research at the War Office was reviewing the whole question of the future of the Special Forces. Brian also had a quiet approach from SIS: '*Would he mind dropping into Broadway when convenient?*' He met his old chum Biffy Dunderdale[138] for a drink at Boodle's and asked him what it was all about. Biffy told him it was probably about Cold War planning. Stewart Menzies, 'C', Chief of SIS throughout the war, had called his regional controllers together, including Biffy who was Controller Special Liaison, and asked them for their views on how special operations of the type carried out by SOE and SAS behind the enemy lines during the war should be developed for the future, given the rapid disbandment of both SAS and SOE.[139] This piqued Brian's interest and he was glad there were others out there thinking on similar lines.

But after six years of war he needed to sort out his personal life, and spend some time with Zoe and Valerie. To that end Brian agreed with Basil Bennett a break from the end of November to the beginning of January 1946, and he went home to Drayton Gardens. Having spent the Christmas holidays together, they discussed how they might organise their lives now that peace had returned. They both felt they would need a country bolthole for weekends out of London. Zoe was a Suffolk girl and Suffolk was easily reached from London. They quickly found an ideal base, Sluice Cottage, on the water at

138 From whom he had 'borrowed' GOODFELLOW for Operation LOYTON.
139 Although SIS had absorbed the pick of SOE personnel.

Broadway Buildings SIS Headquarters

Ramsholt in Suffolk. It was fairly dilapidated but suited them well. Brian bought a boat to potter about in at weekends and invented an ingenious wine cellar. He found an old parrot cage which he would fill with bottles of white burgundy and lower into the well in the garden.

*

In October 1945, at exactly the same time as the SAS was being disbanded, the Director of Tactical Investigation, Major General Rowell,[140] was ordered by the CIGS to investigate the operations of Special Forces during the war and give recommendations for their future. The actual terms of reference were: '*An investigation of SAS techniques, tactics and organisation without prejudice to a later examination of all organisations of a similar nature which were formed and operated in various theatres of this last war.*'

The object of this investigation was to decide whether the principles of operations were correct and if so, what types of units should undertake operations of this nature and how they should be trained and maintained in peacetime.

Mike Calvert grabbed the opportunity and wrote a letter to all those who had commanded Special Forces in the war. The list was impressive and included the Stirling brothers, Paddy Mayne, Brian,

140 Major General Rowell was an Australian, who had been the first Allied Commander to defeat the Japanese on the Koyoda Trail in Papua New Guinea in 1942.

George Jellicoe, David Lloyd Owen and Roy Farran. In the letter he addressed all the criticism of the SAS by the Regular Army[141] and offered some guidance as points for discussion with Brigadier Jack Churchill,[142] Rowell's deputy. Jack knew Brian well from their days in Sicily and one of the results of this consultation was Brian's appointment as adviser to the War Office on future Special Forces operations.

Across at Broadway Buildings a similar process was taking place, hence the request for Brian to *'drop in for a chat'*. On the 1st of January 1946 SOE, like the SAS, had been disbanded and a number of its more effective officers transferred into SIS. Thus special operations and secret intelligence were brought under one roof. This had first been mooted as far back as 1943 in the Bland Report which suggested the absorption of SOE's special operations capability into SIS and that SIS should *'have a small department to preserve and develop expertise in this field of secret action in time of war'*. In February 1946 the Chief of Staff Committee had given SIS the *'task of collating, examining and assisting information bearing on future clandestine operations and the selection of potential objectives for attack by clandestine means'*. In March Sir Stewart Menzies ('C') formed a planning staff, the Directorate of War Planning, within SIS to prepare outline plans for special operations overseas. This would include activities directly against the Soviet Union, now recognised as the new enemy, and activities in preparation for a possible Soviet invasion of Western Europe, so-called 'Stay Behind Operations'. Consideration was also given to subversive threats to British colonies including India, either directly by the Soviets, or Soviet-inspired 'nationalist' movements.

In July 1946, in parallel with General Rowell's review of SAS tactics and techniques, the War Office began an investigation into the *'control of special units and organisations and their relation to MI6 (SIS) activities'*.

141 These included the Private Army; the wasting of Commanders' valuable time; can only be used when the Army is on the offence; overlapping with SOE and other clandestine organisations; not adaptable to all countries; skimming best officers and men from regular units; more expensive; normal infantry would do this work.

142 Jack Churchill DSO and bar, MC and bar, known as 'mad Jack' or 'fighting Jack', had commanded No. 2 Commando in Sicily and later was part of Fitzroy Maclean's mission in Yugoslavia with Evelyn Waugh and Randolph Churchill.

When Brian took up his invitation for a chat at Broadway, he was asked if he would help as an adviser to the War Planning Directorate run by Brigadier John Nicholson, to develop concepts for special operations. Brian was a natural choice as the person most in touch with former SAS soldiers, his operational experiences, and his experiences of the difficulties of working with SOE during the war. Brian's old friend David Smiley,[143] just returned from Warsaw in 1946, found himself '*seconded to MI6 for a year, working most of the time in the office in Broadway ... As a staff officer in the War Planning Section, I had an interesting job for at the time there were proposals for the role of SOE in the last war to be taken over by the SAS in the next one. I worked closely with Brian Franks ...*'

Brian now found himself in an excellent position to push forward his determination to resurrect the SAS as an essential element of the British Army's Order of Battle for future conflict. He was advising and being listened to by both the War Office and SIS.

Brian wasted no time in activating his own network of contacts to help move forward the case for re-forming the SAS. He rapidly enlisted the help of Bob Laycock, Mike Calvert, the Stirlings, General Miles Dempsey and even 'Boy' Browning who was now a full convert, as well as an up-and-coming group of officers who had proved themselves in combat in the war and were not of the hidebound variety, such as Gerald Lathbury, Roy Urquhart, Johnny Frost, in addition to Winston Churchill himself. Much legwork and lunching was done in the clubs of St James's, White's, Boodle's, the Army and Navy and the newly formed Special Forces Club in Knightsbridge. This last, founded by former SOE officers, performed a similar function to the SAS Association, acting not only as a social hub but also maintaining '*a worldwide network which could be activated in the event of a future war*'. While Brian was busy campaigning with his military connections, his work with the SIS War Planning Directorate was also bearing fruit. SIS was directed to:

143 Colonel David de Crespigny Smiley LVO, OBE, MC and Bar. Fought in World War II in Palestine, Iraq, Syria, North Africa with 52 Commando, and with SOE in Albania and Thailand. Later with the Sultan of Oman's Forces, and SIS. He once held the record for most falls on the Cresta Run in one season.

so organise the unified Secret Service that it will be capable in a time of emergency of rapid expansion in order to carry out the requisite S.O. activities in time of war.

To make such preparations as are possible to serve the clandestine operational requirements of H.M. Government abroad, in such cases as the appropriate department of Chiefs of Staff may think fit and subject to the express approval of the Foreign Office.

To study and develop the art of underground warfare and prepare plans for building up subversive movements abroad when such action is authorised by the Foreign Office.

To train reserves of personnel in all forms of clandestine activities so that a rapid expansion of the service is possible in times of emergency.

What was beginning to emerge both in the War Office and SIS was the idea that plans should be co-ordinated so that in time of war an SAS-style military unit should take on SOE's field role. The concept was developing as an important preparation for any possible Soviet military incursion into Western Europe. It envisaged the use of stay-behind parties to form the nucleus of resistance networks, gather intelligence, and conduct surveillance, target acquisition, and reconnaissance, often from pre-prepared hides. In addition the War Office stipulated future roles for this type of unit would include long-range reconnaissance, raiding and that they must be able to operate in any terrain or climate and reach their operational area by any means land, sea or air. Brian was firmly convinced that as most of the wartime Special Forces had the ethos of freethinking 'civilians in uniform', supported by far-sighted regular officers with a maverick streak and taste for adventure, that the Territorial Army might be the best place to create a new SAS regiment. Stewart Menzies thought so too. It would provide a convenient cover to place people who were not full-time SIS officers but had another career, and would be useful in time of war, thus fulfilling the remit to be able to rapidly expand his special operations capability.

In early 1947, in his office at the Hyde Park Hotel, Brian received two phone calls. The first was from General Urquhart, then commanding the TA Airborne Division, telling Brian that his lobbying activities were paying off and that the War Office was minded to create a TA SAS regiment, but that Urquhart thought it should be part of his Airborne Division. Brian listened carefully and was delighted, but privately, with the lessons of 1944 fresh in his mind, was of the view that airborne forces was not the right place, particularly as parachuting was only one way of going to work. He resolved to speak to Laycock, Calvert, Dempsey and if necessary Winston.

His second call was an invitation to lunch from Stewart Menzies at the Carlton Grill in the Carlton Hotel, a very grand establishment on the corner of Pall Mall and Haymarket. When Brian arrived for lunch he was taken to a table for two, placed behind a screen in the corner of the room, which didn't do much for security as it drew the attention of every diner and all the waiters. Brian remembered: '*It seemed to me that every waiter knew we were dreadfully secret and their ears enlarged with each course*.' Over lunch Menzies informed him that authority to form a SAS TA regiment was about to be given, and that he was the obvious choice to command it. The regiment was to act as cover for refresher training for SIS operatives '*in the roughest part of the game*', parachuting training, setting out DZs, demolitions, signals and shooting. This meeting didn't surprise Brian in the slightest as he had had considerable dealings with both SIS and SOE during the war. He took a practical view of both SIS and airborne forces claims on the new regiment, and felt he could navigate his own route to create an SAS regiment that could fulfil all its peacetime training and war roles without being too closely tied to any particular entity.

Once it became clear that authority would be given to re-form an SAS regiment, it would need a home. On and off-the-record discussion took place with the Parachute Regiment, the Rifle Brigade and the Brigade of Guards as possible sponsors of the new regiment, but in the end Brian managed to avoid any arrangement that would entail a quid pro quo. Instead he was able to steer the new home for the SAS towards a regiment with a long, glorious and unusual history: the Artists Rifles.

An explanatory memorandum was issued by the War Office in early April 1947.

It is proposed to include in the post-war Territorial Army a unit that will be trained on lines identical with those of the Special Air Service Regiment in the late war. The Artists Rifles ... has been selected to fill the new role.

As the existing component bodies of the Army Air Corps, i.e. the Glider Pilot Regiment and the Parachute Regiment, are not appropriate to the role of the new unit, it is proposed to reconstitute the Special Air Service Regiment, which was disbanded in 1945, and to transfer to it the Artists Rifles (Territorial Army).

This was followed on the 17th of April 1947 by: '*Authority is given for the formation of the following unit wef 1 May 1947: 21st Special Air Service Regiment (Artists Rifles) (Territorial Army).*' 21 SAS was officially established by Royal Warrant on the 8th of July.

The Artists Rifles had been formed in 1859. They served with great distinction and bravery in the Boer Wars and the First World War, winning eight Victoria Crosses, four DSOs and 822 MCs. During the Second World War it had been employed as an officer training unit. The designation '21' was arrived at by a desire to acknowledge the regiment's antecedents, 1st and 2nd Special Air Service Regiments in the war. '21' is simply 1 and 2 reversed. No doubt having the '2' in front may have had something to do with the former Commanding Officer of 2 SAS. It would in due course be followed by the establishment of '22', the regular regiment and a second TA regiment, '23'.

Brian's hard work, intensive lobbying and political manoeuvring had paid off. The SAS was back and open for business. In the words of David Stirling, '*Had it not been for Brian Franks, we would have been consigned to oblivion.*' Later in 1987 Dare Newell[144] would endorse this: '*In retrospect it is a miracle that the post-war SAS survived, let alone flourish as it does today. Several times it was touch and go. Our salvation depended on a few, very few, dedicated visionaries and persistent champions in the right place at the right time.*'

144 Major Clarence Dare Newell. Wartime SOE in Albania and Force 136 in Malaya and one of the first members of the Malayan Scouts.

*

The cap badge of the Artists Rifles depicts the heads of two Roman gods, Mars the god of war and Minerva, the goddess of wisdom, invention, arts and martial power. It symbolises the blend of warfare and wisdom, quite appropriate to the newly established 21 SAS. Originally the cap badge was worn with the red beret, but was soon replaced by the winged dagger, and eventually in 1956 the red beret, which had caused so much irritation in 1944, was replaced by the original sand-coloured beret.

Brian began his tenure of command on the 1st of May 1947, and the regiment was open for recruiting in mid-September. Major Pat Hart,[145] a regular officer, was appointed Second-in-Command. He had first come to the SAS brigade headquarters in 1944 and then worked as principal staff officer to Mike Calvert at his tactical headquarters in Belgium during the latter stages of the war in Europe. He was an excellent staff officer well versed in the ways and requirements of an SAS operational unit, and an ideal choice to help Brian get 21 up and running.

Questions have been raised as to why Brian was selected to command 21 rather than Paddy Mayne, considering Mayne had more wartime SAS experience with four DSOs to show for it, and was one of David Stirling's originals. He was a fighting soldier *par excellence* but as David Stirling pointed out: '*Brian Franks drew heavily on Paddy's amazing fighting performance in France and Germany when he was creating 21. So Paddy was important, but he didn't know how to cope with officers above him. I had to continuously protect him in that context.*' Mike Calvert agreed, stating that while Paddy knew how to fight, he would not be any good at waging the sort of war required in the corridors of Whitehall. Brian could do both. He had the operational fighting skills and experience, but he was also very well connected and knew how to operate within, and manipulate the system to get what he wanted without treading on too many toes. Given the complexities of the rebirth of the SAS, Brian was the right

145 Major L. E. O. T. Hart, originally from the Rifle Brigade.

choice. He was also closely in touch, via personal contacts and the SAS association, with the most likely potential recruits.

The regiment was established in the artists' drill hall at Duke's Road, Euston.[146] It was to consist of a headquarters and two squadrons, initially A and B. Their role was similar to the SAS in World War II, long-range reconnaissance, and raiding deep in the enemy lines of communication, intelligence gathering, and a new concept of 'Stay Behind operations'[147] in conjunction with local resistance groups. Brian was also very keen to incorporate an SBS element within the regiment. Tom Burt joined as quartermaster, and a regular officer from the Rifle Brigade, Tommy Wallis, was appointed the adjutant. Brian took an early decision that Pat Hart would not fulfil the traditional role of the 21C, organising training, as there were experienced wartime officers who would command and train the squadrons. Hart would devote himself to developing the future structure and longevity of the SAS.

By the end of October 1947 there had been 90 applications to join 21, of which 50 were accepted. The majority were former members of the wartime SAS, but also included 18 of the original Artists Rifles. Recruitment was very much by word of mouth. Tony Greville-Bell, on his way to the 400 Club, dropped into the Hyde Park Hotel one evening to have a drink with Brian, and was immediately recruited. Old faces flocked to the regiment, Ian Lapraik from the SBS was given command of B Squadron, Grant Hibbert took over A Squadron. Others included Henry Druce, Ronnie Grieson, Johnny Cooper, Jim Johnson, Johnnie Wiseman, 'Tanky' Challenor and Stewart Macbeth. Some officers were taken straight away, others had to join as other ranks for a period of time before being commissioned.

The other aspect of 21 SAS, Stewart Menzies's need to prepare people for '*the rougher part of the game*' began as soon as 21 was up and running. Pat Hart described this as '*SOE masquerading as the SAS*'. Within the regiment they were known as the 'Funnies'.

146 It would remain there until 1967 when it moved to the Duke of York's barracks in the King's Road, Chelsea.

147 'Stay Behind' small teams would be concealed in hides, allowing the Soviet Army to roll over them. They would then emerge and carry out operations against lines of communication headquarters and key equipment.

> *We used to get rung up by unknown chaps – a voice would say: 'Have you got a safe in the Hyde Park Hotel? What have you done with Reference Number so and so?' It was too hopelessly inefficient for words. They wouldn't tell anybody what they wanted. It was really quite hilarious. The first few weeks ... we had a constant stream of chaps, coming in, saying: 'I've been told by the War Office to come and see you.' 'Did they say why?' 'No.' 'Any idea what we are doing?' 'No.' 'Are you interested in joining the SAS?' 'No.'*

One such potential recruit was the journalist Malcolm Muggeridge, who had been in SIS during the war, now working for the *Daily Telegraph*. Turning up at Duke's Road he was asked by Brian why he wanted to join. He replied that he didn't really know why he was there, and rather facetiously added '*perhaps to discover myself?*' Brian promptly found him a broom and told him to sweep out the drill hall. He didn't come back.

There were, however, several officers who were 'dual hatted'; they were mostly officers, older and less fit than the former SAS soldiers. A few spoke English with European accents and they kept their distance, conducting their own refresher training. There were also a few 'funny girls'. While this dual arrangement had its more ridiculous moments, Brian understood the requirement, and he and his team were able to make it work.

*

On the 8th of May 1947 Brian had received a very welcome letter from Basil Bennett giving him a salary increase and a place on the board of the Hyde Park: '*The agreement in place between you and the company should be substituted for a new one on terms more favourable to yourself ...*'

Other news was not so good. The one face missing from the flood joining 21 was Roy Farran. At the end of the war Farran had opted to stay in the Regular Army. He became an instructor at Sandhurst.

He was regularly in touch with Brian, keeping him up to date with all the gossip from the Royal Military Academy. Farran was restless. Instructing officer cadets was not the same as 'Jeeping' behind enemy lines. In late October 1946 he had written to Brian outlining a plan to start what nowadays would be called an open source intelligence report focusing on Africa. Brian replied to him on the 20th of November saying that he had written to Ian Fleming '*who is in charge of the foreign correspondents of the Hemsley Press … I know him quite well and have suggested that we have lunch together.*'[148]

This plan was soon overtaken by events much more to Farran's liking. He got a telephone call from 'Boy' Browning summoning him to London, where in a highly classified meeting he was told he was being given what was described as a 'blue ticket' – to conduct special operations against the Jewish underground in Palestine. Behind the request was Lieutenant Colonel Bernard Ferguson, who had fought behind enemy lines in Burma. He had taught Farran at Sandhurst and knew of his reputation with 2 SAS in France and Italy. Ferguson had been seconded from the Army, again by 'Boy' Browning, to head the Palestine Police covert operations, the Police Mobile Force, and he wanted Farran to run a covert operations team.

The Colonial Office, and the Cabinet in London had extended the Defence Regulations for Palestine to include a tougher system of military courts and operational procedures. These were also backed by the new CIGS Field Marshal Viscount Montgomery, who was concerned about the capability and effectiveness of the Palestine Police. He issued a robust directive for British forces in Palestine to take the war to the enemy, after the Irgun[149] had blown up the King David Hotel, the headquarters of British forces in Palestine, killing 91 people, on the 22nd of July 1946.

148 The lunch eventually took place and Farran and Fleming started a publication called *Phoenix Africa*.

149 Irgun Zvai Leumi (Etzel/IZL). A fanatical Zionist paramilitary organisation active in Palestine from 1931 to 1948, conducting attacks against British targets in addition to the Arab population in furtherance of a Jewish state. Infamous for the 1946 bombing of the British headquarters at the King David Hotel in 1946 and the Deir Yassin massacre in 1948, conducted in concert with Lehi (Stern Gang). The IZL commander from 1943–48 was Menachem Begin, Prime Minister of Israel 1977–83.

It was into this very tense environment that Roy Farran flew on the 17th of March 1947 with Alastair McGregor, another of Ferguson's students at Sandhurst who had served in SOE with 2 SAS on Operation LOYTON. They were briefed on their mission by Ferguson, who was clear about the offensive nature of the operation. Farran and McGregor selected their own teams and trained them hard including in 'Tac Tac's' shooting methods. Very quickly the teams made an impact. Ferguson was delighted and reported that *'for three months at the beginning of 1947 the terrorists were to experience counter-terrorism at its most effective'* and *'Roy Farran's actions terrified the terrorists'*.

The terrorists fought back and accused Farran of detaining and murdering a young activist called Alexander Rubowitz. Farran immediately told Ferguson of the incident. Eventually this led to an investigation and a decision to charge Farran with murder. Farran for some reason decided to go to ground in Syria until the heat died down. Ferguson flew to Syria and persuaded him to come back and face the music. After some prevarication and convoluted negotiation which dragged in the Colonial Office, War Office and Foreign Office, Farran returned to Jerusalem and reported to the military authorities at 1300 on the 17th of June, where he was subsequently arrested and charged with murder.

While under house arrest he escaped and disappeared again. There was much excitement in the press, and not a little embarrassment to the administration in Palestine and to the British Government. Eventually Roy Farran gave himself up on the 29th of June. His court martial was set for the 11th of August and it was in the intervening six weeks that Farran's friends swung into action. A number of officers from Farran's old regiment, the 3rd Hussars, started a subscription fund to pay for his defence lawyers. Bob Laycock and Brian immediately formed a powerful and wealthy support group. Co-opting the Stirling brothers as well as former officers of the LRDG they raised money to engage the best lawyers available, Lawrence Collins and Fearnley-Whittingstall Solicitors.

Brian wrote to Bob Laycock on the 4th of July asking for his thoughts and advice on the matter and identifying Bernard Ferguson's concept of operations document, which was approved by his Colonial Office as key to Farran's defence:

> *... a document setting out the whole scheme to the Colonial Office. This document was approved by Creech Jones.*[150] *They are most anxious to get a sight of this and have written twice to the Colonial Office ... but no reply has been received. It follows that the document is fairly hot – can you suggest any means of seeing it? It might make a lot of difference to Roy. I feel that I am too closely connected with the case to do much good either at the Colonial Office or with Browning. I have spoken to Bill Stirling who will probably be in touch ...*

The document in question was Ferguson's memorandum entitled 'Secondment of Army Officers to Palestine's Police' dated the 12th of February 1947. Both Brian and Mike Calvert gave character references. Laycock's on Combined Operations Headquarters headed paper was glowing in praise for Farran: '*... his military record and general character are unimpeachable ... His attributes are patriotism, loyalty and integrity which he possesses in the highest degree. I never met an officer whose character was more thoroughly divorced from anything ignoble.*'

Both Brian and Bob Laycock pulled every string possible to gather supporting testimonials from senior officers, and to get Bernard Ferguson's document released to Roy's lawyers. Unsurprisingly 'Boy' Browning was not particularly helpful, and in a letter to Laycock on the 9th of September 1947 hid behind the process of legally requesting the Ferguson document, saying that a claim of privilege '*would in all probability succeed. I am afraid it would therefore be clearly improper to make any attempt to procure ... that memorandum for scrutiny by the defending solicitors ...*'

In the event Roy Farran's court martial found him not guilty and he

150 Arthur Creech Jones (1891–1964). Labour politician and Colonial Secretary (1946–50); responsible for British policy in Palestine during the final years of the Mandate and the Jewish insurgency. His office dealt with the political repercussions of security operations against Jewish underground groups, during a deteriorating security situation in Palestine.

Roy Farran press conference on return to Britain

was acquitted. Farran returned to Britain on the troop ship *Ordura*, arriving at Liverpool on the 13th of October and, much to his surprise, to a hero's welcome. He was very grateful to those who had stood by him: 'It *was the interest of friends like Brian Franks and Bill Stirling that persuaded me to put up a defence ... the kindness of these friends prevented any feeling of bitterness of my country's official stand.*'

*

Whatever directives Brian had been given about the structure and role of 21, he continued, with the support of his officers, to develop an SAS regiment, able to fulfil any special operation function given to it; if SIS wanted to use the regiment as well that was fine, but it would be on SAS terms.

By June 1948 the regimental strength had grown to 33 officers and 125 other ranks. Training priorities included qualifying all ranks with their eight parachute jumps. The first annual camp split the regiment between three areas – the Commando Cliff Assault Wing at St Ives, the Royal Marines Commando School at Bickleigh on Dartmoor, and Okehampton Camp on Dartmoor for 'Jeeping' operations. The regimental focus was on both Jeep operations using the World War II Jeeps armed with the Vickers K gun, and SBS-style boating operations. The principal objective of the first ever camp was to practise approaches to a target area by land and sea. Brian was keen to ensure that SBS skills were not lost. Surf canoeing, climbing and long paddles in all sea states were practised. Although Brian was of the view that parachuting was only one way to get to work, in September 1948 a balloon jump weekend took place at RAF Upper Heyford. On the Sunday 245 jumps were made, an RAF record for the most done in one day; 46 out of 50 qualified. Much emphasis was placed on all aspects of armed Jeep operations, from driving and maintenance to full-blown raids on airfields and other strategic targets.

Based on their World War II experience, including Brian's own departure from Operation LOYTON, escape and evasion and resistance to interrogation training was a high priority. The police, Security Service (MI5) and SIS all took part. Groups also took part in winter warfare training at the British Army School of Mountain Warfare at Schmelz in the Austrian Alps. The squadron commanders, all wartime SAS officers, ran very realistic and demanding exercises, and by the end of 1948, the mix of experienced and amateur soldiers was being welded by Brian and his team into a unit that had found the *esprit de corps* and comradeship essential to a special operations unit.

*

Across London at Duke's Road 21 SAS continued to evolve. A and B Squadrons were joined by C Squadron, which initially became a holding squadron for 'The Funnies'. C Squadron was commanded by Major Dick Harrison, who had been in SOE during the war. He was a colourful character who on drill nights would send out men from the squadron in plain clothes into Holborn to avoid surveillance by other teams sent out to track them. The drill night would end in the Strand Palace Hotel where '*suitable quantities of liquid refreshment were taken*'. Harrison had ideas of turning A Squadron into an MI9 unit and would regularly involve Airey Neave[151] in his training exercises. Eventually the officers and NCOs of 21 got fed up with 'The Funnies',

151 Airey Neave (1916–1979). Served with the Royal Artillery, was captured in France in 1940, later escaping from Colditz. He joined MI9, specialising in escape-and-evasion organisation, working closely with special operations forces in north-west Europe. He was assassinated on the 30th of March 1979 when a car bomb placed by the Irish National Liberation Army exploded in the House of Commons car park shortly after he had left the chamber. The MI9 Joint Reserve Reconnaissance Unit was converted into 23 SAS.

21 SAS training

thinking they were rather '*long in the tooth*' and should move on. The 'Originals' and new boys were clear that they could do anything 'The Funnies' could do, and probably better. But it was not to be the end of a close relationship between the SAS and the national intelligence agencies.

While training continued at full tilt, accelerated by the Berlin Blockade in June 1948, Pat Hart had been working hard, at Brian's direction, on the ongoing development of the SAS. Having got their foot in the door, Brian wanted to do more. He kept closely in touch with those allies in power both in and outside the Army. Brian was determined that while they probably needed an umbrella of sorts, he would get away '*from anything to do with parachuting or airborne*'. They tried an affiliation with the Brigade of Guards, who were not interested, and the Rifle Brigade who were, but after a disastrous lunch at the 'In and Out' Club[152] with four rather clapped-out senior officers of the Rifle Brigade: Field Marshal 'Jumbo' Wilson and Generals Viscount Bridgeman, 'Squeaker' Curtis and 'Bubbles' Barker, who spent the whole time waffling, Brian lost interest.

Instead he took his problem to Miles Dempsey. Dempsey had

152 The Naval Military Club, popularly known as the 'In and Out' Club from the motto above its entrance, a London gentlemen's club founded in 1862 for officers of the armed services. It has traditionally served as a meeting place for serving and retired officers and for informal professional networking within the services. After 133 years at Cambridge House on Piccadilly, the club acquired the freehold of 4 St James's Square (formerly the home of Nancy Astor) and moved there in 1999.

been asked in March 1948 to be the honorary colonel of 21 and had accepted. His appointment was confirmed and gazetted on the 18th. In August he sent a message to all ranks in 21 SAS. Referring to the war he said:

> *... the Special Air Service Regiment was strongly represented in the Corps I commanded, and from that time onwards ... we had many adventures together ... Great troops, they were full of skill and courage – the sort of men any commander is proud to have under him and doubly glad to have in an emergency ... so when I was invited to become Honorary Colonel I was honoured and delighted to accept. To the present members of the 21st SAS Regiment, I send my best wishes. Their aim is simple ... to carry on the spirit and efficiency of their predecessors who made such a great name for themselves in the Second World War.*

The War Office eventually decided that in future all Special Forces should be in one unit and that it should be a stand-alone corps in the British Army. At the beginning of 1949 the Army was beginning to change its view of the SAS. On the 11th of May Brian wrote to Dempsey, '*As I think you already know, the status of the SAS was altered very much for the better recently ... in that there is now a recognised requirement for it in both peace and war ... I am enclosing a summary of the position which Hart has put on paper after a discussion with me ... I would very much like the chance of discussing it with you ...*' Hart's paper argued that the SAS should be a stand-alone corps with its own Colonel Commandant. On the 7th of July 1949 Brian wrote again pointing out that his command was due to end in May 1950, and recommending Charles Newman VC,[153] the former Commanding Officer of Number 2 Commando, as a suitable successor, and seeking Dempsey's approval.

Brian and Pat Hart's efforts, coupled with Dempsey's pressure in high places, paid off. In 1949 Brian had written a lengthy memo to the

153 Lieutenant Colonel Charles Newman. A pre-war regular officer who was one of the first volunteers for the Commandos. He commanded No. 2 Commando at St Nazaire and was awarded the VC.

War Office and 16th Airborne Division (TA) commanded by General Gerald Lathbury:

> *The fundamental difference between SAS 'units' and other units of the army, which must be grasped if the special needs of the SAS establishment are to be understood, is that the former are not 'units' in the sense generally accepted for the latter. The SAS regiments are NOT organised and can NOT be employed as units; all operations undertaken by SAS troops are carried out by parties especially picked and equipped for the occasion. The strength, composition, equipment and method of employment of each party depends on the exact circumstances of each operation and are only decided when the operation is allotted and examined in detail. It will be seen therefore that the term 'unit' is a misnomer in this case and that the SAS regiment is not a tactical unit. It is merely a force of SAS troops from which a large number of SAS operational parties can be found, controlled and maintained.*

This memo was supported by General Lathbury, who wrote to the War Office on behalf of 21 SAS, reflecting the views of the new, more enlightened breed of Parachute Regiment officers: '*This unit has a role which is unlike any other unit. It is not a parachute battalion and parachuting as such forms only a small part of its role and training. For this reason alone, therefore there is no argument for necessarily bringing this unit into line with any other as regards title.*'

1950 was to be a historic milestone for the SAS. On the 22nd of May 21 SAS became a stand-alone corps within the British Army, promulgated in a Royal warrant: *... our further WILL AND PLEASURE is that the Special Air Service Regiment shall be constituted a separate Corps for the purposes of the Army Act, the Reserve Forces Act 1882 and the Territorial and Reserve Forces Act 1907*'. Corps status meant they were entitled to a Colonel Commandant and Miles Dempsey was delighted to accept.[154]

Simultaneously in May Brian's tenure in command came to an end,

154 Corps status also entitled the SAS to a band!

coinciding with the announcement of the Royal warrant. He was sad to leave but pressure of work at the Hyde Park Hotel had forced his hand. On leaving he addressed the Regiment:

It is with regret that I give up Command of the Regiment after three years. I look back to May 1947, when I was the first recruit to the newly formed Regiment, with considerable pride. I believe that the fact we are now over four hundred strong speaks for itself in showing that the experiment of fusing the Artists Rifles – with its great traditions – with the SAS Regiment – a new arm of the Army founded on experience of the last war – has proved successful. I am very pleased to know the Regiment's future will be in the capable hands of Charles Newman, and I could wish for no better or wiser successor.

Brian was disappointed to have missed the formation of M Squadron, which was to be mobilised to fight in the Korean War. Due to the changing tide of the war, the deployment of the squadron, under command of Tony Greville-Bell, was switched to Malaya. The Malayan emergency had broken out in 1948. Mike Calvert had been tasked with formulating a plan to counter communist insurgents. Part of that plan involved setting up a special long-range penetration unit to be known as the Malayan Scouts. The unit comprised three squadrons: A Squadron recruited from regular units in Malaya, B Squadron the redesignated M Squadron from 21, and C Squadron made up of Rhodesian[155] volunteers. Of the three, B Squadron proved the most effective. With all the high level of experience and standards of training and discipline instilled by Brian in 21, it was a highly professional and well-drilled team. In mid-1951 Brian would be appointed Honorary Colonel of the Regiment (21) replacing Miles Dempsey, who was to become the first Colonel Commandment of the new SAS Corps. As part of the process of giving the SAS corps status, the Chiefs of Staffs had directed that all British Special Forces units be designated SAS, therefore the Malayan Scouts would be renamed

155 This Squadron eventually became C Squadron 22 SAS and after the Rhodesian Unilateral Declaration of Independence in 1965 formed the nucleus of the Rhodesian SAS Regiment.

22 SAS in 1951. Nine years later, in 1959, the Reserve Reconnaissance Unit, a descendant of the wartime MI9, would be redesignated 23 SAS, a second TA SAS regiment.

The war criminals who had murdered his soldiers in 1944 were, all but one, detained and punished, and the SAS was properly re-established in the Order of Battle. Brian had done his job and achieved both his ambitions, but he was not quite ready to finally hang up his boots.

Relaxing after a training night at Duke's Road. Brian back row, fourth from right

CHAPTER 14 – HEYDAY

> 'Like many of the upper class, he liked the sound of breaking glass.'
>
> Hilaire Belloc, 'About John' from *New Cautionary Tales*

As the war had dragged on the Hyde Park Hotel had grown shabbier by the day. Carpets became threadbare, paint peeled and the gilt was faded and dull. Even the vast marbled walls seemed to have lost their shine. Many of the key staff had gone to war, including Brian and Basil Bennett, and it was only the efforts of those like Mary Shiffer that kept things going, in spite of the shortages and difficulties of wartime rationing. It wasn't just food rationing; by 1944 paper was in short supply and in particular lavatory paper. Notices were put up on all the loos asking guests to be '*sparing with the toilet facilities*'. Four sheets were suggested: '*one up, one down, one across and one to shine*'. Using newspaper was banned, as it blocked the drains.

On VE Day the blackout was taken down amid a shower of dust and dead insects. The hotel was in an extreme state of dilapidation. Basil Bennett gave a rallying talk to the staff saying, '*We must get back to where we were before the war ... we must make it the same or even better, we need the monarchy back. That is how we will survive.*'

Bennett had already agreed with Brian that he would come back as General Manager after clearing the decks at Wivenhoe Park. He also understood and agreed with Brian's extracurricular activities with the War Office, SIS and Eric Barkworth's War Crimes team. He was also happy that the hotel should become a meeting place and watering hole for those in the clandestine world. Another Etonian, Tom Sawyer, was brought in as Brian's assistant. Brian described what he found on his return:

> *The hotel was in a dreadful state. We had to rely totally on the black market for many kinds of food and the staff had slipped into many strange wartime habits. The old manager, for instance,*

Brian and Tom Sawyer

could be seen cooking up his own kippers in the service lift and the wine cellar seemed to have become a free social club. The heating was as idiosyncratic as some of the staff. Trucks of coal had to be taken down to the boilers, which were like angry, unpredictable monsters. They were, in fact, boilers from an old battleship and the boiler room was almost identical to its shipboard counterpart. About the only stable influence in the hotel seemed to have been Mary Shiffer – who had been a kind maid-of-all-work in the Hyde Park since before the First World War ... She was very popular with the guests, particularly the few we still had in residence. The staff liked her too, despite the fact she treated them like erring children, calling all the Italian waiters Macaronis.

Brian's first hire was Ronald Massara, as Catering Manager. Massara had remained at the Mayfair until conscripted in 1941.[156] He recalls the hotel in 1945 as:

Full of rats with hardly any clients. We were told that we had three months to pull the place together. It was no easy job. Unbelievably there were no serviettes – and all the plates were cracked – the few that had survived the war years, that is. The staff were very

156 Ronald Massara had been called up in early 1941. Luckily for him he was spotted in some run-of-the-mill jobs by General Butterworth, Commander of the 78th Infantry Division, who had known Massara before the war and employed him as cook at his headquarters.

old, very set in the ways of pre-war days. When I asked if they had any ice buckets they stared at me in bewilderment. Everyone was on the fiddle and I'm sure this is how most of the stuff had disappeared. The hotel was a shell, and without any money, we had to fill it – to bring it alive again. Our objectives were three – firstly to bring back the Monarchy, secondly to bring back the very top aristocracy, thirdly to bring back the debs – but twice as glamorously as before. Overall we were to restore the Hyde Park to the height of fashion. As we tried to lick the battered old place into shape I used to face every day as a new fight. It was good – a glorious way to live.

Ronald Massara's single-minded devotion to his career had ensured his rapid rise to success in the hotel business. He was suave and debonair with a great deal of charm and charisma, he had worked at the Savoy and the Ritz in Paris, and had made a real success of his time at the Mayfair. His 'foreignness', once considered a drawback, was now considered exotic and a distinct advantage. He had become a 'character' on the London social scene, and when he married, the *Daily Express* further enhanced his image with a report headlined *EX-WAITER WILL MARRY HEIRESS*. In fact he married a lady called Joan Marshall from a 'very well to-do family', not quite an 'heiress'; but why let the truth get in the way of a good headline?

From his office on the first floor,[157] Brian set about working all his contacts. He also knew that he needed some glamour to attract the young, so he brought back Tommy Kinsman and his orchestra as the house band. Kinsman's big break came in the 1930s when he was hired as the resident band at the fashionable Ciro's Club in Bond Street. He then played at the Ritz, where the Prince of Wales ensured his success in the mid-thirties by patronising the band, enjoying and dancing its tangos, and inviting Kinsman to his table. Suddenly Tommy Kinsman was 'in'. Brian knew that by hiring Kinsman he could attract both Royalty and the debs: '*Tommy was the debs' delight and we knew, if we had Tommy playing in the ballroom, we'd*

157 With the aforementioned large oriental rug that used to 'belong' to Frau Goering.

Ronald Massara

Tommy Kinsman

be back where we were. It wasn't just the debs who liked him – it was Royalty too. He played in a way that was very easy to dance to for them. Nothing too fast, nor too loud. And the tempo allowed for anyone with two left feet – which a lot of them had.'

The first test for Brian and his team came on Victory Day, the 8th of June 1946, with a lunch of three courses with Algerian wine at 15 shillings a carafe. It was followed in the evening by dinner and dancing to Tommy Kinsman and his band. Brian and Basil Bennett were delighted; it was a roaring success. The future for the Hyde Park looked bright.

The next significant event due to be held at the hotel was the first SAS Association dinner on the 17th of December 1946, organised by Brian. However demand to attend was so great that the Hyde Park couldn't accommodate it and the venue was changed at the last minute to the Connaught Rooms in Great Queen Street. The event was described as '*Cheerful bandits to meet again*' in the *Observer* newspaper. David Stirling, Paddy Mayne and over 300 British, French and Belgian SAS veterans attended.

The hotel would soon become the 'unofficial' headquarters of the SAS, just as it had been throughout the war. Other departments of the secret world favoured it, as it was both stylish and discreet. MI5 and SIS would regularly hold dinners and post-war reunions there, and undoubtedly used the hotel from time to time for operational purposes with the full knowledge and co-operation of the General Manager.

First association dinner

The critical year for the Hyde Park Hotel was 1948. Throughout 1946 and 1947 Brian's management team had worked hard to get the hotel back on the map, but what they needed was a full-blown test. The opportunity to do just that came in 1948 with the silver wedding anniversary party of Lady Doris Vyner, the daughter of the Duke of Richmond and Gordon. She had decided to hold it at the Hyde Park Hotel. As she had been a bridesmaid to Queen Elizabeth, whose silver wedding anniversary was almost at the same time, she decided to invite the King and Queen.

This sent Brian and his team into overdrive. While the party was exactly what they needed, the stakes were high as the hotel was still in a state of extreme decay, and in no state to receive Royal guests. Although the occasion was to be a private one, Brian had no doubt that it would be heavily reported in the press, principally because the King and Queen had not been into a hotel since the war – and had rarely been into one before. Massara had persuaded Lady Vyner to leave everything to him. While supremely confident on the outside he, like the duck, was paddling madly under the surface.

He had to swallow his pride and borrow extensively to make up for the shortfalls at the Hyde Park – china from Royal Doulton, rugs from Harvey Nichols across the street to cover the holes in the carpets – and he recruited waiters from every hotel in London. Brian stood back and watched as Massara thoroughly briefed everyone – the waiters, wine waiters, the chef, sous chefs, flower arrangers and the hotel security staff. Nothing must go wrong. Tommy Kinsman meanwhile was also having his problems. Very aware that this was

SPECIAL AIR SERVICE REGIMENTAL ASSOCIATION

DINNER

President:- Lieut. Col. David Stirling, D.S.O.

December 16th, 1946

Connaught Rooms, Great Queen Street

Tom Burt

make-or-break night for the Hyde Park, he was determined that nothing should go wrong. Having been hired to play during dinner only, Kinsman sent Lady Vyner a list of light classical numbers that he thought would be suitable background music. However Lady Vyner was anxious that the party should be informal and she returned his programme with a request for his light classic repertoire to be replaced by nostalgic and modern dance numbers.

When the night came, all seemed to go according to plan. Tommy Kinsman, having played throughout dinner, was wondering how long he would have to continue: '*a message arrived from the Queen to ask whether we knew a rather lurid party piece called "Civilisation". The song had recently come from America and started with the words "Bongo, bongo, bongo". Although I never dreamed the King and Queen would ask for it at a dinner party, I had the sheet music with me.*'

Worse was to follow. The Royal party insisted that Kinsman sing it to them. Tony couldn't sing a note, and neither could anyone in his band. Realising how much was at stake for the Hyde Park, Kinsman waved the sheet music at the King and Queen, imploring them to lead the singing. Brian, Basil Bennett and Massara were watching from the back of the room, and beginning to sweat. Suddenly Mary Shiffer marched up to the Royal couple and told them she knew the tune. She joined the group surrounding the Queen, who held the lyrics up for them. 'Bongo, bongo, bongo' won the day.

George VI asked Lady Vyner if the carpets could be rolled up for dancing. Lady Vyner asked Massara. Realising this would expose all the holes, Massara reluctantly agreed. George VI, forgetting protocol in the excitement of an unexpected treat, helped him, dragging aside the Harvey Nichols rugs and ignoring the mess below. Meanwhile, Mary was asked by the Queen to stay. Soon the party really began. The Kinsman orchestra played foxtrots, waltzes, and eventually the royal favourite, the hokey-cokey. The King spent some time reminiscing with Tommy Kinsman about nightlife before the war, asking him about Royal musical favourites. When the King later played the accordion with Kinsman's band, Brian and his team knew they had passed the test.

The party ended around 5 a.m. with a conga which snaked through most of the ground floor of the hotel. The Royal partying and enjoyment instantly brought back the 'debs'.[158] The fashion and society magazine *Queen* wrote: '*Because no courts were held during the war there are now eight times as many applicants for presentation as there were in 1939.*' Such was the demand for coming-out parties that the Hyde Park held three or four each week. Despite rationing, Brian produced pigeon, venison and game sent in from his friends' country estates, black-market eggs and strawberries without cream. The Hyde Park was back in business.

158 'Debbery' refers to the 'debut' or 'coming out' of a young woman usually with an aristocratic or upper-class background who was of marriageable age and was ready to meet eligible bachelors from a similar background. This event usually occurred at a Debutantes Ball.

*

Brian had had to relinquish command of 21 SAS due to the pressure of work mounting in his day job at the Hyde Park. While Basil Bennett and the management board were fully behind Brian's involvement with 21, he knew he couldn't do both. However everyone was happy for the hotel to remain in full support of the SAS and other agencies.

Lady Vyner's Silver Jubilee party had set the tone for the revival of the Hyde Park: 1951 opened with the Festival of Britain, the keynote of which was '*fun, fantasy and colour*'. It would set the tone for the next 20 years of roaring success for Brian and his team.

Change was in the air. In October 1951 the Labour Government called an election, and Winston Churchill swept back into power. On election night he moved into the Hyde Park for two weeks while both his own townhouse and Number 10 were redecorated. On the 5th of February 1952 the King died and his daughter Elizabeth acceded to the throne. When the Coronation took place on the 2nd of June 1953, the Hyde Park was filled with visiting Royalty. Brian had spent the last several years overseeing the hotel's complete refurbishment and it was now fully restored to its pre-war glory. As ever Evelyn Waugh, who stayed there regularly when in London, had something critical to say complaining about the '*ingenious hideousity*' of a newly decorated suite, although it didn't stop him coming back for more and indulging himself in typical impish tricks such as muddling around all the guest shoes left outside their rooms for cleaning.

Other regular users and guests included Sir Max Aitken, Giles the cartoonist,[159] King Hussein of Jordan, the Crown Prince of Norway, the Grand Duke of Luxembourg, Lord Montagu of Beaulieu, Bette Davis, Elizabeth Taylor, John Wayne, Cary Grant, Field Marshal Slim and Winston Churchill. It became a 'home from home' for many of Brian's wartime comrades, Bob Laycock, the Stirlings, Christopher Sykes, Evelyn Waugh and many others, and it also became the venue for the SAS association annual general meetings and dinners.

Max Aitken felt that Brian and Ronald Massara '*gave the place a unique club atmosphere, making it different to any hotel in London by*

159 After lunch one day at the Hyde Park, Max Aitken took Giles to Barclay Brothers in Berkeley Square and bought him a Bentley.

sheer force of personality'. It was a formidable team, '*no wonder the hotel has excelled itself under such men*'.

The Hyde Park was also *the* place for debutantes' 'coming out' balls during the London season when they were presented at Court. An article in *The Times* summarised the debutante season:

> *The English are great students of Form where their twin passions, debutantes and racehorses, are concerned and from now until the end of the season we shall avidly follow the progress of the debs, read their comments and opinions, observe their stamina, speed and staying power, speculate on their escorts, and cast our private votes for that minor modern mythological figure, ritually slain at the end of each summer, the Deb of the Year.*

The deb balls at the Hyde Park were regularly attended by the younger members of the Royal Family, including the Duke of Kent, Princess Alexandra and Princess Margaret, who tended to stay until the end at about 5 a.m.

Sometimes the parties would get very rowdy, losing the stylish sparkle of the early 1950s. The debs' escorts were mostly Guards officers or young men working in the City. '*It was all a bit rowdy, with people behaving as they imagined people did in* Vile Bodies,'[160] causing Evelyn Waugh to complain when staying at the Hyde Park: '*Sometimes I think I created these people, God help me.*' Mary Shiffer would also have mixed feelings about the season at Hyde Park: '*It was all very glamorous, but often the girls would look absolutely miserable. But it was when they behaved badly – like hooligans – that I got really cross.*' Eventually the debs season came to an end in 1957 with an announcement by the Lord Chamberlain: '*The Lord Chamberlain gives notice that there will be no presentation parties after 1958. The Queen proposes to hold additional garden parties in order that larger numbers may be invited to Buckingham Palace.*' The run of balls and parties continued for the next fifteen years or so, but without the Royal cachet, eventually petering out in the late 1960s.

160 *Vile Bodies*. Evelyn Waugh (1930), satirising London's post-First World War 'Bright Young Things'.

The Balaclava Ball

Perhaps the high spot of Brian's transformation of the Hyde Park came on the 26th of November 1954, hosting '*a ball the likes of which had not been seen outside Court circles since the turn of the century*'. The Balaclava Ball celebrated the centenary of the Charge of the Light Brigade during the Crimean War in 1854. Brian had used all his military contacts within the five cavalry regiments that had taken part. All officers wore full dress uniforms and the Colonel of the 11th Hussars, Major General Combe, wore the original tunic and pelisse worn by the Earl of Cardigan during the charge. The Royal party, the Queen, the Duke of Edinburgh and the Queen Mother arrived at 10 p.m. The Queen inspected a Guard of Honour and then started the dancing with Air Marshal Sir John Baldwin. The Royal party danced for most of the evening, leaving at 1 a.m. It was a resounding success. The Hyde Park had pulled off its most historic occasion. Brian was extremely pleased to see his success reflected in the lead story in the Court Circular for the 26th of November 1954: '*Her Majesty and the Duke of Edinburgh accompanied by Queen Elizabeth, the Queen Mother, were present this evening at the Balaclava Centenary Ball at the Hyde Park Hotel.*'

The meteoric success story that marked Brian's return to the Hyde Park was marred by the tragic death of Paddy Mayne in December 1955. On the 13th of December Paddy, after an evening of heavy drinking first at the Friendship Masonic Lodge in Newtownards and later with friends in Bangor, left to drive home in his red Riley Roadster at

Paddy Mayne's funeral

about 0400hrs in the morning of the 14th. Driving down Mill Street in Newtownards he hit a parked car and was killed instantly.

The funeral took place two days later on the 16th. The service was held at his family home, Mount Pleasant on Scrabo Road in Newtownards. After the service, he was buried in the Mayne family plot at Old Movilla Abbey Cemetery. Fraser McLuskey took the service and Brian, in David Stirling's absence in Africa, was the senior representative of the SAS and gave the eulogy which was printed in *The Times* the following week. Many members of the wartime SAS attended.

*

Brian's personal life settled into a more relaxed routine. Every morning, dressed in an immaculate suit, wearing a bowler hat from Lock's, and carrying a furled umbrella from Brigg's, he would set off with his children Valerie and George, who had been born in 1947, dropping them off at school, Valerie at Glendower at 87 Queen's Gate, and George at Wagner's across the road at number 90. He would set off at a fast clip and Valerie remembers almost having to run to keep up. If the weather was bad they would use Brian's black cab. He had always wanted to own a black cab, thinking that if you had to drive in London it was the speediest and least stressful way of getting around.

After a particularly successful year, the Bennetts, besides giving him a bonus, asked him what he would like as a present. The answer was a black cab. He employed a driver, a Mister Croft, and later in 1971 put the taxi to good use during the three-month-long national postal strike, by implementing a regular courier service between all the hotels in the Trust House Group.

After dropping the children at school he headed for his office at the Hyde Park where he would light up the first of his sixty-a-day Senior Service untipped. Brian's doctor once ordered him to stop smoking cigarettes and try cigars instead, but gave up in exasperation when Brian told him he had been inhaling the cigars just like the cigarettes.

At 1200hrs sharp, whether at work or at home, he would have a gin and French,[161] followed by lunch, usually with old friends or comrades from the SAS and Commandos. Bob Laycock, the Stirling brothers, Philip Dunne and Evelyn Waugh were regulars, as were Roy Farran when he was in London,[162] Lord Beaverbrook, Max Aitken, Giles, and Osbert Lancaster, the cartoonists, Ian Fleming, who was George's godfather,[163] and on occasion Winston Churchill. Brian had a very wide circle of friends, most of whom shared his love of good food and wine. His love of food goes back to his days at Eton and the Thursday Breakfast Club. This was soon to be reincarnated as what became known as the annual 'Franks Feast', held just before Christmas at the Hyde Park. It started life as a reunion for his wartime chums, but soon grew to include his ever-widening circle of friends. The food was exotic, regularly starting with caviar and moving through many courses, always accompanied by excellent wine and finishing with vintage port, another of Brian's favourites. His great friend Ronnie Chittenden would always write a poem, which was printed on the menu:

161 Gin and French vermouth with a twist of lemon, slightly less punchy than a dry martini.
162 He had emigrated to Canada in 1950.
163 Ian Fleming, as was his style, would often introduce his friends into his Bond novels. Hillary Bray became a genealogist from the Royal College of Arms in *On Her Majesty's Secret Service* in 1963, and Brian made an appearance as Peter Franks in *Diamonds are Forever*. James Bond assumes his identity to infiltrate a diamond-smuggling pipeline.

COLONEL FRANKS' XMAS PARTY

(Advice to a new boy)
Never, never let your tum
Get the better of your bum,
Though it should unloaded be
Before you go to Brian's spree.

If twixt you and neighbouring guest
Caviar should come to rest,
Swallow back your sweet saliva,
Every spoonful costs a fiver.

By now someone's always farted
Before the meal has really started,
So let this maxim e're be thine
'Mix well thy vodka with thy wine'.

Mousse de Hommard's the next course
(It's really lobster with some sauce),
'Pas mal' someone describes this food
For me, I think it's bloody good.

Birds that flew and beasts that ran
Including Alsace Ortolans –
An endless stream of high endeavour
Why can't this party last for ever!

Château d'Yquem fifty-seven
Flown straight here direct from Heaven,
Someone said 'the bottle's corked'
What *dreadful* nonsense Cobbold[164] talked.

164 Ralph Cobbold. Fellow Etonian, cricketer, joined Justerini and Brooks in 1935, Coldstream Guards during the war. Returned to Justerini after the war, lived near Brian in Suffolk.

That's the last thing I remember
On the fourteenth of December
Or was I just about alive
To drink some Taylor '35.

The brandy and the coffee mix
To take you on till half past six,
And that my boy is not a hunch
It's what I call a damned good lunch.

And so my story is unfurled
No better party in the world,
Name? Address? They do so tell
Brian Franks. Hyde Park Hotel.

Brian and Basil Bennett

'That was your father ringing from the bar at White's just to let us know that he is putting in an extra half hour for Britain.'

CHAPTER 15 – IN THE BAR AT WHITE'S

Just over a mile to the east of the Hyde Park Hotel at 37–38 St James's Street lies White's. White's is London's oldest club, founded in 1693 by Francesco and Elisabetta Bianco as a coffee house with a gambling room at the back. It became a club – White's from the anglicised version of Bianco – in 1736. Algernon Bourke, on writing a history of the club in 1892 noted, '*White's: all the Prime Ministers from Walpole to Peel, and most of their colleagues, have been at one time or other elected members, and a large number of the great generals and captains who have executed the schemes of these statesmen in all parts of the world, have spent their leisure in the club rooms.*'

The bar at White's only became a feature in 1938. Before that drinks were dispensed from a serving hatch. The bar rapidly became the hub of the club and such a feature that an American guest visiting the club, chatting to a barman, asked what were the opening hours of the bar, only to be told, '*It hasn't been closed for 300 years.*'

To many, White's seems to be an '*unbending institution of unshakable tradition*'. In fact it is a '*living organism*', which is able to maintain its high standard and strong traditions, while adapting to the changing circumstances brought about by war, economic crises and social upheaval. White's is special – *primus inter pares* in London club land, and its members are utterly devoted to it. It is well known for operating along the intersection between government, the intelligence services, the military and the aristocracy, its connection being so effective that it was sometimes known as *Le Reseau Blanc.*[165]

165 Le Reseau Blanc – sometimes used to describe the White's network – '*an interconnected system of linked elements, sharing resources, information in a complex interwoven structure*'. Reseau was often used in the war to describe intelligence or sabotage networks run by SIS or SOE.

Brian was put in the book[166] for White's in 1951. He was proposed by Seymour Berry[167] and seconded by David Stirling. His page in the White's book shows a large number of signatures for the time, more than 70, and includes Bill Stirling, Bob Laycock, Sandy Scratchley, Evelyn Waugh, Christopher Sykes, Johnnie Astor, Basil Bennett, Peter le Poer Power and Philip Dunne; 25 of the signatures were of those who had served with Brian during the war. Brian was elected to full membership in October 1952. With just over a year in the book, it was a very swift election indeed. He had had use of the club earlier through wartime reciprocal membership with Boodle's, of which he became a member before the war, or through a special dispensation given to certain members of the secret world during World War II, and it was '*in the bar at White's*' that Brian had interviewed and subsequently 'borrowed' Robert de Lesseps, GOODFELLOW, from SIS for Operation LOYTON. The phrase '*recruited in the bar at White's*' has slipped into the mythology of the clandestine world, but it is not without some substance. It has always been home to a core of the more adventurous-spirited, and those with an appetite for '*free-lance adventures of a cloak and dagger nature*', Rudyard Kipling's *Gentlemen Rovers Abroad*.

White's is secure – so secure that Sir Stewart Menzies had most of his secret correspondence delivered to the club because he believed, probably quite rightly, that the porter's desk at White's was more secure than the post rooms at the War Office, Foreign Office and Broadway.

The membership of White's reads like a catalogue of the Intelligence Services and Special Forces of World War II, and many of these highly successful organisations can trace their pedigree to White's. Early in the war David Stirling and Brian Mayfield, both Scots Guardsmen, had joined the short-lived 5th Scots Guards Ski Battalion, which included many other members of White's. Peter

166 'Put in the book' in White's speak means being put up for membership. The candidate's name is recorded in a book and other members sign it indicating support for the candidate. When a certain number of signatures have been gathered, this candidate goes before the membership committee for election.

167 Seymour Berry, 2nd Viscount Camrose. At Eton with Brian. Wartime service in the Royal Artillery. Deputy Chairman *Daily Telegraph*, member of the House of Lords.

Kemp had fought in the Spanish Civil War and was to join Fitzroy Maclean, Billy McLean, Julian Amery, Evelyn Waugh and Randolph Churchill, all members, on SOE operations in Yugoslavia and Albania. Paddy Leigh Fermor, who in 1944 kidnapped the German commander of Crete, General Kreipe, was also a member.

David Stirling and many others first found out about the Commandos from Robert Laycock in the bar. Laycock then formed 8 Commando, the Guards Commando, otherwise known as the White's Commando. Lord John Manners of the Life Guards was recruited in the bar for 2 SAS and so the list of 'gentleman adventurers' goes on. It was to those that Winston Churchill's rallying cry appealed; '*Enterprises must be prepared, with specially trained troops of the hunter class, who can develop a reign of terror down these coasts of occupied Europe leaving a trail of German corpses behind them.*'

It was not just Special Forces but included pilots for the Battle of Britain and 'The Air Squadron' or 'Legion', the County of London Fighter Squadron of the Auxiliary Air Force. This was founded by Lord Edward Grosvenor in 1924 at a dinner in White's. One of its most exotic members was Rupert Belville, who had twice been challenged to a duel and had flown in the Spanish Civil War.

It has been said that the war was the making of White's, and certainly many of its members had distinguished war records in the Commandos, Special Forces and Intelligence Services, as well as the more conventional military. White's features heavily in Evelyn Waugh's *Sword of Honour* trilogy, thinly disguised as 'Bellamy's'.[168] Standards were maintained at all costs. David Bruce, the wartime Head of OSS in Europe, remembers going there for dinner in 1944 and dining on smoked salmon, lamb, prune tart, Château Margaux '24 and some excellent vintage port.

Much of the planning and plotting for the revival of the SAS took place in White's and the Hyde Park Hotel.

In 1963, Nicholas Elliot, an SIS officer, and member of White's, had started dropping hints to David Stirling in the bar that '*something needed to be done about Yemen*', and on Wednesday the 3rd of

168 This has been adopted as the name for an excellent restaurant in London run by Gavin Rankin, a member of White's, and 'home from home' for many other members.

April Brian was asked to join a lunchtime meeting at White's. The other participants were David Stirling, Lieutenant Colonel Neil 'Billy' McLean, Julian Amery the Minister for Air, and Alec Douglas-Home, the Foreign Secretary.

*

The background to the meeting in White's has its origins seven years before, in the ignominious circumstances of Suez. The forced British, French and Israeli withdrawal encouraged General Nasser to further his policy of Arab nationalism, anti-monarchy and anti-British. He set his sights on the Royalist Imam of North Yemen, Saudi oil and the ultimate prize, the British protectorate of Aden.

Aden with its strategic position on the approaches to the Red Sea and Suez Canal, its port and oil refinery, had been identified as one of the linchpins of British defence policy, in the Defence Review of 1962. Its protection and security were fundamental to British interests in the Middle East. Implicit in the security of Aden was support to the Royalist tribes in North Yemen. Nasser had instigated a coup, with Russian backing, against the Imam of Sanaa. Aden was directly under threat but the British Government was vacillating over recognising the new Republican regime in North Yemen. King Hussein of Jordan flew to London[169] to urge the government not to recognise the regime, and to provide support to the Royalists, who were fighting back.

Alex Douglas-Home had asked SIS for an assessment. The SIS station in Aden was unable to provide it. The Head of Station, Hubert (Terry) O'Bryan-Tear, had little or no capacity, as intelligence regarding Aden was the responsibility of MI5. An exasperated Foreign Secretary tasked Billy McLean, adventurer and MP for Inverness, to conduct a full reconnaissance of Yemen and report back. McLean made three trips to Aden, Saudi and Yemen, and reported back that with some modest but robust support Sharif Saleh Bin Hussein of Beihan could conduct an effective resistance: '*With a little bit of help the tribes now fighting with the Imam could hold off the Egyptians.*'

169 He stayed at the Hyde Park Hotel.

Dick White, who had taken up the post of 'C' in 1956, had told the Foreign Secretary that SIS would not be able to set anything up in Yemen for at least six months. He was opposed to his service '*going on the offensive*' and '*should stick to the job of intelligence gathering*'. He was overruled.

Hence the meeting at White's. David Stirling was told that the operation would not be officially recognised, and would be '*off the books*', but fully supported by the British Government. It was also made clear that the SAS could not be involved 'officially'. Money would be provided by the Saudis, and in an unlikely alliance, Mossad would arrange arms drops to the Royalists. David was asked to provide the operators to support the Royalists in a war of attrition, which would drain Egyptian resources and tie down large numbers of Egyptian troops. Britain's involvement would be '*arm's length*'.

Brian being the most current and closely in touch with the SAS, as Honorary Colonel of 21 SAS, was asked who he thought might be the right person to run the operation. He suggested Jim Johnson, a commodity broker working for Thomas Nelson at Lloyd's. Johnson had served in the Welsh Guards during the war, fighting in Normandy, Belgium and Germany. More recently he had just finished commanding 21 SAS.[170] Johnson had asked Brian if he could join 21 SAS as an officer in 1947. Brian had explained that he was inundated with former SAS officers waiting to join, but if he wanted to join the ranks as a trooper he could.

Brian telephoned Jim Johnson from White's and asked him if he could '*come round and have a glass of brandy?*' When he arrived Brian got straight to the point, explaining that he had just come from a meeting at White's with Alec Douglas-Home, Julian Amery, David Stirling and Billy McLean. Billy, just returned from Yemen, had written a report for the Prime Minister. The gist of the report was that the Royalists were fighting back hard, but needed help, particularly with the destruction of Egyptian aircraft. '*How would you like to take*

170 Colonel Jim Johnson OBE (awarded for 'classified work'). Later became ADC to the Queen. Johnson would go on to found KMS, the second of what would come to be called PMCs, the first being David Stirling's Watchguard. In the 1990s there would be others: DSL, Hart, Sandline and Aegis, all founded by White's members, many of whom coincidentally were, like David Stirling, in the Scots Guards.

Jim Johnson

Johnny Cooper

on the job of burning all the Egyptian aircraft on airstrips in Yemen?' Johnson replied that *'he didn't have much on that week'* and would be happy to take on the job. Brian explained the full background, and that this was to be a covert operation sanctioned by the British Government but with no overt involvement.

The next meeting took place at Julian Amery's flat, with Brian, David Stirling, Billy McLean present. Jim was introduced to Ahmed Shami, the Foreign Minister of the Yemen, who was in London to secure British support. Money to fund the project did not seem to be a problem, and Shami handed over a cheque for £5,000 (worth approximately £160,000 today). Brian agreed to provide the initial use of one of the Hyde Park Hotel's bank accounts to run the funding of the project and that cash would be held in the hotel safe for use by Jim as required.

Jim Johnson had agreed to head up the project but realised that he couldn't organise and manage it as well as at the same time being the ground commander in Yemen. Johnny Cooper,[171] who had been one of David Stirling's original 'L' detachment, now serving in the Sultan of Oman's Armed Forces, was identified as a potential Commander. Described as *'sinewy with sun-blackened skin and the features of a Greek bandit'*, he was the ideal choice and readily agreed.

171 Johnny Cooper, one of the SAS 'originals'. David Stirling's driver in North Africa. Fought with 1 and 2 SAS until the end of the war and was recruited by Brian Franks as one of the first officers in 21 SAS. Served in M Squadron in Malaya, 22 SAS in Oman, then Sultan of Oman's forces.

*

In September 1962 the Egyptians had backed a military coup against the Imam Muhammad al-Badr. The coup was led by Brigadier al-Sallal and behind the coup were age-old tribal and religious tensions. The Republicans consisted mainly of the Shafi'i Sunni tribes from the centre and south of the country. The monarchists were Shia Zaidi tribes from the mountains in the north and east. Behind this were the wide politics of the Middle East. The Kingdom of Saudi Arabia felt threatened by Nasser's Arab Nationalists and felt that he had his eye on Saudi oil. Nasser was supported by the Russians, who also had their eye on Saudi oil, and Aden. The Israelis, unlikely partners with the Saudis and Shia tribes in Yemen, were as ever pragmatic. Anything that aimed at weakening Egypt was fine by them.

The British Foreign Office urged the government to recognise the Republicans. SIS had little or no capacity in Yemen, but there was a strong grouping in government demanding action against Egypt and the Republicans. This was largely led by Julian Amery and Peter Thorneycroft, the Defence Minister, who wanted '*decisive action to sabotage intelligence centres and to kill personnel engaged in anti-British activities*'. Brian knew Thorneycroft well; they had been at Eton together. They were supported by the robust and hardline High Commissioner in Aden, Sir Kennedy Trevaskis. Collectively they saw themselves as the guardians of British security policy in the Middle East and were also determined to avenge the humiliation of Suez.

Billy McLean had undertaken a tour of the area in October 1962 which included Yemen, Jordan and Saudi Arabia. He submitted his report to the Cabinet, which caused them to rethink any recognition of the Republicans in Yemen. Still uncommitted to full support for military action, they were happy to initiate the clandestine action envisaged at the White's meeting, provided funding would come from elsewhere and not be traceable to HMG. As a result Billy McLean undertook his fourth mission to the region, this time taking David Smiley with him.

David Smiley, a regular officer in the Blues, had spent the war in SOE working in the equally complex tribal environment of Albania

David Smiley

and subsequently worked with Brian for the war planning directorate of SIS. This trip was to deliver a full military appreciation and plan for the Saudis, in order to secure funding for the operation.

*

Back in London the structure for the operation was shaping up. Both Brian and David Stirling had been busy helping to put together an effective team. They formed a strategic planning committee which would be based in London, consisting of David and Brian, Jim Johnson, Billy McLean and Tony Boyle. Tony, an RAF jet pilot, had recently been ADC to the High Commissioner in Aden, had left the RAF after being recruited by David Stirling, and was to be very useful as part of the team liaising between London and Aden.

Johnny Cooper was the Ground Force Commander. David Smiley would have a roving commission operating in both Yemen and liaising direct with the Saudis. He would establish operational teams initially based in Khawlan, Nihm, and al-Jauf with a rear link at Beihan working back to Aden where Major Peter de la Billière working as a Staff Officer in the British headquarters and the newly appointed SIS Head of Station John de Silva would facilitate the passage of personnel and equipment through Aden to Beihan, and onwards into Yemen.

Jim Johnson set up shop in the basement of David Stirling's office at 21a Sloane Street. David found him Fiona Fraser, Shimi Lovat's daughter, as his personal assistant. He also would soon use the cellar at his Sloane Avenue house for the storage of weapons, radio and medical equipment. This would give rise to some amusing incidents. His wife Judy mistook someone delivering a large box for one of the team and directed him to the cellar, where a Hoover vacuum cleaner delivery man was very surprised to find several muscular military types degreasing German Schmeisser submachine guns, which had just arrived from the large store of 'unattributable' foreign weapons held in the SAS armoury at Hereford. The movement of large packing cases in and out of Sloane Avenue also gave rise to rumour and speculation that this was one of the hideouts of the 'Great Train Robbers'.[172] Maurice Green, the Editor of the *Daily Telegraph*, lived next door and knowing what was going on, he remained both silent and supportive, and would be very helpful in due course.

Although official support was very much 'on the nod', Brian and David Stirling approached the Commanding Officer of 22 SAS, John Woodhouse, to see if he could help with some specialist manpower, particularly in the field of support weapons, communications and medical skills. Woodhouse, knowing full well he would face a court martial if caught, agreed. He summoned three serving SAS soldiers to see him in his office, Sergeant 'Geordie' Dorman, Corporal 'Taff' Chidley and Trooper Jimmy Richardson: '*I've called you three here to ask if you would be willing to go on a secret mission. It could be very dangerous and your chances of survival are about 50-50. It will be though for the good of your country.*' They didn't hesitate and agreed immediately. '*Good. Johnny Cooper who is also involved will meet you outside camp this evening, take you to London and brief you.*'

Woodhouse took a huge risk releasing three specialist SAS soldiers 'on leave'. Woodhouse himself would soon join the Yemen operation on leaving the Army after finishing his tour as CO 22 SAS. There was also a fourth SAS man involved in the operation, Bill Condie, who was one of the regiment's best Arabic linguists. He was sent from Oman and attached to the Imam's headquarters.

172 The Great Train Robbery had taken place on the 8th of August 1963. £2.61 million (£70 million now) had been stolen from the Royal Mail train travelling from Glasgow to London. It became a *cause célèbre* at the time. Most of the men were eventually caught but the money remained unrecovered.

Roger Faulques

Bob Denard

Cooper and Stirling also flew to Paris to meet the SDECE,[173] the French Foreign Intelligence Service, and to recruit some former French Special Forces operators with experience from Indo China and Algeria led by Roger Faulques and Bob Denard.

While David, Brian and Johnny Cooper were busy recruiting, Jim Johnson was writing the operational plan which included the mission statement '*to assist the legal government of the Yemen to reassert its authority over the country*', with the general outline for the delivery of the plan as follows:

a) To establish and maintain a regular supply of arms and ammunition to the Royalist forces in the field. This must be done by:
   1. Parachutage or, if this is impossible (or the political situation changes)
   2. Overland delivery from Saudi Arabia, the Yemen coast or Beihan
b) To deny the Hedeida road to the Egyptians and assist the Royalists in other acts of sabotage which may periodically seem desirable.
c) To help the Royalists with skilled advice and practical assistance whenever it is sought.

With the first team set to go Johnny Cooper, the three SAS men and three French men, all en route to Yemen via Aden, suddenly the

173 Service de Documentation Extérieure et de Contre-Espionnage. Formed on the 28th of December 1945, renamed Direction Générale de la Sécurité Extérieure (DGSE) on the 2nd of April 1982.

Peter de la Billière (right) and team in Aden

British Government panicked and got in touch with Stirling and Brian and told them to cancel the operation. Jim Johnson was furious and with a characteristic Nelsonian approach sent them anyway.

The Aden end of the operation, Peter de la Billière and Tony Boyle, completely unaware of the government change of attitude, ensured their safe passage through Aden. '*I would meet someone off the London Comet, make what arrangements I could to ease his passage through customs, and – to avoid being seen in contact – pass him a typewritten note asking him to book in at a certain hotel, where I would meet him for lunch next day. Then I would send him up to Beihan, either by a Dakota of Aden Air, or by Land Rover, and he would slip through the Yemeni frontier at night.*'

Gradually things settled down and the government had yet another change of heart and followed an arm's length policy of support, allowing Peter de la Billière, Tony Boyle and John de Silva to provide covert support. But Peter was getting concerned: '*With traffic building up fast, I became anxious that people would cotton on to what we were doing, and when I heard that the immigration authorities had been told to take a special interest in travellers heading for Beihan, I suggested ways of improving security: people on their way out should break their journey somewhere in Africa, so that they did not appear to come from Britain.*'

The covert operation in Yemen would continue becoming more and more effective. The supply line set up by Peter de la Billière and

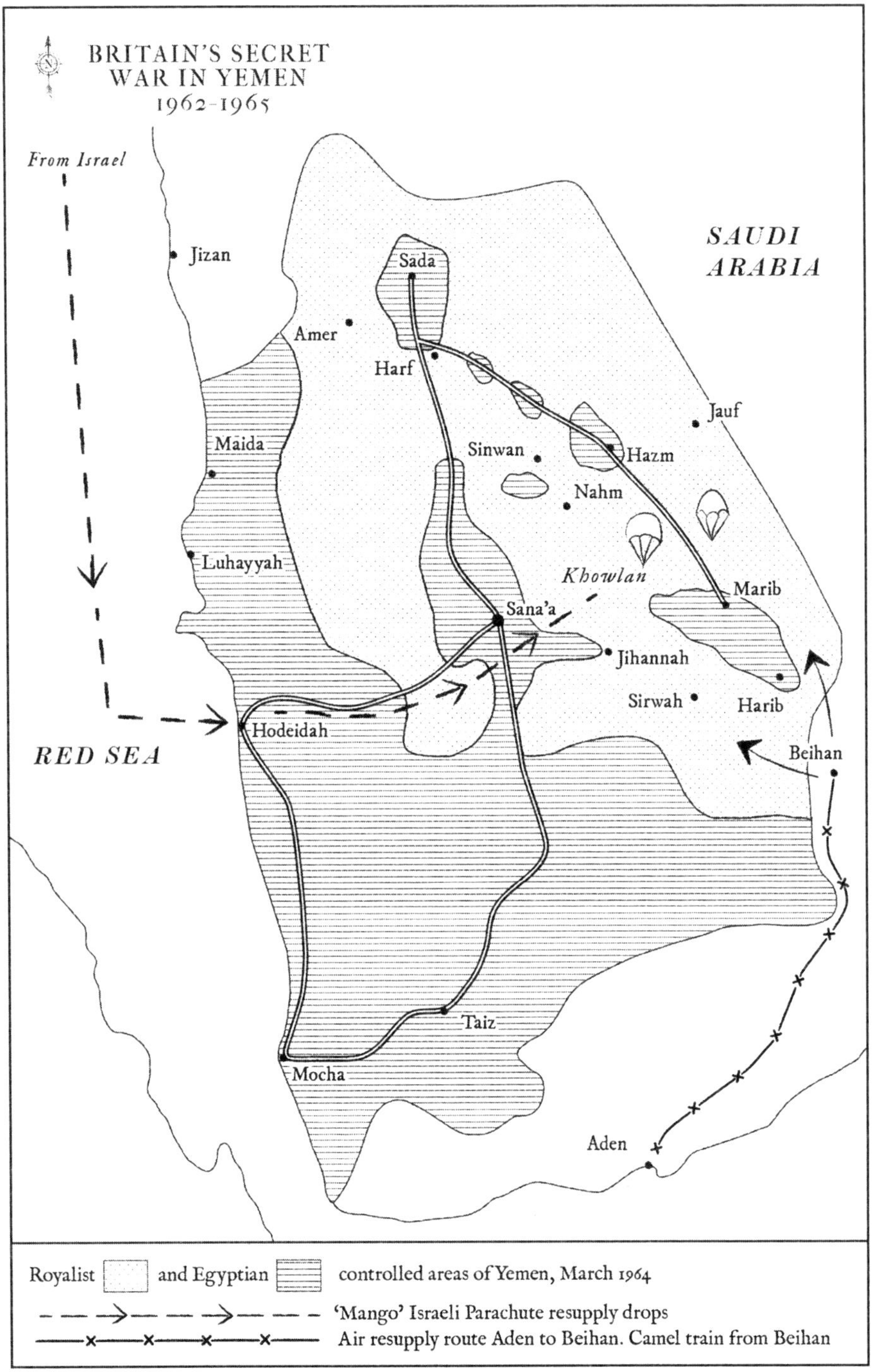
BRITAIN'S SECRET
WAR IN YEMEN
1962–1965
From Israel
Jizan
Sada
SAUDI
ARABIA
Amer
Harf
Jauf
Maida
Sinwan
Hazm
Nahm
Luhayyah
Khowlan
Marib
Sana'a
Jihannah
Sirwah
Harib
Hodeidah
RED SEA
Beihan
Taiz
Mocha
Aden
Royalist
and Egyptian
controlled areas of Yemen, March 1964
'Mango' Israeli Parachute resupply drops
Air resupply route Aden to Beihan. Camel train from Beihan

Royalist tribesmen and SAS

The Imam

Tony Boyle would be maintained but increasingly only for the transit of personnel. Camel trains for weapons supplies were replaced in 1964 by air drops of suitably deniable weapons and ammunition by the Israeli Mossad, codenamed 'MANGO' operations, reminiscent of wartime drops to the French Resistance.[174] These had been set up by David Smiley and Tony Boyle visiting Tel Aviv using alias passports provided by SIS.

Cover stories for the British and French going in and out of Yemen became more and more ridiculous. David Smiley went under journalistic cover – as a reporter for *The Guards Magazine* and the Yemeni line was that individuals are '*one of many British historians who are enquiring from us about contemporary events in Yemen*'. Other stories involved '*locust control*' and '*the distribution of television films*'. Smiley continued to make trips to Yemen and eventually, in agreement with Johnson and Roger Faulques, would take control of the whole operation. By 1965 Egypt had lost 15,000 men killed in Yemen. The combined Royalist, British and French force was being very effective, but gradually both British and – more importantly – Saudi support ceased.

Assessments were varied about what this intrepid band of former and serving British and French Special Forces achieved, but the official Joint Intelligence Committee report concluded with the following:

174 There were 13 'MANGO' air drop operations between 1964 and 1966.

Sabotage school

ACHIEVEMENTS OF THE MERCENARIES

119. The contribution made by mercenaries to the Royalist military effort in the Yemen Civil War was out of all proportion to their small numbers. They helped to sustain the morale of the Royalist princes in the field and encouraged them to keep up the struggle against the Egyptians and Republicans. We would not go so far as to say that the latter, had there been no mercenaries, would have been able to extend their control over the whole of the Yemen; tribal factors would probably have made this as impossible for them as for almost all previous rulers of the Yemen. But had it not been for the mercenaries, who trained the Royalist tribes, organised their supplies and ran their communications, the Royalists would not have been able to inflict so much damage and so many casualties on the highly-mechanised and air-supported Egyptian army and their Republican allies. Indeed, the military setbacks which the Egyptians suffered, and which were partly the result of the important support given to the Royalists by the mercenaries, were one of the main reasons why in the late summers of 1963, 1964 and 1965 they showed readiness to make concessions to the Saudis in order to achieve some kind of settlement.

In 1970 the whole story including the Israeli involvement in clandestine air drops and co-operation with the Saudis was in danger of being exposed by a *Sunday Times* Insight Team investigation. David

Stirling got wind of this and decided to pre-empt it by contacting Maurice Green, the Editor of the *Daily Telegraph*, who had known about the operation. Green instructed one of his experienced reporters Ian Colvin to conduct an interview with Jim Johnson to 'scoop' the *Times* article. David Stirling wrote to Lord Thompson of Fleet, the proprietor of the *Sunday Times*: '*The story of the British participation in the Yemen which all concerned would have far preferred to remain under wraps, had to be paraded in three articles in the* Daily Telegraph *in order to avoid the infinitely worse evil of allowing your Insight team to make its claim of Arab–Israeli collusion.*'

All those involved in the covert war in Yemen, Jim Johnson, Johnny Cooper, David Smiley and later Mike Gooley,[175] were all quite clear they were not in it for the money. For them it was about the undercover advancement of British interests. As Mike Gooley later said: '*We were all invited to take part. Our services were for and in the interests of the nation. We had to be released from regular service to make the operation unattributable.*'

Today, many would criticise David Stirling, Brian, Jim Johnson, David Smiley, John Woodhouse and Mike Gooly for becoming involved with a 'mercenary' operation. The word 'mercenary' became a pejorative term rather than a noble calling after the involvement of mercenaries in the Congo in 1960 which highlighted the complex interplay of colonial legacies, Cold War politics and post-colonial instability. As former colonies became independent nations, the existing colonial structures including the military were dismantled. Consequently, the establishment of new national armies was necessary, and internal conflicts often arose in these transitional phases. To address these difficulties, the governments of these newly independent countries often sought out professional military personnel with combat experience.

Modern opinions and stereotypes were formed as a result of the employment of mercenaries in the Congo even though they kept order, fought vicious rebel groups, protected innocent civilians and strategic assets, and at times assisted the UN and other peacekeepers.

175 Sir Mike Gooley CBE – Founder of 'Trailfinders' travel company.

No one could give a bad name to the 50 or so British and French mercenaries who operated in the Yemen. They were supported by the British and French governments, initially completely covertly but later more openly. They were paid by a legitimate government, the Kingdom of Saudi Arabia, and worked closely with an ally, Israel, all in support of a legitimate government which had been overthrown by a military coup instigated by Egypt and Russia. Both were enemies of Britain who wanted to take control of Yemen and southern Arabia with an eye on Saudi oil and the strategically important British protectorate in Aden. They worked in furtherance of British interests but eventually had to pull out when Saudi funding dried up and the Israelis lost interest after their victory against Egypt in the Six-Day War. The Israelis were however grateful that 50,000 Egyptian troops were bogged down in Yemen when they launched their lightning attack. The final factor for the end of the Yemen operation was the British withdrawal from Aden in 1967.

David Smiley, who was eventually commanding the Yemen operation, was clear on the issue, a view shared by the instigator of the Yemen involvement, Billy McLean:

> *A hired soldier in foreign service is the Oxford Dictionary's definition of the term, and so it must include fine infantrymen such as the Gurkhas and such distinguished British soldiers as General Gordon and, in our own day, Glubb Pasha. I am very happy to be in such company. Although mercenary excesses in the Congo brought discredit to our calling, I maintain that it can still be an honourable one – with the important provisos that the mercenary's own conduct is honourable, and that what he is doing is in the interest of his own country or in the defence of his own ideals. Speaking for myself, I was – and am – certain that what we were trying to do was in the interest of Britain.*

Brian maintained his involvement throughout but kept it low key. Valerie Franks had left school in 1959 at 16 to learn languages, first with a year in Austria learning German, then a year in Paris. She returned to London and attended a secretarial course where she was

David Smiley and the Imam

talent spotted and recruited by SIS. By the time of the secret war in Yemen, she was working for one of the regional directors. A story is recounted in several books that she was called in by her director one day and asked to have a quiet word with her father to tone down his involvement because he was appearing in too many intelligence reports.

This is totally untrue. SIS were fully aware of Brian's role in this operation. He had worked for them and kept in touch. Brian undoubtedly kept them informed and after their initial misgivings, SIS had become fully involved and would have known exactly what was going on.

Brian still continued to support Jim Johnson with advice and behind-the-scenes support from the hotel when needed, such as meetings with SIS, Mossad and Saudi contacts. They would also use White's for discreet lunches or dinners. He also used his considerable ability at high-level influence-building, on behalf of the operation in Yemen, and also the SAS.

The surprise win for Labour in the October 1964 General Election ushered in an era of defence cuts. The Defence White Paper published in February 1966 announced that Britain would give up Aden by 1968. It's never a good idea to signal your intention to your enemy, and this clearly had a lot to do with the ideology of the Labour Party insisting on withdrawing from any vestiges of Empire. In spite of Labour's ideological stance, Brian wanted to get to know the new Minister of Defence, Denis Healey. John Woodhouse when he was commanding 22 SAS tipped him off that Healey was a great supporter of specialist parts of the Army such as the Gurkhas and SAS, and described him as '*a very intelligent man and obviously a clear thinker, I was impressed*'. Brian scented an ally, and invited him to the 1967 SAS regimental dinner at the Hyde Park Hotel. In a break with protocol and to everyone's surprise, he accepted, saying that it was '*an unusual step in my position*'. The evening was a great success and Brian could chalk up another victory for the SAS in Whitehall.

CHAPTER 16 – BOARDROOM BATTLES

> 'It's not the size of the dog in the fight, it's the size of the fight in the dog that matters.'
>
> Mark Twain

For the next ten years, although Brian continued to remain close to all matters SAS, it was increasingly his personal life and the machinations of the hotel trade that were to come to prominence again. Brian and Zoe maintained their lifestyle of weekdays in London and weekends in Suffolk. Zoe was what might be described as a 'lady of leisure', employing a nanny to look after Valerie and George. After school on Friday afternoon she would pack the children, nanny and her whippets into their Morris Traveller estate and drive to Sluice Cottage. Brian would take the train to Woodbridge later on and Zoe would pick him up. In 1958 Zoe and Brian decided on a change of emphasis on the housing front. They would sell their large mansion flat in Drayton Court and buy a smaller London flat in Marsham Street. At the same time they would sell their relatively small Sluice Cottage and buy the Old Vicarage in the village of Sutton, which was in need of serious attention, having been empty since the end of the war.

One SAS-related event showed (like Roy Farran's trouble in Palestine) Brian's loyalty and his consistent support for his soldiers and friends. After the war 'Tanky' Challenor MM, hero of Operation WALLACE, had joined the Metropolitan Police, rising quickly through the ranks to become a feared and respected member of 'The Sweeney' or Flying Squad, working against organised crime gangs in Soho. As a Detective Sergeant at West End Central Police Station, he became known for his aggressive pursuit of criminals.

In July 1963 'Tanky' arrested several demonstrators protesting at the visit of Queen Frederica of Greece, claiming that they had been carrying house bricks and intended to use them as offensive weapons. Forensic evidence produced at their trial proved that the bricks could not have been in the suspects' pockets and that in all likelihood they had been planted. The resulting police enquiry found that 'Tanky' had been '*fitting up*' – planting evidence – on numerous suspects over a long period. 'Tanky' as part of due process was referred for a mental health assessment. He was diagnosed with paranoid schizophrenia and declared unfit for trial. He spent several years in a mental hospital but eventually recovered. Brian and others, notably Roy Farran and the SAS Association, supported 'Tanky' with money, loyalty and close friendship throughout and played no little part in his eventual recovery.

*

Brian's personal life didn't take a back seat during his frenetic development of the Hyde Park, nor did his work with Jim Johnson and David Stirling. In 1961 *Tatler* reported: '*Thursday 1st June 1961 Mrs Brian Franks and Mrs Miles de Zoete for Miss Valerie Franks and Miss Sarah de Zoete at the Hyde Park Hotel.*' The coming-out ball for Valerie was to be one of the last presentations to the Queen. By this time she was working for SIS and George was at Eton. Nine years later, on Saturday the 22nd of June 1968, Valerie married William Richards, a lawyer.

Due to his hard work and success at the Hyde Park, combined with other directorships and some astute investments on the stock market, Brian began to make a fair bit of money. His daughter Valerie maintains that she and George '*were educated courtesy of the stock exchange*'. In 1949 he fulfilled a lifelong ambition and bought a race horse, Moss Rose, which enabled him to become one of the hosts at Goodwood race week that year alongside, among others, the Duke of Norfolk, Sir John Jarvis, Major Graeme Whitelaw and Lieutenant Colonel Bernard Hornung. Hosting at Goodwood would be an annual event for Brian and Zoe until 1972. His choice of horses and his long association with racing came about through his friendship with Basil Bennett, who had always been a racing enthusiast. When Brian was commanding 21 SAS he would ask Basil, given his wartime experience, to sit in on interviews, particularly for administrative posts such as adjutant or quartermaster.

One candidate for the post of adjutant was a young cavalry officer, Tommy Wallis, who was mad keen on racing and the interview became primarily a study of runners at Windsor that afternoon. Tommy, who was also a capable soldier, got the job. A few months later Tommy was at Sandown Park when he bumped into Basil who was with his attractive daughter Vivien.[176] They hit it off immediately and their shared interest made them perfectly matched. They were married in 1949.

Tommy was a regular soldier and was periodically posted to Germany but would regularly come back to Britain, and they would stay with Vivien's parents at their country house, High Comfield Stud Farm at Ewhurst in Surrey, which Basil had bought after the war. Between them the Bennetts and Wallis found Moss Rose for Brian, which went on to win many races and eventually become a very valuable brood mare. Tommy Wallis reached the rank of colonel before retiring and becoming managing director of Racecourse Holdings Trust which owned most of the race courses in Britain. Brian's love of racing also kept him in touch with two of his close wartime friends John Hislop and Sandy Scratchley, both excellent jockeys and breeders.

Another of Brian's sporting interests was greyhound racing, and in 1962 he was asked to join the board of the Greyhound Racing Association. It was here that Brian very nearly became an early rock music entrepreneur. He got the GRA board to agree to host an Elvis Presley concert at White City dog track to raise money for the association. All was going well until Presley announced that he had taken against flying and would not be able to come over from the USA. It was more likely that the plan was scuppered by Elvis's manager Colonel Tom Parker, who had entered the US as an illegal immigrant and didn't have a passport. He actively prevented Elvis performing overseas as Parker was terrified of being caught without a passport, being deported from the US, and losing the Presley gravy train.

176 Vivien Wallis, lifelong racing fanatic who raised large amounts of money for charity and never missed a Royal Ascot since 1948. She became such a feature at Ascot race course that she would walk across the turf every day with her dogs. Nobody was allowed to do this, but nobody dared stop her as she was such a legend.

*

Things were also moving in the hotel sector. The Bennetts had formed a company, Queen Anne's Mansions and Hotels Ltd, which owned the Hyde Park. In 1953 Leonard Bennett, Basil's father, retired but retained a seat on the board. Basil was appointed Chairman and Brian Managing Director. In 1954 Alastair McGregor, one of Brian's officers from 2 SAS who had been on LOYTON and in Italy with Roy Farran, joined them as Sales Manager. The company, building on the success of the Hyde Park, started to expand. In 1963 Queen Anne's Hotels bought the Cavendish Hotel when Rosa Lewis died. They planned to demolish it and build a modern 260-room hotel on the site.

Brian and Evelyn Waugh had kept up their friendship after the war. Evelyn would stay at the Hyde Park in London but usually eat at White's with the one exception of Brian's annual 'Franks Feasts' in December. He also kept up a stream of letters to Brian, the majority of which were amusing and tongue-in-cheek:

> *September 1957*
> *Dear Brian,*
> *Have you ever, when inspecting your premises, been shown a lightless and airless cell numbered 315, with walls so thin that every fart can be heard from the next-door prisoner and a bed so narrow that if one dozes one falls out? I am sure not. It is the kind of thing that is hidden from commanding officers. It was in this cell that in your absence your henchmen sought to confine your old comrade in arms.*
> *E. Waugh.*
> *Even Harry (Lord Stavordale), who is constantly and cruelly persecuted has never, he says, seen anything like the horror of 315.*

When Waugh heard of the purchase of the Cavendish he wrote to Brian on the 28th of May 1963 insisting that '*it is essential that the Jermyn Street studio façade and the lounge remain undisturbed whatever you do behind them*', and '*it is highly desirable that Rosa's parlour remain intact*'. When Evelyn heard that the whole hotel had been demolished with no trace of the original left, he sent a furious letter to Brian accusing him of being a vandal. This caused Christopher Sykes, Waugh's biographer, to write to Brian:

How very silly of Evelyn to consider you a vandal for knocking down the old Cavendish Hotel. I am sure that Harry could have knocked it down with ease and it was of no architectural or other aesthetic value whatsoever. It could not have had any nostalgic memory for Evelyn as he was forbidden the house by Mrs Lewis. Shortly after Vile Bodies *was published I heard the old lady say, 'There are two people I am not allowing in here. One is that little swine Donegal and the other is that dirty little Evelyn Waugh.'*

The new Cavendish opened, fully booked, in July 1966. Evelyn would not see the opening, which was probably a good thing. He had started to become withdrawn and depressed. Brian continued to hold his annual Christmas dinners and in December 1965 invited Evelyn, which elicited the following response:

Dear Brian,

It is very good of you to remember your old comrade in arms. I shall think of you all with envy on December 14th but, alas, I can't be there. The truth is that I am no longer sociable – deaf, toothless, without appetite, reduced to extreme exhaustion by travel. I should only be a bore and a burden. But thanks awfully for asking me. My love to Bennett & all old friends.

I enclose a book I wrote which won't amuse you but will stand as a token of affection.

Yours ever,
Evelyn

Brian replied with an offer of free accommodation.

Dear Brian,

I am deeply touched by your wish to have me at your banquet and by the offer of rooms on 13th & 14th to rest my decayed body.

I accept with gratitude & the repeated warning that I can only be regarded as ghost. People get a macabre pleasure in observing the decay of their contemporaries. That is the only pleasure I can hope to give the assembled company. I shall have great pleasure in seeing you all. I can't hope to hear you.

Yours ever,
Evelyn

He sat opposite Brian and Christopher Sykes and next to Bob Laycock. He had felt too ill to join for drinks before lunch. He didn't eat or drink, and stayed silent throughout. Sykes caught a glance from him which clearly said '*you see the state I'm in* ...' He died of a massive heart attack in Combe Florey in Somerset on the morning of Easter Sunday, 10th of April 1966. Later that year Basil Bennett also died. The previous year, luckily as it turned out, the Bennetts' company Queen Anne's Hotels was sold to the Trust House Group. Brian was kept on the Trust House board. This would eventually lead to a boardroom battle every bit as tricky as the machinations and wrangles he had faced with the Army Staff both during the war and later in reviving the SAS. In the meantime, in October 1966, he and Zoe took an extended holiday to Ceylon prompting Ronnie Chittenden to pen another witty little rhyme:

Brian and Zoe are off to the tropics,
Full of scotch and antibiotics.

Brian also caused quite a stir when he went down to Eton to take George and some of his friends out to lunch. Accompanied by Ian Fleming, George's godfather, they drove down in a bright yellow Ferrari that Fleming had 'borrowed' from the set at Pinewood of one of the early Bond films. Needless to say George's 'street cred' soared.

*

The Trust House Group was formed in 1904 by Lord Grey with the intention of saving the traditional English coaching inn from extinction. By the end of the First World War, the company operated 100 small hotels and inns across the country. The company expanded during the 1920s and 1930s, reaching a peak of 222 hotels just before World War II. Dividends for shareholders were kept low so that profits could be ploughed back into the company. However most of the original funding was put up by eminent or aristocratic families in each county. Collectively they only formed 1 per cent of shareholders, but controlled the corporate administrative and management and were able to outvote the other 99 per cent of shareholders. During the war quite a few of the Trust House properties were requisitioned but never returned. Nevertheless by 1970 they were operating 181 hotels, totalling 10,300 rooms with an enviable reputation for quality and British tradition. They had also begun to diversify into the contract catering business, in 1966 buying John Gardner Catering. Gardner had been a Victorian butcher expanding into ships chandlery and provisioning. During the war John Gardner was contracted by the government to run factory canteens that needed to feed workers 24 hours a day. After the merger in 1966 the catering arm was called Gardner Merchant.

Enter Charles Forte, an entrepreneur with a decidedly different background and approach to business than the aristocratic and old-school-style management of Trust House.

Forte was born in Italy in 1908. His father had emigrated to America but came to live in Scotland in 1911 and set up an ice cream manufacturing business. They started a successful café called the Savoy in Alloa, which soon developed into a chain across Scotland. Carmine changed his name to Charles Forte and joined his father in Weston-super-Mare after a period of studying in Rome. By 1935 young Forte had his sights on London, borrowing money from his father to set up a milk and ice cream bar on Regent Street. By 1939 he owned a total of nine restaurants in London but in spite of being an anglophile, and having applied but not been granted citizenship, on the outbreak of war he was interned as an enemy alien for three months.

Forte's business survived the war and in 1949 he bought the Criterion Brasserie in Piccadilly Circus and two years later won the catering contract for the Festival of Britain. His business continued to thrive. In 1954 he bought the Café Royal in Mayfair and established the first food concession at the new Heathrow Airport in 1955. He set up roadside catering services that would be known as Little Chef, modelled on American style fast-food chains.

Forte moved into the luxury hotel business in 1958 when he bought the Waldorf Hotel and in 1960 he bought three luxury hotels in Paris, the George V, Plaza Athénée and the Hôtel de la Trémoille. The purchase by a '*foreigner who sold hotdogs and hamburgers*' sent shockwaves through the hotel industry.

The Trust House Group now owned the Hyde Park, Cavendish, Grosvenor House and Brown's Hotels. They were an attractive target for Charles Forte, particularly as they were linked to another contract catering business. In 1970 Forte began his campaign for a merger, pitching the idea to the Chairman of Trust House, Lord Crowther. Crowther was not receptive: '*Trust Houses is a very different sort of company from yours. I greatly doubt we could do business together.*' Forte also had a line of communication to Michael Pickard, the CEO of Trust Houses, who he thought might be more receptive to a merger. He also knew that Crowther listened to him. Pickard was an accountant with a clear understanding of figures and a sharp mind. He agreed that the merger was logical and beneficial to both sides.

Eventually Crowther came round to a deal. The negotiations lasted three weeks and both sides managed to keep them completely secret. At a stroke they had almost overnight created the largest hotel and catering company in Britain and one of the largest in the world, together owning 215 hotels in Britain and others in 13 countries. They also had 250 restaurants, 43 pubs and seven motoring service stations, in addition to airport catering, amusement parks and theatres. Trust House also had a stake in Travelodge in America and Australia.

Crowther undoubtedly saw the advantage of the merger but firmly believed he would retain control and from the outset there was a degree of friction almost certainly due to a clash of culture and style, and disagreements over major commercial decisions. It soon became apparent there was an unbridgeable gulf regarding approach and delivery. The Trust House directors were old-school, believing that a business, while it should be successful, should be gentlemanly and fun as opposed to totally focusing on the bottom line.

It had been agreed in principle that Lord Crowther would remain as Chairman of the merged company for a year and then step aside to allow Forte to take over. Soon it became clear that Crowther had no intention of stepping down, stating there was no enforceable agreement in place. Forte believed there had always been a plan to keep all effective control out of his hands.

Friction continued on a daily basis, and ultimately came into the open with Crowther confirming he was not going to step down because '*the staff don't like you*'. Forte threatened to sue him. Brian, the only professional hotelier on the Trust House board, was stuck in the middle. He didn't like Forte one bit, but he didn't like Crowther much either. He was once quoted as saying: '*I hate Charles Forte even more than I hate Crowther.*' He probably didn't like Crowther's lack of competence and business acumen, and he certainly didn't like Forte's business style. There was an atavistic clash of cultures and background. There may also have been a direct confrontation over the disbursement of the important and exclusive wine cellar at the Hyde Park Hotel, which Brian had built up over the last 20 years.

Relations continued to be very fractious, not helped by the fact that Trust Houses directors were in informal discussions with Allied Breweries for a takeover bid. A formal approach came on the 18th of October. The approach was discussed at the board meeting of the 22nd of October 1971 and rejected. On the 29th Allied Breweries withdrew their interest. Crowther went public with an article in the *Sunday Times* on the 21st of November entitled '*Crowther goes to war*'. Two days later Allied Breweries renewed their offer. The boardroom battle dragged on until the 11th of January. Allied finally withdrew their bid, and Crowther and his other Trust House supporters resigned. Forte had won.

Brian had become completely fed up with all of them. On the 2nd of December 1971, he resigned as Managing Director of Trust Houses Westminster but would stay on the main board of Trust House Forte. A week later on the 10th of December he resigned from the main board of Trust House Forte as well. He was replaced by Michael Chapman, who had been in Trust Houses since their purchase of the Imperial Hotel, Torquay, in 1969. He was also the recently appointed director of the Mediterranean and Barbados Division of Trust House Forte. Brian was reported in the press as saying, '*Since the major reconstruction at Grosvenor House and the Hyde Park Hotel has been virtually completed, I feel this is the moment to go. While there have been differences between myself and other members of the board, I now believe I am leaving the company under good management and I am extremely pleased that Sir Charles Forte has appointed another Trust Houses man to succeed me.*'

Brian held one final 'Franks Feast' Christmas lunch on the 12th of December 1971. His invitation also made it clear he was resigning and this would be the last 'Feast'. The regular poetic missive from Ronnie Chittenden was to the point:

Your letter arrived as my Master was lunching
And sending down bites of the muck he was munching
The news it contained sent me all of a quiver
And I dreaded to think I would have to deliver
This shock to all workers no matter the costs
From crapulent throttle to noisy exhaust.

I swallowed a double to bolster my mettle
And after two more felt in good enough fettle
To ring Mr Jaw who was rinsing the roof
Of his mouth and his tonsils – and gnashing his tooth
I'm sorry I said, oh alas, and alack,
Old Mustard[177] *contrived to be given the sack.*

It went on to make less than complimentary references to the new management, in the next three verses. The row was widely known about in SAS circles and Brian was more than a little amused and touched by a telephone call he received one day. One of his wartime sergeants had heard that '*someone in the hotel world*' had taken some action to the '*Colonel's disadvantage*'. He was perfectly serious when he asked: '*Shall I rub him out, sir?*' Brian acknowledged the

177 As in Colonel Mustard from the Cluedo board game.

kindness of the thought but suggested it would be better if no action were taken.

Brian was delighted to go, but the whole saga had seriously upset him and it took him a long time to get over his anger and irritation. But it did allow him to follow his country pursuits, fishing in Iceland, Scotland and Norway, stalking and lots of shooting with his faithful black labrador Nick, and of course racing. He could spend more time with his children and Zoe. His excellent lawyers had negotiated a very favourable exit package for him, including protecting his pension, enabling him to have a comfortable lifestyle. It also allowed him to continue his support of the SASthrough the association and later on as Colonel Commandant.

*

Behind the boardroom battles raging in the hotel world, Brian was fighting another boardroom battle in the corridors of the SAS establishment. Brian's tenure as Honorary Colonel of 21 SAS, was due to come to an end early in December 1972. Brian and the regimental hierarchy wanted Jim Johnson to succeed as Honorary Colonel 21 SAS. The then DSAS, Roderick 'Fergie' Semple, who had been a wartime Parachute Engineer and not served in the SAS, was rather

Front row: Maj P.C.B. Davissen TD, Capt A.M. Scrase-Dickens (Adjt), Brigadier J.D. Frost DSO, MC (Bde Comd), Lt Col D.G.C. Sutherland MC (CO), Col B.M.F. Franks DSO, MC, TD (Hon Col), Maj J.M. Woodhouse MBE, MC (2i/c) Maj E.T. Pinnock MM (QM)

nervous as to the publicity this might attract due to Jim's recent involvement in Yemen. Brian was of the opinion that this was a weak attitude and saw no reason why Jim, a perfect candidate in most people's view, should not be given the job.

As a result Brian was asked to stay on for another year to allow the fuss about Jim to blow over – and for the DSAS to move on, which he accepted, writing to Ian Davies, an eminent barrister and the last non-regular Commanding Officer of 21 SAS, at his chambers on the 14th of December.

Dear Ian,

My word, you can write a persuasive letter – which is no doubt why you are such a successful Barrister.

If you really think, as it seems you do, that I will be helping the Regiment by remaining as Honorary Colonel for one more year I will be delighted to do so. It seems to me that that is about the right time. The Brigadier, thank God, will have gone and I should think any opposition to Jim's appointment would have gone also, but things by then may have changed anyway.

I take it you will put this particular bit of machinery in motion. I will call you in on the new Commanding Officer early in the New Year and see how he goes. In the meantime, thank you for all you have done for the Regiment in the last three years.

Sadly, in the end 'funk' prevailed and Jim was not given the job, much to Brian and many others' disgust.

Ian Lapraik (left) and Ian Davies

CHAPTER 17 – COLONEL COMMANDANT

> Leventeia 'Greek': High spirits, humour, quickness of mind and action, charm, generosity, love of living dangerously, readiness for anything.
>
> 'In our desert days we used to say the regiment is the man and the man is the regiment.'
>
> David Stirling

When Brian stepped down from Trust House Forte he was delighted to be away from the rather unpleasant in-fighting of the last two years in the Trust House Forte boardroom. However, he felt he was a in bit of a vacuum. Gone were the days when the Hyde Park was a haven of civilisation, gone too were the 'Franks Feasts' and the SAS dinners, the Thursday lunches in Brian's private dining room to debate and develop the future of the SAS. Being the robust character he was he didn't let it bother him for long, although on occasion he was known to let rip about Charles Forte, the takeover and style of management.

Being very popular and capable, he had a number of lucrative directorships to keep the wolf from the door, and he was an astute investor. However he now had the time to throw himself fully into the SAS Association, of which he was still chairman.

Ever since its inception in 1945, the Association Committee was mainly made up of retired World War II veterans of the SAS and SBS and the Commanding Officers of the three SAS regiments with Brian still chairman. In 1972 Dare Newell, who was a staff captain in SAS headquarters in charge of 'A' or personnel matters, took it upon himself with Brian's approval to bring the association closer into the centre of the SAS world by juggling some of the staff positions combining the role of secretary of the association with the post of regimental adjutant and establishing a new official post of assistant secretary, a post then immediately filled by Chris Dodkin, who had been working as a civilian in the orderly room of HQ SAS. Dodkin's memories of this period, of Brian when he came to visit Dare Newell and himself, are of '*a true gentleman always supporting Dare in his endeavours to improve the association, particularly the finances*'. It was Brian's view that the association should become a charity and be able to accept donations and carry out fundraising in order to help and support SAS veterans.

On the 17th of May 1972 an incident took place which was to be the start of a decade of events which would change the profile of the SAS for ever, an era through which Brian – first in the capacity of chairman of the association, and later as Colonel Commandant – would help steer the regiment.

At 1500hrs the telephone on the Cunard Finance Director Charlie Dickinson's desk rang. A muffled voice demanded US$350,000 or six bombs hidden on the *QE2* would be detonated by two accomplices on board, a former convict and a terminally ill cancer patient. The *QE2* was halfway across the Atlantic heading for Cherbourg with 1,438 passengers and 800 crew. On board the captain, William Law, on his first journey as master, ordered all watertight doors sealed and instituted a search. When news reached London, Cunard immediately contacted the Police Special Branch and Ministry of Defence. The MOD contacted DSAS and a team consisting of an SBS officer, Captain Richard Clifford; an ATO,[178] Captain Robert Williams; an SAS sergeant, Cliff Oliver and Corporal Thomas Jones of the SBS, were ordered to stand by to parachute into the Atlantic alongside the *QE2*.

On the 18th of May the team parachuted from an RAF C-130. Weather conditions were very poor with 20-knot winds and heavy waves. Williams had never parachuted before but all arrived on board safely. Three suspicious suitcases were found and destroyed. No bombs were found and the incident declared a hoax. The FBI arrested the perpetrator, who was sentenced to ten years in prison. Clifford's team were all awarded the Queen's Commendation for Brave Conduct.

This had a significant effect on the SAS. It was the first time that they were put on public display, igniting a debate within the regiment

178 ATO – Ammunition Technical Officer – Bomb disposal expert.

"Well, as they are here, we'll only charge them one way!"

Robert Williams, Richard Clifford, William Law

about the pros and cons of publicity and media relations. There were those totally opposed to any exposure or media engagement. Others, like John Woodhouse and Brian, felt that the regiment should not hide its successes providing there were no security implications. This debate would rumble on and still continues today. The media would soon loom large for Brian during his tenure as Colonel Commandant, in six years' time.

There is no doubt that the SAS was creeping into the national consciousness, from now on helped by JAK. JAK was the pen-name of Raymond Allen Jackson, the cartoonist of the *Evening Standard* from 1952. He had a great affinity for the Army and in particular the SAS. Brian had been friendly with the cartoonists Osbert Lancaster and 'Giles' (Carl Giles), who were both regulars at the Hyde Park Hotel. Brian soon got to know JAK and he was regularly invited to regimental and association dinners, and in the 1970s and 1980s, the SAS would become regular subjects of his cartoons. The regiment quite enjoyed this form of notoriety, delivered as it was with good humour. There was even a private dining club, 'JAK's Black Pudding Club', which held a lunch once a year which many serving and past members of the SAS attended.

In 1976 Brian was asked if he would take over from Viscount Head PC, GCMG, CBE, MC[179] as Colonel Commandant of the SAS. He had

179 Anthony Head, 1st Viscount Head PC, GCMG, CBE, MC. At Eton with Brian, Life Guards in World War II. Secretary of State for War 1951–56.

no hesitation in accepting. This meant he would have to step down as chairman of the association after 31 years, resigning at the Annual General Meeting held at the Duke of York's headquarters.

> *The Commander directs that the attached Order of the Day be published in Unit Orders, in the case of 22 SAS on January 24 1977, in TAVR units in the first order succeeding that date. The Viscount Lord Head PC, GCMG, CBE, MC retires as Colonel Commandant today. He is succeeded by Colonel B. M. F. Franks DSO, MC, TD.*
>
> *CLD Newell*
> *R02*
> *For Director.*

The SAS had become firmly established, more widely accepted and respected throughout the Army, and service with the regiment was something for soldiers to aspire to. The need to fight for survival had passed. SAS operations were now of a national strategic nature and often very sensitive. It was essential to have a director of sufficient rank, experience and ability in London close to the Ministry of Defence, the Intelligence Community and other parts of government such as the Home Office and increasingly the Northern Ireland Office.

The regiment also needed a strong, effective and respected Colonel Commandant who could complement the serving director working the corridors of power, by providing advice based on experience and at the same time take responsibility for the image of the regiment. The role of a Colonel Commandant in the British Army is that of a respected elder statesman for his regiment, ensuring its heritage is guarded, bridging the gap between its history and the operational present, acting as a voice for the regiment, and providing guidance on significant matters and future policy based on considerable experience. Brian's appointment was unanimously greeted with enthusiasm with a message from the director: '*Everyone in the SAS is delighted and proud that you have taken this on.*'

In 1976 the Prime Minister Harold Wilson had rather ill-advisedly made a public statement that the SAS would be deployed in South

Armagh. Very soon the IRA would start a full-blown black propaganda or smear campaign directed at the SAS. One of Brian's first tasks was to manage the fallout of what became known as the Dunloy Incident. On the 11th of July 1978 the SAS had deployed a two-man observation team to watch a weapons hide in a grave in Dunloy cemetery. At some point during the stakeout John Boyle approached the hide and took out a weapon which he appeared to point at the concealed SAS man. They opened fire and killed him.

The IRA and Sinn Fein went into propaganda overdrive, publishing photographs of the much younger Boyle as a choirboy and making him out to be an innocent victim of a shoot-to-kill policy. A pathologist, Doctor Press, examined the body and pronounced that he had been shot in the back. There were clearly two very different versions of events, the soldiers saying that they had shot him face on when he pointed the weapon at them.

The newly appointed Director Special Forces Brigadier Peter de la Billière, an old friend of Brian's, and supported by Brian, immediately approached the Adjutant General, General Sir Robert Ford, to get hold of the best lawyers available to represent the soldiers. Once the lawyers interviewed the soldiers, they believed them and thought they would have a credible defence. A second pathologist's examination of the body was commissioned, this time carried out by Doctor James Cameron, a well-known and renowned pathologist who regularly worked on complex cases for the Metropolitan Police.

His report indicated that the first round fired hit Boyle in the front of the head. Two more shots then hit him in the back as his body spun from the impact of the first round.

> *The Lord Chief Justice of Northern Ireland, Sir Robert Lowry, summing up the case described Dr Press as a most important Crown witness, whose evidence was a clear indication that the deceased was shot in the back and that the defence of self-defence ... could not possibly stand up. But defending counsel, Mr Michael Lavery, had cross-examined Dr Press with such a wealth of convincing anatomical and scientific detail as to cause the gravest possible doubt on the reliability of his [Dr Press's] principal conclusion.*

In the event the soldiers were acquitted, and it has never been proved one way or the other whether he was an IRA volunteer or an innocent victim of a tragic accident.

The next incident, which would involve Brian more directly, came in early 1979. In March the *Daily Telegraph* ran a story that an SAS sergeant had raped Elizabeth Irwin, the wife of a doctor in Belfast, Doctor Robert Irwin. It was followed by an editorial on Saturday the 17th of March, which demanded an official enquiry by Northern Ireland Minister Roy Mason. This had all the hallmarks of a fabricated propaganda story. Peter de la Billière checked with the Commanding Officer of 22 SAS, who confirmed that there were no SAS in the area of the alleged rape at the time stated and there was no one matching the description given in the Province. De la Billière knew that they had to act quickly to kill the story, but if he as Director of the SAS issued the statement via the MOD, it would not be believed nor have the desired effect. So he telephoned Brian on Sunday morning asking for help.

Brian immediately saw the point and agreed to issue a press statement under his own name. They would need to craft the statement carefully and it would need to be issued to the Press Association and Reuters that day, in order to make Monday's papers. Brian agreed to the suggestion that Peter fly up by helicopter from Hereford in spite of the very poor weather conditions – snow and fog. Brian was due to have a house full of guests for lunch whom he could not put off. He offered Peter lunch and promised to work on the press statement immediately afterwards and get it out in time. The helicopter, after a hair-raising journey, landed on the lawn. After lunch they produced the statement and in the absence of fax or email in those days, George Franks took the statement to Reuters that evening. Brian and Peter knew it would cause a stir. It made both the 9 o'clock and 10 o'clock news as the lead item.

Frantic phone calls ensued from the MOD Director of Public Relations trying to muzzle Brian. He ignored them and the next morning his statement was in every national and regional newspaper.

> *SAS chief rejects rape report. The head of the crack Special Air Service regiment has denied that any of his men were involved in the alleged rape of a doctor's wife in Belfast.*

Col. B. M. F Franks made an unprecedented statement.

I believe the time has come to rebut the ever-growing, ill-informed comment in the press and elsewhere about my regiment. In particular, of course, I refer to the spurious reports suggesting an SAS soldier was involved in the rape ... in Belfast in 1979. At that time, no SAS soldier is known to have been in Belfast. Evidence is quite conclusive on this point and the whereabouts of every man in the regiment serving in NI at that time has been checked and accounted for. Some newspapers have suggested that the culprit was 'spirited out' of NI. So far as the SAS is concerned I am satisfied that there is no vestige of truth in this allegation. I am disturbed at the increasing tendency to report on the SAS as if it were some secret undercover organisation. In fact, it is a corps of the British Army subject to both military and civil law in exactly the same way as any other corps listed in the Army List.

Brian got an angry call from the Chief of the General Staff Field Marshal Sir Roland Gibbs, who gave him a severe ear bending. Ever his own man, Brian was delighted. The call from Gibbs caused him a great deal of amusement, and satisfaction in beating the IRA at their own game, but it also made him a marked man and he would need to be careful.

Later in a letter to Brian's second wife Bridget on Brian's death, Peter de la Billière would say that '*all his characteristics which made him the man we all loved and admired came out in this episode. His personal courage, his delicious sense of humour, his disregard for authority, and the orthodox – his considerable intellect and of course that most endearing characteristic, his love for other people and his regiment.*'

Brian, David Stirling, Jim Johnson, and the regiment would become regular targets for *Time Out*[180] magazine, necessitating a number of robust lawyers' letters to the Editor, Tony Elliott.

Towards the end of 1979 Brian started to think about his successor, who was due to take over in May 1980. Brian discussed this matter

180 *Time Out* started life in the late 1960s as a useful entertainment guide to London. In the 1970s it became very left-wing and politicised.

with his predecessor Anthony Head who wrote to him on the 8th of November.

> *Dear Brian,*
>
> *Further to our talk on Tuesday, I entirely agree with you that for the SAS, more than almost any other regiment, it is very important that they should have someone of influence and standing as their Colonel Commandant, who can represent their point of view at the highest levels.*

I appreciate that it is not easy to find somebody of this calibre, and of a suitable age and who has both experience and independence of mind. After thinking the matter over, I feel absolutely convinced that your suggestion of the present Adjutant-General is far and away the best.

Also early in 1980 Roy Farran wrote to Brian from Canada bringing back a ghost from 1944 in the shape of Raymond Lee, who had been court martialled for his behaviour during Operation HARDY/WALLACE, where he was accused of desertion and smuggling an enemy alien into Britain disguised as an SAS soldier. Lee had died of liver cirrhosis in 1978 and his widow had written to Roy in a fit of guilt pleading that Lee was not dishonourable but misunderstood. She felt that it was her fault as she was working for the Home Office aliens' department at the time. When Lee was persuaded to take the German to Britain he asked his wife to clear it with the Home Office. Scared that MI5 would never understand, she did nothing, and he was court martialled.

Farran went on to say, '*The trouble is that I fought with him and I know he had lots of guts. He was amoral, sadistic, reckless, twisty, and everything else. But he didn't run away ... Surely a fighting soldier and colourful character like this deserves more than contempt. If you felt like writing to his widow to ease her guilt she lives in Swansea ...*'

Brian, ever big-hearted and compassionate, particularly with regard to his soldiers, wrote her a letter focusing on his bravery, which he hoped would go some way to easing her guilt.

*

Zoe had been diagnosed with emphysema in 1976, which was unsurprising since both she and Brian were heavy smokers. She died in 1978 and during the autopsy it was found that her lungs showed evidence of TB scarring. It was believed that she had contracted it during the war when driving the London Fire Brigade Commander during the Blitz.

Zoe and Brian had employed a housekeeper at the Old Vicarage. After Zoe died, for some reason she became increasingly difficult

Arthur Barnard

Brian and Michael Rose

and unbearable. Not one to suffer fools, Brian fired her. To replace her, Brian found a local man in Sutton, Arthur Barnard, who was an excellent cook and known to the family as 'chef'.

He and Brian became close friends. He did the cooking and they both smoked like chimneys while watching the racing on TV. At Christmas he would put on his chef's whites and toque, and cook a wonderful Christmas lunch. He stayed with Brian until he remarried.

Brian's time as Colonel Commandant was running out; he was due to hand over to General Sir Robert Ford on the 19th of May 1980. On the 30th of April armed terrorists seized the Iranian Embassy in Prince's Gate. The SAS counter-terrorist contingency plans swung into action. Peter de la Billière moved to COBR[181] and Michael Rose the Commanding Officer of 22 SAS sped from Hereford to London with his standby counter-terrorist squadron. Brian knew there was little he could do except provide moral support, somewhat frustratingly, but he knew he had to leave it to his two key commanders who were both outstanding soldiers and knew their jobs backwards. Brian was clear that his regiment was in capable hands.

For six days the country and most of the world were glued to their televisions. At 1923hrs on the 5th of May, after the terrorists had killed a hostage and thrown his body out into the street, the police handed over control of the operation to the Army, and Mike Rose gave the

181 COBR – Cabinet Office Briefing Room: the government centre of operational planning and response, with all relevant departments and agencies represented.

Brian and Bridget

order to initiate the assault. The country watched the assault live on television. David Stirling and Brian happened to be in White's having a drink. The television was on in the billiard room and they rushed through from the bar to watch, causing David Stirling to remark '*we don't often kill our fox in the open*'.

The operation lasted 17 minutes. Five terrorists were killed and one captured. All the hostages were rescued. After the assault the SAS team returned to Regent's Park Barracks to receive congratulations from the government, including the Prime Minister Margaret Thatcher and Home Secretary William Whitelaw in person. A few days later Brian visited the team at Hereford to congratulate them on a job well done.

The embassy siege would also bring another series of JAK cartoons. On the 19th of May Brian handed over the role of Colonel Commandant to Robert Ford. He went home to Suffolk, where he married his second wife, a lifelong close friend, Bridget Nicholson – the widow of an old friend from the wine trade. They were devoted to each other. Sadly they were to have only two very happy years together.

*

On the Parade Square at Stirling Lines there is a clocktower. It is the regiment's war memorial, inscribed with the names of SAS soldiers killed on operations or training. There is a saying in the regiment that surviving a dangerous and tricky moment on operations was known as 'beating the clock'.[182] The clock ran out for Brian on the 6th of May 1982 in Ipswich General Hospital. He had begun to feel unwell in the evening after a fun day at Newmarket Races and checked himself in to hospital. Dare Newell, his old friend and comrade, was at his bedside with him when he died. Brian was suffering from lung cancer brought on by his fondness for Senior Service. Incredibly there had been no previous diagnosis and he was spared a long and painful demise.

Barely a month before he died, the Argentinians had invaded the Falkland Islands. Sadly Brian would never know of the outstanding success of the regiment there. It was sad he could not welcome them home and congratulate them on a job well done.

*

David Stirling was always clear about the standards necessary for admission into the SAS, and what was required of every man who passed through the gates of Stirling Lines: '*The very survival of the regiment, in a society wary of elitism, depends on the calibre of each individual man recruited. This was, is and must always remain the cornerstone. I know the regiment believes in this and must always do so.*' He set out four clear principles for Special Forces officers: the unrelenting pursuit of excellence; the maintenance of the highest standards of discipline; a classless but not rankless structure and the maintenance of a sense of humour and humility at all costs. These principles are still used as a benchmark for officer selection into the Special Forces today.

Brian Franks lived up to these principles his entire life. He was an inspiring leader, whether in the Vosges Mountains or the marbled halls of the Hyde Park Hotel. Other than the Stirling brothers, Brian was probably the most original thinker produced by the SAS during the war. He was the driving force for the survival of the SAS, taking up the mantle from the Stirlings, ensuring that the SAS returned to

182 After a popular TV game show from the 1950s and 1960s, 'Sunday Night at the London Palladium', which featured a 15-minute game-show slot called 'Beat the Clock'.

the order of battle of the British Army, and helping the regiment to become what it is today. Brian lived to see it used in the way that he, the Stirlings and Paddy Mayne had fought for in the days before D-DAY. It is now one of Great Britain's most vital strategic assets, revered and feared throughout the world.

Brian was buried with a small family funeral in Sutton church next to his home, the Old Vicarage, on Tuesday the 11th of May. A memorial service was held at St Columbus's Church, Pont Street on Wednesday the 26th of May, which was conducted by Fraser McLuskey and attended by Brian's extended family and many of his friends. Almost the entire Army Board was there, including his successor as Colonel Commandant Robert Ford, as was the SAS aristocracy represented by David Stirling, Peter de la Billière, Ian Lapraik, Jim Johnson, Dare Newell and Tom Burt among others. Bridget received hundreds of letters of condolence, including one from David Niven which said, '*We were friends from the age of eight, and he never seemed to change.*'

Brian was tough, courageous, resolute and determined. He sometimes didn't suffer fools and in the words of his daughter Valerie '*could give one a really furious bollocking*'. Fraser McLuskey recalls that he first met Brian in a formation headquarters in Germany in 1945. He was irately tearing into a staff officer, who had committed some heinous offence against Brian's beloved regiment. But beneath it there was a gentler spirit with much understanding and compassion for human weaknesses and failings. He was an unusual man with rare and encouraging qualities and a specialist in the art of the impossible. Above all he loved having fun and in all likelihood would have summed up his life in the words of his friend the cricket commentator Brian Johnston, '*What fun it all was.*'

In the words of Roy Farran, who knew him better than most: '*Brian was loved by us all as a real fighting colonel who took an interest in every single man in the unit. As a leader of men he was a prince of a guy.*' And Dare Newell: '*Without his wisdom, his charm, his drive and vitality, there would be no SAS today. We owe him almost everything.*' Fraser McLuskey again: '*His friendship and loyalty, so generously bestowed, enriched us all. His lightness of touch kept us from taking ourselves too seriously. His courage made it easier for us to be brave.*'

The final word must go to Tom Burt, the quartermaster of 2 SAS: '*I will say that I am very proud to have had the honour to have served with such a fine example of an English gentleman.*'

We are the Pilgrims, master; we shall go
Always a little further: it may be
Beyond that last blue mountain barred with snow
Across that angry or that glimmering sea ...
'The Golden Road to Samarkand', James Elroy Flecker (1913)

EPILOGUE

While researching this book, several people asked me if I thought that, given his long friendship with Evelyn Waugh, Brian was a model for one of the characters in the *Sword of Honour* trilogy. Tommy Blackhouse comes to mind, but it is dangerous to ascribe specific models to fictional characters. Rather like James Bond, Tommy is more likely to be a pastiche, which includes Bob Laycock, Bill Stirling and Brian.

Brian had a very wide circle of friends from all walks of life, both civilian and military. He kept closely in touch with them through his Thursday lunches and Christmas Franks Feasts at the Hyde Park Hotel, at White's, and also through both the Commando Veterans and the Special Air Service Regimental Associations. It would be difficult to keep track of all of them, but here is a snapshot of 'what happened next' to some of the cast of characters in this story.

David Niven: Having given up his promising career in film, to return to Britain to fight for his country, he resumed his Hollywood career. He became one of the best-known and loved actors of the twentieth century, starring in 92 films. He retired to Switzerland and died in 1983 from motor neurone disease aged 73.

David Stirling: Left the Army in 1947 and moved to Rhodesia. He founded the Capricorn Society which aimed to fight racial discrimination in Africa. It didn't work out and closed in 1959. Always the innovator, his next adventure was Watchguard International, the first private security company and the forerunner of the modern private security industry. During the 1960s and 1970s his offices were at 22 **S**outh **A**udley **S**treet! He was knighted in 1990. He died later that

year. In 2002 a statue of him was unveiled on the Hill of Row near his family home at Keir.

Bill Stirling: Returned home to Keir after his run-in with 'Boy' Browning and took no further part in the war. He remained on the held strength of the Scots Guards as a reserve officer until 1961. He was appointed Forestry Commissioner for Scotland by King George VI. He also farmed in Tanzania, but lost his 4,000-acre estate when it was 'nationalised' by President Julius Nyerere in 1974. He sold the family estate in Scotland and moved to London. In December 1982 he fell and broke a leg at his home in Park Lane. He was undiscovered for 36 hours and subsequently died on the 1st of January 1983.

Robert Laycock: Remained as Chief of Combined Operations until 1947. In 1954 he was knighted and appointed Commander in Chief and Governor of Malta, during a very tense period of relations between the British and Maltese Governments, a post he held for five years. From 1960–66 he was Colonel Commandant of the SAS. He died on the 10th of March 1968.

Several SAS officers became involved in Antarctic expeditions including **Paddy Mayne** and **John Tonkin**. Mayne was killed in a car accident in 1955. John Tonkin retired to Australia and died in 1995.

John Durnford-Slater: Remained with the Commandos for the rest of the war, taking part in the D-DAY landings and operations in Holland and Germany. He retired after the war and became bursar of Bedford School. He was killed on the 5th of February 1972 when he fell under a train at Haywards Heath Station.

Evelyn Waugh: Demobbed in September 1945 and resumed his '*tempestuous lifestyle*'. Although continuing to be a very successful author, his physical and mental health was unpredictable. In 1960 he was offered a CBE but turned it down, believing he should have been given a knighthood! He remained close friends with Brian but his health took its toll and he died of a heart attack on Easter Sunday, 10th of April 1966.

Christopher Sykes: Went to work for the BBC in 1945. He was also a freelance journalist for, among others, the *Spectator* and the *Observer*. He wrote 15 books, a mix of fiction and biographies, including that of Evelyn Waugh in 1975. He died in 1986.

John Hislop: Having won an MC in 1945, returned to the world of racing and was described as '*probably the finest amateur jockey of all time on the flat*', riding the winners of 102 races. He also became a very successful breeder. He bred Brigadier Gerard, one of the greatest race horses of the post-war era. He was also an accomplished author and journalist, racing correspondent of the *Observer*, *News of the World* and *Sporting Chronicle*. He died in 1994.

Roy Farran: After his return from Palestine, he left the Army and lay low on Bill Stirling's estate in Scotland. During that time the Irgun sent a parcel bomb to his home address. His younger brother opened it and was killed by the explosion. Roy spent time in Africa, returning to Britain to run as a Conservative candidate in the 1950 General Election. He was unsuccessful and emigrated to Canada, where he had both a successful business and political career culminating in being Solicitor General of Alberta. He died in 2006.

Henry Druce: Returned to SIS after the war serving in London, Holland and Indonesia. After retirement in 1951, he emigrated to Canada and built up a shipping business in Newfoundland, Quebec and the Cayman Islands. He retired in 1981 and died in January 2007.

John Manners: Lord John Manners's last job in the Army was to escort Grossadmiral Karl Dönitz to the Nuremberg Trials. Dönitz was so charmed by Manners that he presented him with an oriental carpet. Manners returned to Belvoir Castle and after several eccentric business ventures started the successful Belvoir Fruit Farms. He also spent a lot of time at his other family property, Haddon Hall, where he continued to develop the magnificent gardens, and was often seen on the estate fishing '*with a cigar in his mouth and a labrador by his side*'. He died in December 2001.

Eric Barkworth: Left the Army in 1949. He married his German secretary, who had worked with him at Villa Dengler. They emigrated to Australia where he worked in Queensland helping to settle foreign immigrants. He died in July 1985.

Dusty Rhodes: Returned to his native Barnsley and worked for the council in the parks department. He continued to feel very strongly about his murdered comrades and gave many interviews about them. He died in 1990.

Yurka Galitzine: Left the Army in 1949 and set up a public relations company. He developed several successful businesses and was closely involved in some of David Stirling's ventures. He died in 2002.

Robert de Lesseps – GOODFELLOW: Left the British Army in December 1945 being transferred back to the French Army. He then joined the French Intelligence Service SDECE (later DGSE) and worked both for the World Bank and European Development Bank. He died in 1981.

Tom Burt: Stayed in the Army after the disbandment of the SAS, becoming Senior Quartermaster of the British Army of the Rhine. He retired to Wivenhoe and was not only the SAS Association Secretary but also a welfare officer at Colchester Military Prison. He died in November 1987 aged 92.

Anthony Greville-Bell: Joined 21 and 22 SAS. He became a screenplay writer, of which five were made into films. In the 1980s he became a sculptor. His bronze of a wounded soldier being helped to safety is in the SAS Memorial Garden. He died in 2008.

John 'Jock' Easton: After the war served in both 21 and 22 SAS. After leaving the Army, he started a film double and stunt agency with Joe Powell, a former Army Commando. They stood in for many famous actors with Jock doubling for Gregory Peck in *The Guns of Navarone*. Powell tried his hand at acting, playing Sergeant Windridge in *Zulu*.

Bob Walker-Brown: Stayed in the Army after the SAS was disbanded. He then joined 21 SAS as training major and 22 SAS as Second-in-Command before commanding 23 SAS. He served on the Defence Intelligence Staff and retired in 1964. He died in 2009.

Basil Bennett: Retired after the sale of the Hyde Park to Trust House. He spent his time at his stud farm near Ascot and died in 1966.

Hilary Bray: After the war he went back to stockbroking for Row and Pitman, which he didn't take that seriously. He was made a senior partner, which he appeared to have accepted subject to three months' holiday a year. Some thought this rather much and they met to discuss it without him. At the end, they said delightedly that all was well and his condition was unanimously accepted. '*What was accepted?*' asked Hilary. '*Three months off a year,*' they said. '*Oh no,*' he replied, '*you've got it wrong. I said three months on and nine off.*' Hence his early retirement, about which he was very happy as it gave him more time for his preferred life of skiing, cricket, golf and fishing, and for many amusing lunches and dinners with Brian, Ian Fleming and Evelyn Waugh. He died in 1980.

'Tanky' Challenor: After his trial and detention in a mental hospital he worked for the firm of solicitors who had defended him. He retired to Cornwall and he died in 2008 aged 86.

Jim Johnson: After the Yemen operation he set up one of the first and most successful private security companies, KMS, together with David Walker, a regular officer in 22 SAS. One of their first major contracts was to set up and train the Sultan of Oman's Special Forces with the full approval of the British Government. He died in 2008.

Philip Dunne: Left the Commandos in 1946. He loved racing and became a breeder, as well as entering politics as a Conservative MP. Shimi Lovat wrote that '*he had a kind of twinkle that sometimes debunked and seldom reassured his superiors*'. He died in 1965 aged 61.

David Smiley: After the Yemen operation he wrote three books: *Arabian Assignment*, *Albanian Assignment* and *Irregular Regular*. He died in 2009.

Abbé Gassman: Remained as the parish priest of Moussey until his death in 1973. He was instrumental in preserving the memory not only of his parishioners who had been killed in the war, but also the memory of the SAS men of LOYTON. He is buried in the Moussey Cemetery alongside the graves of several of the SAS.

*

The memory of the events of the autumn of 1944 remains very strong in Moussey and the surrounding area. The LOYTON Association, formed in 2022, is dedicated to preserving the legacy of the operation and those involved in it, both British and French. They continue to work on on-site memorials and have plans to turn the Château de Belval, the former Gestapo headquarters, into a museum.
https://operationloyton1944.org

In Britain the events of Operation LOYTON are remembered in the Special Forces Memorial Grove at the National Memorial Arboretum. The Special Forces Memorial Grove was the brainchild of Len Owens MM, who escaped with Brian Franks (See Chapter 10), and Mike Colton. Since 2003, under Mike Colton's guidance, the Special Forces Grove has developed into a very special place. On the 1st of May 2026 a new memorial, the Moussey Memorial, was dedicated in the grove.
https://alliedspecialforcesmemorialgrove.org/
https://thenma.org.uk

ANNEX A – DAVID STIRLING'S SPEECH AT THE OPENING OF STIRLING LINES, 30TH JUNE 1984

What a magnificent gathering; it moves me to conclude that our regiment has a special magic in generating for itself an intense loyalty in all who have served it. Indeed we are more than just a regiment – we are a family.

In the SAS it is a tradition never to be heard in public boasting about our regiment's past or present performances. Today, because this is strictly a family occasion, I am going to break that rule – in a modest way.

Almost to the day 43 years ago as a second lieutenant and known to be something of a 'cheekie laddie', and of dubious value to the Army, I submitted to Field Marshal Auchinleck's Chief of General Staff a paper setting out in my own nearly illegible handwriting the SAS proposition. Within days I was authorised to raise and command a 65-man unit to be called L Detachment, SAS Brigade; and within minutes of getting that favourable nod, the SAS was underway.

Most survivors of the original SAS foundation unit – and I understand we are known in the regiment as the Dirty Dozen – are here today (and in spirit alongside me). Perhaps you can understand our astonishment, and how proud we are, in looking around this mighty throng.

After L Detachment's first disastrous parachute operation on a moonless and stormy night in November 1941, L Detachment was reduced to only 27 men; but it was more than enough to get on with proving the SAS role.

In January 1942 during our drive for recruits we were joined by Georges Bergé and his Free French unit. From this group eventually were born the French SAS Regiments. Bergé's men were of superb quality and they were the bravest of the brave.

In those early days we came to owe the Long Range Desert Group a deep debt of gratitude. The LRDG were the supreme professionals of the desert and they were unstinting in their help. Here among us today is David Lloyd Owen, a wartime Commanding Officer of this magnificent unit. We are proud to regard the Long Range Desert Group as honorary members of our SAS family.

By February 1943, L Detachment had prospered at the enemy's expense and had become the first SAS regiment. By then we had acquired our full establishment of Jeeps and supply vehicles, and we had consolidated our maritime capabilities by incorporating, under George Jellicoe, the Special Boat Squadron. Thus, sub-units of the regiment could arrive at a selected target area by air, by sea or by land.

Shortly after I was nabbed by the enemy and after a hiccough or two the command of the 1st SAS Regiment passed to the great Blair 'Paddy' Mayne.

In the meantime the 2nd SAS Regiment has been formed by my brother, Bill, and commanded by him until he had a bitter quarrel with the High Command who insisted on his regiment being used in a semi-tactical role for which it had not been trained. Although he had to resign he won the argument. He was succeeded by Brian Franks, who was allowed to revert to the true SAS strategic function – of operating deep behind the enemy lines. At the end of the war Paddy Mayne was still in command of the 1st SAS and Brian Franks of the 2nd SAS and the SAS Brigade from the end of 1944 was under the command of Mike Calvert; while in the Middle East, George Jellicoe had been succeeded by David Sutherland in command of the Special Boat Squadron.

You will all know of the prodigious range of SAS operations carried out in the Western Desert, Italy, France, Norway, Germany and the eastern Mediterranean. A senior general, Miles Dempsey, who commanded 13 Corps, in writing to the commanding officers of the 1st and 2nd SAS Regiments, summarised his views on the SAS as follows:

'In my military career, and in my life, I have commanded many, many units but I have never met a unit in which I had such confidence as I have in yours. And I mean that.' Surely a marvellous accolade coming from such a famous soldier.

After the war the anti-climax – we were disbanded. Had it not been for Brian Franks we would have been consigned to oblivion – just a meagre footnote in the history of the Second World War. With admirable tenacity of purpose he persuaded the military establishment to form 21 SAS as a Territorial unit. By 1951 the 22nd SAS was being formed in Malaysia and the regiment soon thereafter regained its proper status.

With John Woodhouse and his successors in command there began the post-war heyday of the regiment. Campaigns were fought in Malaysia, Borneo, Aden, Oman, Northern Ireland, South Georgia and the Falkland Islands – campaigns often operationally complex and each of them studded with episodes demanding the full range of SAS skills.

During the post-war period the SAS family was further enriched by the forming of the Australian, New Zealand and Rhodesian squadrons. Each of them has merited splendid chapters in the history of its own country. The Australian and the New Zealand SAS retain the strongest links with Hereford. The Rhodesian SAS, sadly now disbanded, had its roots in 22 SAS as C Squadron. Their roll of honour stands alongside that of 22 SAS within these Lines.

At this point I want to emphasise that I have always felt uneasy in being known as the founder of the regiment. To ease my conscience I would like it to be recognised that I have five co-founders: Jock Lewes and Paddy Mayne of the original L Detachment; Georges Bergé who started the French SAS; Brian Franks who re-raised the SAS flag after the war and John Woodhouse who created the modern SAS during the Malayan Campaign by restoring to the regiment its original philosophy.

There are so many others who have played vital parts in the SAS story like Mike Calvert, Ian LaPraik, Eddie Blondeel (who raised and commanded the Belgian SAS), Christodoulos Tzigantes and his Greek Sacred Brigade, a squadron of which fought gallantly alongside the SAS in the Middle East, Pat Riley, Bob Bennett, Johnny Watts, Geordie Lillicoe, Peter de la Billière, Fitzroy Maclean, Johnny Cooper, Tankie Smith, Tom Burt, Roy Farran and 'Mr SAS' himself, Dare Newell – but to mention them all would be almost like calling the roll.

I must specially commend to you the wise words of Neville Howard on the standard of the SAS man. I would go further. The very survival of the regiment, in a society of elitism, depends on the calibre of each individual man recruited. This was, is and must remain the cornerstone. I know the regiment believes in this and must always do so.

There is a further imperative which the SAS has traditionally imposed upon itself. The regiment must never regard itself as a corps d'élite, because down that road would lie the corruption of all our values. A substantial dash of humility along with an ever-active sense of humour must continue to save us from succumbing to this danger. Only then can we be sure of consolidating the foundations of these splendid new Lines and shielding the spirits and integrity of those setting out from here on their exacting tasks.

The sum total of all that has been accomplished in all those campaigns waged during the regiment's 43 years; the sacrifices of all those who have died, been disabled or wounded, from the time of our first casualty in the Western Desert to the last just two months ago on Mount Everest; the grief and anxieties caused to the wives and families throughout those years; all this must be added together for us properly to grasp the scale of our investment in the regiment as it stands today. We are deeply proud of our regiment and we are confident that in the crucial years ahead, as we advance towards our fiftieth anniversary, the SAS will further enhance that standing and thereby its ability to serve our Queen and Country.

And, now, on behalf of the entire SAS family – with a chest fit to bust in sheer proudness, I declare open the Stirling Lines.

ANNEX B – ORDER OF THE DAY

Letter from General Eisenhower to Brigadier McLeod, S.A.S. Brigade

Supreme Headquarters
Allied Expeditionary Force
Office of the Supreme Commander

SHAEF/17240/2/4/Ops(C)
GCT 370.2-4/Ops (C)

25 Sep. 44

Dear McLeod,

I wish to send my congratulations to all ranks of the Special Air Service Brigade on the contribution which they have made to the success of the operations of the Allied Expeditionary Force.

The ruthlessness with which the enemy have attacked Special Air Service troops has been an indication of the injury which you were able to cause to the German armed forces both by your own efforts and by the information which you gave of German dispositions and movements.

Many Special Air Service troops are still behind enemy lines; others are being re-formed for new tasks. To all of them I say, 'Well done, and good luck.'

Yours sincerely,

DWIGHT EISENHOWER
Brigadier R.W. McLeod,
Commander, SAS.Bde

ANNEX C – CITATIONS

Military Cross: Termoli Italy 3–7 October 1943
At TERMOLI between Oct. 3rd and 7th Major FRANKS carried out the duties of Brigade Major SS Bde. Throughout the period this officer showed a fine sense of initiative and complete disregard of personal danger. Early on he saw movement in the station and went forward by himself and captured two German soldiers. Later he was continually visiting the most forward troops making any necessary adjustments and exposing himself fearlessly. During the critical counter-attacks period his personal example and steadiness were an example to all ranks, did much to save the situation, particularly on the extreme right, where he personally organised and placed the troops. He was continually leading and encouraging the men and his resolute manner and confidence were a most important factor.

Distinguished Service Order: France August to October 1944
Lt-Col B.F.M. FRANKS dropped by parachute behind the enemy lines in the VOSGES on 31 Aug. in order to organise SAS operations in that area. In spite of repeated enemy attacks which forced the SAS parties to move continuously, Lt-Col FRANKS succeeded in organising successful operations including the reception and employment of armed Jeeps. Owing to his courage and initiative a large party of uniformed troops were able to operate in a strongly held enemy territory and inflict great damage on the enemy with little or no assistance from local partisans. The parties successfully withdrew through the lines on 11 Oct., Lt-Col FRANKS being wounded during the process. Throughout most of the period the SAS parties were within twenty miles of the front lines in an area constantly patrolled and searched by the enemy. Weather conditions were appalling and prevented regular resupply by air. By his coolness and cheerfulness throughout a long-drawn-out period of danger and hardship, with little food, Lt-Col FRANKS was an inspiration to all under his command without which the men could not have carried on.

Légion d'Honneur – Knight. Vosges Mountains September–October 1944
Lieutenant Colonel Franks, a highly qualified Commander of a SAS Regiment, was given the difficult and dangerous mission of parachuting into the western Vosges region in order to disrupt the enemy. He was steadfast throughout the mission, showing great courage and resolve, despite the significant slowdown in the Allied advance. He worked closely with the local Maquis who he had equipped and armed in achieving the objectives assigned to his unit from mid-August to October 1944. Despite the brutal response of the enemy he inflicted severe losses in personnel and equipment on the enemy during repeated attacks. He was wounded in action.

In addition Brian held many other decorations...

- Croix de Guerre
- North Africa Star
- Italy Star
- France and Germany Star
- 1935–45 Star
- Defence Medal
- 1939–45 War Medal
- Territorial Decoration
- Queen Elizabeth II Coronation Medal
- Queen Elizabeth II Jubilee Medal

ANNEX D – HITLER'S COMMANDO ORDER – KOMMANDOBEFEHL

This order was signed by Hitler on the 18th of October 1942 and issued with a covering letter from General Jodl, the Army Chief of Staff, on the 19th.

HEADQUARTERS OF THE ARMY	*SECRET*
No.55 1781/42 g.k. Chefs W.F.St/Qu.	*F.H.Qu. 19.10.42*

The enclosed Order from the Führer is forwarded in connection with destruction of enemy Terror and Sabotage-troops.

This order is intended for Commanders only and is in no circumstances to fall into Enemy hands.

Further distribution by receiving Headquarters is to be most strictly limited.

The Headquarters mentioned in the Distribution list are responsible that all parts of the Order, or extracts taken from it, which are issued are again withdrawn and, together with this copy, destroyed.

Chief of Staff of the Army
JODL

The Führer	*SECRET*
No. 003830/42 g.Kdos.OWK/Wst	*F.H.Qu. 18.10.1942*

1. *For a long time now our opponents have been employing in their conduct of the war, methods which contravene the International Convention of Geneva. The members of the so-called Commandos behave in a particularly brutal and underhand manner; and it has been established that those units recruit criminals not only from their own country but even former convicts set free in enemy territories. From captured orders it emerges that they are instructed not only to tie up prisoners, but also to kill out-of-hand unarmed captives who they think might prove an encumbrance to them, or hinder them in successfully carrying out their aims. Orders have indeed been found in which the killing of prisoners has positively been demanded of them.*
2. *In this connection it has already been notified in an Appendix to Army Orders of 7.10.1942. that in future, Germany will adopt the same methods against these Sabotage units of the British and their Allies; i.e. that, whenever they may appear, they shall be ruthlessly destroyed by the German troops.*
3. *I order, therefore:*

   From now on all men operating against German troops in so-called Commando raids in Europe or in Africa, are to be annihilated to the last man. This is to be carried out whether they be soldiers in uniform, or saboteurs, with or without arms; and whether fighting or seeking to escape, and it is equally immaterial whether they come into action from ships and aircraft, or whether they land by parachute. Even if these individuals on discovery make obvious their intention of giving themselves up as prisoners, no pardon is on any account to be given. On this matter a report is to be made in each case to Headquarters for the information of Higher Command.

4. *Should individual members of these Commandos, such as agents, saboteurs etc, fall into the hands of the Armed Forces through any other means, for example, through the Police in one of the Occupied Territories, they are to be instantly handed over to the S.D. To hold them in military custody – for example P.O.W. Camps, etc only as a temporary measure, is strictly forbidden.*
5. *The order does not apply to the treatment of those enemy soldiers who are taken prisoner or give themselves up in open battle, in the course of normal operations, large scale attacks; or in major assault landings or airborne operations. Neither does it apply to those who fall into our hands after a sea fight, nor to those enemy soldiers who, after air battle, seek to save their lives by parachute.*

6. I will hold all Commanders and Officers responsible under Military Law for any omission to carry out this order, whether by failure in their duty to instruct their units accordingly, or if they themselves act contrary to it.

A. Hitler

ANNEX E – 2 SAS SOLDIERS MURDERED ON OPERATION LOYTON

Trooper Christopher ASHE
Trooper Frederick L. AUSTIN
Trooper James W. R. BENNETT
Lieutenant James D. BLACK
Trooper Selwyn P. BROWN
Lieutenant Geoffrey C. CASTELLAIN
Trooper Reginald S. CHURCH
Trooper John J. CONWAY
Trooper Jack S. CROSIER
Lieutenant David G. DILL
Trooper James F. DOWLING
Lance Corporal John H. ELLIOT
Sergeant Michael B. FITZPATRICK MM
Trooper Maurice A. GRIFFIN
Lance Corporal James HALL
Sergeant Ralph HAY
Trooper Richard IRELAND
Corporal Thomas IVISON
Corporal George KING (Kasperoritch)
Trooper Donald LEWIS
Trooper Leonard E. C. LLOYD
Sergeant Robert LODGE DCM
Trooper Peter McGOVERN
Sergeant Walter H. E. NEVILL
Trooper Frederick PUTTICK
Captain Denis B. REYNOLDS
Lance Corporal George ROBINSON
Lieutenant Joseph ROUSSEAU
Trooper James SALTER
Lieutenant James L. SILLY
Sergeant Frank E. TERRY-HALL
Sergeant Percy R. THORPE MM
Trooper Edwin T. WEAVER
Captain Andrew R. WHATELY-SMITH
Corporal Harry WINDER

TEAM JACOB HQ Special Forces
Captain Mavrick BOISSARIE
Captain Victor GOUGH

PHANTOM Detachment
Private Peter BANNERMAN
Sergeant Gerald DONOVAN
Private George JOHNSTON

ANNEX F – RESISTANCE SUPPORT TO 2 SAS – OPERATION LOYTON

Camilla Sykes, wife of Captain Christopher Sykes, Intelligence Officer of 2 SAS on Operation LOYTON accompanied her husband to Moussey in August 1945 for the first memorial service. On her return she wrote this article:

I have just returned from a visit to Lorraine where my husband was parachuted last year. I have been touring the Vosges towns, visiting the families who helped our SAS troops when they fought in the area behind the German lines before the liberation in November. At the moment, it is a very sad part of France. We went through the Blitzkrieg in England, the anxiety and terror of the V-1 and V-2, but I wonder if anywhere in England we suffered agony comparable to that inflicted on the people of Lorraine by the Germans. Let me give you an idea of what eastern France did for our men and at what cost.

In August, the Americans were rapidly advancing towards the Moselle. The Vosges Maquis answered the call for liberation and rose up. At that moment, nobody understood that it was a fatal error. They had risen up too soon. They had not yet received the weapons and they had not been trained. The Germans attacked in force and the Americans were stopped on the Moselle. Early in September, the Maquis was dispersed by the Germans with terrible losses.

The Germans thought they had swept away all resistance in the Vosges.

And yet they were singularly mistaken. The remnants of the Maquis continued to fight and eventually received their weapons. In the meantime, the SAS had been able to build up a certain force and could now give the Maquis extra weapons, of those they had received from their own headquarters. This small corps of Maquis operated so successfully that the Germans, until November, did not dare to go into the woods without being in large numbers and therefore with great noise.

But by November it was too late. The SAS had been able to get organised and attack. In July and August, the Vosges is usually an ideal holiday destination. But in September and October the nights are freezing and the rain often lasts for long days. Replenishment of SAS supplies was often interrupted for long periods and the Germans had begun to fortify the slopes. It thus became necessary to rely on the local people for food and shelter, and to rely entirely on their loyalty and courage, for one word of indiscretion or treachery would have sealed the fate of all the partisans. That word was never uttered. The local families resisted all threats of reprisals and torture. In some cases, they were actually tortured, but no one ever gave us up.

I went to see many of these people and was moved by their courage and self-sacrifice. What courage these French women showed, wives of farmers or workers whose husbands had almost all been in the Maquis.

One woman had Germans billeted in her house, and three British paratroopers hidden in a pile of hay. She managed to feed the British in her kitchen and at the same time cooked for a large number of German officers. A 20-year-old girl went every evening by roundabout ways to bring food to soldiers at a British base in the forest, miles away. She considered it all a terribly exciting and rather comical adventure. Alas, these good people paid dearly for their tenacity.

On the edge of the Vosges there is, or rather there was, a beautiful old town on the Meurthe: Saint Dié. It is famous because it was there that in 1507 a book was published about the explorations of Amerigo Vespucci, in which the name of America was mentioned for the first time. Saint Dié is called the Godmother of America. Today this city hardly exists. It was not bombed or shelled. No. It was burned by the Germans out of hatred. They systematically burned the city, street by street, house by house. Today it is a mass of ruins as deserted and as desolate as the worst parts of the city of London. There are streets where you get lost because there are no houses to guide you through the rubbish blocking the way.

It was there that the bishop asked the German commander to spare the church. He gave the Bishop his word of honour that it would not be burnt. But instead he blew it up. You get used to seeing houses burnt down in the Vosges. You see everywhere farms where the SAS or the Maquis were attacked. And yet this destruction of property is only a small part of the tragedy of Lorraine and the price paid by the people of the Vosges for the help they gave us. Worst of all was the loss of their young men.

Continuing their brutal policy of destruction and looting, the Germans deported all the young men they could find. This is how they were taken: on 24 September, they were inspected by the Germans in the market square. The senior German officer told them: 'You can all go home on condition that those who have information about the parachutists come forward.'

Not one of them moved. The result was not long in coming.

My husband told me that when he returned in December, these people who had suffered so much to help his regiment felt no bitterness or regret, but on the contrary received them with every possible care. What more can you ask of an ally? When you meet these people, you begin to understand how they accomplished these feats. They possess more than anywhere else the irresistible French cheerfulness. In one house, I noticed some ugly stains on the wall in the living room of the lady of the house. So, we asked her how it happened. She laughed and said: 'The Germans were so greedy! They loved eggs. So I put a small, appetising pile of rotten eggs in the middle of the table. The Germans were furious.'

Key members of the Resistance who provided support to 2 SAS:

Blaison, Joséphine
Cherrier, Alcide
Clerc, Marcel
Colmant, Rose
Doutrey, René
Folcher, René
Freine, Albert & Irene
Gander, Lucien
Gassman, Abbé Achille
Gaston, Petit- Jean
George, Fernand
Georges, Victor
Gourrier, Paul
Granjon, Jean
Helle, Paul
Huin, Jean-Baptiste
Launay, Clément
Launay, Henri
Lequeux, Henri
Lequeux, René
Malaise, Yvonne
Mallens, Étienne
Marchal, Leon
Ploussard, Gaston
Py, Jules
Renault, Marie
Roland, Myrhiam & Frederic
Suchet, Roger
Thirion, Marie
Thomas, Jacques
Tisserant, Andre & Marcelle
Toussaint, Charles & Margueritte

SOURCES AND BIBLIOGRAPHY

The research for this book began at the end of 2024, almost as soon as *A Suspicion of Spies* had been published. One book flowed from the other, the common denominator being Robert de Lesseps, working for Biffy Dunderdale and being 'borrowed' from SIS by Brian Franks for Operation LOYTON. Brian Franks's story has never been told, and it was clear to me that this needed to be put right. His family, the Special Forces community and his huge circle of friends wanted his achievements to be recognised. They were all unstinting in their support. As a result I was lucky to have total access to private papers, correspondence and archives, and to be granted many personal interviews. Much was uncovered but one document eluded me – Bill Stirling's resignation letter, in spite of extensive searches at the National Archives, the SAS and Scots Guards Archives, and the Stirling family papers.

PRIVATE PAPERS, PERSONAL INTERVIEWS AND CORRESPONDENCE

Valerie Richards
Ingrid Franks
Jamie and Susie Lowther-Pinkerton
Franks family archive
Marc and Bruno de Lesseps
General Sir Peter de la Billière, KCB, KBE, DSO, MC, DL
General Sir Michael Rose KCB, CBE, DSO, QGM, DL
Martha Mlarnic: The Papers of Major General Sir Robert Laycock KCMG, CB, DSO
Charlie Maxted
Michael Orr
Patrick Baty
Pip Birtwistle
Peveral Manners
Eddie Manners
Amy Crossland
David Farran
David Anderson
Philippe Get
Archie Stirling
Johnny Stirling
Xan Smiley
Rupert Johnson
Chris Dodkin
Richard Mead
Rupert Alison
David Walker
Bertie Wetherall
Damien Lewis

Rob Hann
Mark Miller-Mundy
Alan Hoe
Gavin Rankin
Clive Jones
Jason Philips
Lady Dunne
Nicky Dunne

PRIVATE PUBLICATIONS

Operation LOYTON: 2 SAS in the Vosges. Phillipe Get
Wiltons 1742–1992
Operation WALLACE, France 1944: The Missing Patrol. Pip Birtwistle
COPP to Normandy 1943/44. Major General Logan Scott-Bowden CBE, DSO, MC. *Royal Engineers Journal* Vol. 108. No.1. April 1994
Unpublished History of 21 SAS. Barry Gregory

THE SPECIAL AIRSERVICE REGIMENTAL ARCHIVE

Operational reports: DEVON, SPEEDWELL, DUNHILL, DEFOE, TRUEFORM, GAFF, RUPERT, HARDY, HOUNDSWORTH, WALLACE, LOYTON, PISTOL, ARCHWAY, GALIA, TOMBOLA, APOSTLE
The Regimental Journal. Mars and Minerva
The Regimental Identity, Insignia and Traditions
War Diary
Personal file of Lt. Col. BMF Franks DSO, MC
Historical Archive 21 SAS (V)

SCOTS GUARDS REGIMENTAL ARCHIVE

Bill Stirling Personal File

IMPERIAL WAR MUSEUM

Documents.21759: TVS, SAS Interviews
Documents.16000: Private Papers of Captain Y. Galitzine

THE LONDON ARCHIVE

LCC/FB/WAR/04/012-014
LCC/FB/WAR/04/035-039
LCC/FB/STA/03/034 All relating to London Fire Brigade

BEMBRIDGE SAILING CLUB ARCHIVE

Various articles and photographs

KING'S COLLEGE LIBRARY

LAYCOCK 2/7	Instructions for signalling training exercises, Mar. 1941, with related papers.
LAYCOCK 2/8	Commando training notes and orders, Jan. 1941–Jun. 1942.
LAYCOCK 3/5	Memo, Feb. 1941, on the organisation and training of LAYFORCE.
LAYCOCK 3/8	Extract from the war diary of LAYFORCE HQ, 14–20 Apr. 1941 relating to the planning of a raid at Bardia (Ad Bardiyah).
LAYCOCK 3/14	List of personnel involved in a LAYFORCE operation in Egypt, 14 Jun. 1941.
LAYCOCK 3/19	Papers, Sep. 1941–Jan. 1942, on the reorganisation of Special Service Brigade forces in the Middle East after the disbandment of LAYFORCE.
LAYCOCK 5/1	Report and notes, 19 Apr.–7 May 1941, on Operation ADDITION raid on Bardia (Ad Bardiyah).
LAYCOCK 5/2	Order and report, 19–26 Apr. 1941, on Operation ADDITION for the raid on Bardia (Ad Bardiyah).
LAYCOCK 5/5	Diary kept by Laycock and official report, Apr.–Jun. 1941, relating to the evacuation of Crete.
LAYCOCK 5/26	Notes by Laycock on Special Service Brigade operations, 1941–44.
LAYCOCK 6/20	Official correspondence, May–Jul. 1943, on subjects including Captain Evelyn Waugh leaving Special Service Brigade, and reorganisation.
LAYCOCK 6/21	Official correspondence, Aug. 1943, on subjects including the restructuring of Special Service Brigade, and the invasion of Sicily.
LAYCOCK 6/22	Official correspondence, Sep. 1943, on subjects including recommendations for honours.
LAYCOCK 6/23	Official correspondence, Oct.–Dec. 1943, on subjects including Laycock's appointment as Chief of Combined Operations and future plans.
LAYCOCK 6/25	Official correspondence, 1964, as Colonel Commandant Special Air Service (SAS), on topics including the possible use of British special forces in East Africa.
LAYCOCK 6/27	Correspondence, 1947, about the trial of Captain Roy Farran for murder.
LAYCOCK 9/2	Memoirs, 1942 and 1945 by members of 'G' Troop, 7 Commando, gathered by Mrs Cornell, mother of Captain Jocelyn Nicholls, killed in action in 1941.

NATIONAL ARCHIVES, KEW

WO 169/68	1 Cavalry Division: Signals (Sigs). 1939 Sept.–1940 Dec.
WO 169/84	1 Cavalry Division: Headquarters 6 Cavalry Brigade. 1939 Aug.–1940 Dec.
WO 169/424	Royal Signals: F Troop 1 Middlesex Yeomanry Signal Section (Sigs) 1940 Nov.–Dec.
WO 106/2042	Plan M.C.D: move of 1st Cavalry Division to Palestine from U.K. 1939 Dec.–1940 Feb.
WO 169/68	1 Cavalry Division: Signals (Sigs) 1939 Sep.–1940 Dec.
WO 169/82	1 Cavalry Division: Headquarters 5 Cavalry Brigade. 1940 Feb.–Jul., Sep.–Dec.
WO 169/84	1 Cavalry Division: Headquarters 6 Cavalry Brigade. 1939 Aug.–1940 Dec.
WO 169/1226	Cavalry Division: Signals (Sigs). 1941 Jan.–Feb., Jun.–Jul.
WO 169/1224	Cavalry Division: General Staff (GS) 1941 Jan.–Jul.
WO 169/1262	6 Cavalry Brigade: Headquarters. 1941 Jan.–Jun.
HS 8/257	MI(R): functions and organisation (war establishment).
HS 8/258	MI(R): functions and organisation 1940.
WO 215/1	Phantom Way Diary 1939 Oct.–1940 Jun.
WO 215/10	Phantom HQ Jun.–Dec. 1940.
WO 215/11	Phantom Reconnaissance reports Sep. 1940.
WO 260/8	Special training centre at Inverailort Jun. 1940.
WO 218/8	8 Commando 1940 Jul.–Nov.
WO 218/170	8 Commando ('B' Battalion, Layforce) Jan.–Mar. 1941.
WO 218/168	Layforce 'A' Battalion. 1941 Jan.–May.
WO 218/169	Layforce 'B' Battalion 1941 May–Jun.
WO 218/170	8 Commando ('B' Battalion, Layforce) 1941 Jan.–Mar.
WO 201/714	Layforce: signal organisation 1941 Mar. 19–Jun. 11.
WO 201/715	Layforce: stores and organisation 1941 Mar.–Jun.
WO 201/718	Layforce: signal equipment with blueprint 1941 Mar. 1–Nov. 17.
WO 218/99	Special Raiding Squadron, 1 Special Air Service Regiment. 1943 Jul.–Oct.
WO 218/106	'M' Detachment 1 Special Air Service Regiment and 'M' Detachment, Special Boat Squadron, 1 Special Air Service Regiment. 1943 Feb. 6–21; 1943 Jun. 1–Jul. 12.
WO 218/96	1 Special Air Service Regiment. Includes war diary for B Squadron, 1 SAS Regiment for Oct. 1942. 1942 Oct.–Dec.
WO 219/2878A	Future operations: planning papers, appreciations and general correspondence. 1944 May–1945 May.
WO 218/61	2 Special Service Bde. 1944 Jan.–Dec. (Airborne Corps).
WO 218/59	1 Special Service Bde. 1944 Jan.- Dec. (Airborne Corps).
WO 171/369	Airborne H.Q. Tps. Main War Diary 1944 Jan.–Jul.
WO 171/425	G Branch 6th Airborne Div 1944 Feb., Apr., Jun.–Dec.

WO 219/2332	Special Forces Headquarters: operational directives. 1943 Mar.–1944 Oct.
WO 219/2195	Raids and reconnaissances: proposed programme, employment of airborne troops, reports on raids carried out and general policy. 1943 Dec.–1944 Mar.
WO 219/2994	Airborne Forces: organisation, operations memoranda, standing operating procedure, establishment of Combined Airborne H.Q. and cables concerning employment, movement, etc. 1944 Jan.–Dec.
WO 218/114	H.Q. S.A.S. Tps. 1944 Feb.–Aug.
WO 218/189	Operational employment of SAS forces. 1944 Apr.–1945 Jul.
WO 218/194	Employment of SAS troops. 1944 Jun.–1945 Apr.
WO 219/3468	SHAEF HQ G Div. France: information summaries, reports, records of discussions and analysis of correspondence. 1943 Dec.–1944 Jun.
WO 219/2875	Allotment of British and U.S. airborne division: memoranda, correspondence, discussions. 1944 Jun.–1945 May.
WO 219/222	Operation OVERLORD: employment of airborne forces policy. 1943 Jul.–1944 May.
WO 219/223	Operation OVERLORD: employment of airborne forces policy. 1944 Jun.–1945 Dec.
WO 219/2994	Airborne Forces: organisation, operations memoranda, standing operating procedure, establishment of Combined Airborne H.Q. and cables concerning employment, movement, etc. 1944 Jan.–Dec.
WO 205/195	Airborne operations: plans. May 1944.
WO 205/196	Airborne operations: plans. 1944 May, Jun.
WO 171/392	SHAEF G Div. 1944 Jan.–Aug.
WO 219/1418	Airborne units: miscellaneous papers on organisation and administration. 1944 Jun.–1945 Jan.
WO 219/2860	Formation of 1 Allied Airborne Army 1944 May 1945 May.
WO 205/78	Operation OVERLORD: organisation of airborne forces. 1944 Mar.–Oct.
WO 219/2861	Operation OVERLORD: overall planning for employment of airborne units. 1944 Feb.–Jun.
WO 106/4355	21 Army Group directives. 1944 Jun.–Jul.
WO 219/3951	2 Army: demi-official letters to 21 Army Group. 1944 Jun.
WO 218/173	L Detachment SAS Brigade (later 1 SAS Regt): formation, training and report of operations in Mediterranean area.
WO 218/98	Headquarters, Raiding Forces (including Special Raiding Squadron, Special Boat Squadron, 1 Special Air Service Regiment and 1 Special Boat Service Regiment). 1943 Feb., May–Jul., Sep.–Dec.; 1944 Jan.–Mar.
WO 204/8277	Operations in Italy: reports of battles at Termoli and on the River Trigno 1943 Oct.

WO 218/199	2 SAS Regt: operations reports 1944 Jul.–1945 Apr.
WO 218/202	Operation LOYTON: report.
WO 218/206	2 SAS Regt: operations log 1944 Sep.–1945 Apr.
FO 371/41904	Special operations in France: arming and maintenance of the Maquis.
WO 205/652A	Reports on Special Air Services and special forces. 1944 Jun.–Sep.
HS 6/218	SAS operations 1944.
WO 361/730	France: special operations by the SAS (Special Air Service); post operation investigations into Operations LOYTON and Pistol; includes interim report on missing personnel of the 2nd Special Air Service Regiment captured by the Germans in Eastern Europe in the Autumn of 1944.
WO 219/2389	Operation OVERLORD: Special Air Service operations 1944 Feb.–Aug.
WO 219/2398	Strategic planning for resistance and Special Air Service operations 1944 May–Sep.
WO 205/93	Reports on Special Air Service operations Sep. 44 to Apr. 45
CAB 101/301	Unpublished narrative, Resistance and Special Air Service Operations in North West Europe, 1944–1945, S. Passant.
WO 218/198	Operations signal book 1944 Jul.–Sep.
WO 218/216	2 SAS Regt: operations log. 1945 Mar.–Aug.
WO 218/197	2 SAS Jeep Sqdn: reports on operations in France. 1944 Jul.–Sep.
WO 218/44	1Special Service Bde. 1943 Jan.–Dec.
WO 218/194	Employment of SAS troops. 1944 Jun.–1945 Apr.
WO 218/195	HQ SAS Troops: reports, notes and correspondence on operations. Includes 4 photographs depicting: Jeeps: modifications to armour, mountings, magazine clips, luggage rack and petrol supply. Dated 1945. 1944 Jun.–1945 May.
WO 218/203	SAS Reports on operations in Belgium. 1944 Aug.–Dec.
WO 219/2674	Special Air Service: command and control, war establishments equipment and deployment including French and Belgian units. 1944 Mar.–1945 May.
HO 405/16506	GALITZINE, G Date of birth 18.02.1919. Naturalisation. 1937 Jan. 01–1938 Dec. 31.
WO 311/762	Captain Galitzine (Royal Northumberland Fusiliers): appointment as staff captain to AG 3 (VW).
WO 309/659	Noailles, France: killing of five Special Air Service Regiment personnel.
WO 309/660	Noailles, France: killing of five Special Air Service Regiment personnel.
WO 311/627	Special Air Service (SAS) War Crimes Investigation Team France and Germany Mar./Apr. 1946.
WO 311/628	Special Air Service (SAS) War Crimes Investigation Team France and Germany 1946 Mar.–Oct.

WO 311/629 Special Air Service (SAS) War Crimes Investigation Team France and Germany 1946 Dec.–1947 Aug.

WO 361/653 Special Air Service Regiment (SAS), War Crimes Investigation Team (WCIT) weekly situation reports Nos 3, 4 and 5 Feb.–Mar. 1946.

TS 26/898 Murder of parachutists in North East France, Aug.–Oct. 1944: report prepared for 2 SAS regiment.

WO 235/559 Notes on trial. Place of Trial: Wuppertal.

WO 311/89 La Grand Fosse, France: killing of British soldiers. 1945 Dec.–1946 Sep.

WO 309/474 Special Air Service Regiment war crimes cases: situation reports and general correspondence.

FO 1093/370 Cold War planning 1948. 1948 Jun. 16–1948 Dec. 21.

FO 1093/194 Future of secret services: part 2; post-war planning. 1943 Mar. 01–1944 Apr. 26.

FO 1093/563 Cold War: UK strategy in Eastern Europe. 1949 Apr. 18–1949 Jul. 30.

FO 1093/360 Special Operations: future planning. 1947 Jun. 16–1947 Jul. 02.

WO 32/10921 ARMY ORGANISATION: Other Arms (Code 14(J)): Formation of Special Air Service Regiment. ARMY ORGANISATION: Airborne (Code 14(P)): Formation of Special Air Service. 1944–47.

DEFE 2/1621 (1950/51) Weekend training of 21 Special Air Service Regiment (Artists Rifles) Territorial Army at Amphibious School RM; visit of LCT 4063 to France: history of Special Boat Sections and proposed use of title SBS for part of the RM.

WO 32/15620 21 SAS (TA) request for authorisation of colours 1947–55.

WO 32/18094 21 Special Air Services Regiment (Artists Rifles) (TA) 1952–67.

WO 279/864 The Special Air Service 1955 Jan. 01–1955 Dec. 31.

FO 1093/388 Publication of information on special operations. 1949 Nov. 25–1949 Dec. 29.

WO 32/16612 Special Air Service Regiments: mobilisation, training etc 1954–1961.

FO 371/162957 Yemen: Internal political situation, including revolution. 1962.

DEFE 13/710 Aden/Yemen situation 1964–65.

DEFE 13/569 Aden/Yemen situation 1964.

DEFE 13/570 Aden/Yemen situation 1964.

DEFE 68/775 Assistant Defence Attaches, Saigon: Detailed Report number 36; The Special Air Service Regiment in Vietnam. 1968 Mar. 6–1968 Mar. 6.

DEFE 68/779 Assistant Defence Attaches, Saigon: Detailed Report number 37; Special Forces. 1968 Jul. 17–1968 Jul. 17.

SERVICE HISTORIQUE DE LA DÉFENSE CHÂTEAU DE VINCENNES

All files relate to members of the Resistance in the Vosges
GR 16 P 364766
GR 16 P 364767
GR 16 P 364768
GR 16 P 387300
GR 16 P 82051
GR 16 P 82052
GR 16 P 82054
GR 16 P 82055
GR 16 P 82056
GR 16 P 82058
GR 16 P 54711
GR 16 P 54712
GR 16 P 572290
GR 16 P 572300
GR 16 P 82046
GR 16 P 82048
GR 16 P 82049
GR 16P 82050
GR 28 P 2 345
GR 28 P 4 296 (14)
GR 16 P 190052
GR 16 P210790
GR 16 P210791
GR 16 P 234462
GR 16 P 268265
GR 16 P 268271
GR 16 P 369633
GR 16 P369634
GR 16 P 482243
GR 28 P 4 447 (2)

ETON COLLEGE ARCHIVE

Papers relating to Brian Franks 1921–29

SHERBORNE SCHOOL ARCHIVE

CCF wartime relations with Special Service Brigade
Papers relating to Henry Druce

WEBSITES

https://www.britishnewspaperarchive.co.uk/
https://www.newspapers.com/
https://en.wikipedia.org/
https://hannbooks.com/sas-operation-galia
https://www.specialforcesroh.com/index.php
https://www.commandoveterans.org/commando_roll_of_honour_search
https://operationloyton1944.org
https://alliedspecialforcesmemorialgrove.org/
https://thenma.org.uk
https://www.evelynwaugh.org
https://britishonlinearchives.com/

BOOKS

Alcock, Graham (2024). *SAS Operation Pistol: Raindrops in Alsace*. Pen & Sword Military.

Armstrong, David (2013). *At Close Quarters: SOE Close Combat Pistol Instructor Colonel Hector Grant-Taylor*. Fonthill Media

Baedeker, Karl (1911). *The Rhine, Including the Black Forest & the Vosges: Handbook for Travellers* (17th ed.). K. Baedeker.

Bennett, Gill (2006). *Churchill's Man of Mystery – Desmond Morton and the World of Intelligence*. Taylor and Francis.

Billière, General Sir Peter de la (1994). *Looking for Trouble: SAS to Gulf Command – The Autobiography*. HarperCollins.

Bower, Tom (1995). *The Perfect English Spy: Sir Dick White and the Secret War, 1935–90*. William Heinemann Ltd.

Card, Tim (1994). *Eton Renewed: A History of Eton College from 1860 to the Present Day*. John Murray Publishers Ltd.

Cesarani, David (2009). *Major Farran's Hat: Murder, Scandal and Britain's War Against Jewish Terrorism 1945–1948*. William Heinemann Ltd.

Challenor, Tanky and Draper, Alfred (1990) *Tanky Challenor: SAS and the Met*. Leo Cooper.

Cooper, Johnny (1991). *One of the Originals: Story of a Founder Member of the S.A.S*. Pan Books.

Dorril, Stephen (2000). *MI6: Fifty Years of Special Operations*. Fourth Estate.

Dupont, Marc (2020). *Faulques: L'homme aux mille vies: L'homme aux mille vies*. INDO.

Durnford-Slater, John (1953). *Commando*. Kimber.

Farran, Roy (1960). *Operation Tombola: Special Forces Library*. Collins.

Farran, Roy (1948). *Winged Dagger, Adventures on Special Service: Special Forces Library*. Collins.

Fielding, Daphne (1964). *The Duchess of Jermyn Street: The Life and Good Times of Rosa Lewis of the Cavendish Hotel*. Eyre & Spottiswoode.

Fielding, Xan (1990). *One Man in His Time: Life of Billy McLean*. Macmillan.

Flamand, Roger (1990). *L'Inconnu de French Squadron*. R. Flamand, La Bussière.

Foot, M.R.D. (2008). *Memoirs of an SOE Historian*. Pen & Sword Military.
Ford, Roger (2003). *Fire from the Forest: The SAS Brigade in France, 1944*. Cassell.
Forte, Charles (1986). *Forte: The Autobiography of Charles Forte*. Sidgwick & Jackson.
Geraghty, Tony (2007). *Guns for Hire: The Inside Story of Freelance Soldiering*. Portrait.
Gold, Mary Jayne (1980). *Crossroads Marseilles: A Memoir.* Doubleday.
Hann, Robert (2009). *SAS Operation Galia*. Impress Books.
Harding, John (2009). *Roads to Nowhere: A South Arabian Odyssey, 1960–1965*. Arabian Publishing Ltd.
Hart-Davis, Duff (2011). *The War that Never Was*. Century.
Helm, Sarah (2006). *A Life in Secrets: Vera Atkins and the Lost Agents of SOE*. Little, Brown.
Hill, R.J.T. (1951). *Phantom was There*. Edward Arnold.
Hislop, John (1965). *Anything but a Soldier*. Michael Joseph.
Hoe, Alan (1992). *David Stirling: The Authorised Biography of the Founder of the SAS*. Little, Brown.
Hoe, Alan (2019). *Keystone of 22 SAS: The Life and Times of Lieutenant Colonel J M (Jock) Woodhouse MBE MC*. Pen & Sword Military.
Holland, James (2020). *Sicily '43*. Bantam Press.
Jerome, Lilianne (2024) *Quatre Petits Maquis*. Self-published.
Johnston, Brian (1974). *It's Been a Lot of Fun*. W.H. Allen.
Jones, Clive (2004). *Britain and the Yemen Civil War, 1962–1965: Ministers, Mercenaries and Mandarins – Foreign Policy and the Limits of Covert Action*. Sussex Academic Press.
Jones, Clive (2019). *The Clandestine Lives of Colonel David Smiley: Code Name 'Grin': Intelligence, Surveillance and Secret Warfare*. Edinburgh University Press.
Jones, Tim (2005). *SAS: The First Secret Wars: The Unknown Years of Combat and Counter-Insurgency*. I.B. Tauris.
Kemp, Anthony (1991). *The SAS at War: The Special Air Service Regiment, 1941–45*. John Murray Publishers.
Kemp, Anthony (1994). *The SAS: Savage Wars of Peace, 1947 to the Present*. John Murray Publishers.
Lewis, Damien (2015). *The Nazi Hunters*. Quercus.
Lewis, Damien (2020). *SAS Band of Brothers: The Last Stand of the SAS and Their Hunt for the Nazi Killers*. Quercus.
Lewis, Damien (2025). *SAS The Great Train Raid: The Most Daring SAS Mission of WWII*. Quercus.
Lewis, Damien (2018). *SAS Italian Job: The Secret Mission to Storm a Forbidden Nazi Fortress*. Quercus.
Masters, Anthony (1979). *Inside Marbled Halls: Life Above and Below Stairs in the Hyde Park Hotel*. Sidgwick & Jackson.
Messenger, Charles (1985). *The Commandos: 1940–1946*. Kimber.
Monaghan, Shannon (2024). *A Quiet Company of Dangerous Men: The Forgotten British Special Operations Soldiers of World War II*. Viking Press.
Mortimer, Gavin (2023). *The SAS in Occupied France: 2 SAS Operations, June to October 1944*. Pen & Sword Military.

Niven, David (1971). *The Moon's a Balloon*. Hamish Hamilton.
Phillips, Alan (2023). *An Oral History of Bembridge, Isle of Wight: I'm Not Blessed Well Jokin'!*. Countryside Books.
Pryce-Jones, David (ed.) (1973). *Evelyn Waugh and His World*. Weidenfeld & Nicolson.
Ross, Hamish (2003). *Paddy Mayne*. Sutton Publishing Ltd.
Saunders, Hilary St. George (1949). *The Green Beret: The Story of the Commandos 1940–1945*. Michael Joseph.
Smiley, David (1975). *Arabian Assignment: The Extraordinary Life of Colonel David Smiley* (Vol.2). Cooper.
Smiley, David (1994). *Irregular Regular: The Extraordinary Life of Colonel David Smiley* (Vol.3). Cooper.
Smith, Michael (1996). *New Cloak, Old Dagger: How Britain's Spies Came in from the Cold*. Weidenfeld & Nicolson.
Spicer, Tim (2024). *A Suspicion of Spies: Risk, Secrets and Shadows – the Biography of Wilfred 'Biffy' Dunderdale*. Barbreck Publishers.
Stafford, David (2011). *Mission Accomplished: SOE and Italy 1943–1945: David Stafford World War II History*. Bodley Head.
Sykes, Christopher (1975). *Evelyn Waugh: A Biography*. Collins.
Sykes, Christopher (1946). *Four Studies in Loyalty*. Collins.
Taylor, Derek and Bush, David (1974). *David: The Golden Age of British Hotels*. Northwood Productions.
Trenowden, Ian (1995). *Stealthily by Night*. Crecy Publishing.
Walker, Jonathan (2005). *Aden Insurgency: The Savage War in Yemen 1962–67*. Spellmount.
Waugh, Evelyn (1976). *The Diaries of Evelyn Waugh* (Michael Davie ed.). Weidenfeld & Nicolson.
Waugh, Evelyn (1980). *The Letters of Evelyn Waugh* (Mark Amory ed.). Weidenfeld & Nicolson.

PHOTO CREDITS

Amy Crossland: 77, 229
Artists Rifles archives: 257, 261, 305, 306
Authors collection: 33, 35, 51, 53, 63, 67, 69, 72, 76, 79, 80, 81, 86, 92, 98, 101, 107, 112, 114, 117, 140, 168, 184, 193, 195, 212, 213, 220, 227, 255, 286 back cover
Bembridge Sailing Club: 26
Birtwistle family archive: 149, 165
Brandstaetter Images via Getty Images: 53
de Lesseps family archive: 150, 198
Dunne family archive: 65, 81
Eton archive: 36, 37, 38, 39, 40, 41, back cover
Express Newspapers / Hulton Archive via Getty Images: Back cover
Franks family archive: Front cover, title page, 7, 29, 31, 32, 46, 48, 49, 55, 56, 59, 61, 94, 105, 217, 218, 219, 224, 316, 317, 319, 333
Galitzine family archive/Damien Lewis: 228, 239
Hambro family archive: 87
Hawkins via Getty Images: 52
Hulton Archive via Getty Images: 52
Imperial War Museum: 64, 109, 243
Johnson family archive: 282, 314
Laycock family archive: 83, 93, 99
Mandarin Oriental: 275
Manners family archive: 324
Massara family archive: 263, 265, 268
Museum Vliegbasis Deelen collection: 218
Noonans, Mayfair 241
Paul Popper/Popperfoto via Getty Images: 271
Philippe Get: 174, 176, 177, 179, 183, 202, 203, 204
Popperfoto via Getty Images: 265
Rob Hann: 209
Scots Guards Regimental archive: 121
Smiley family archive: 284, 293
Special Air Service Regimental Association: 101, 111, 123, 125, 127, 133, 135, 157, 159, 164, 166, 187, 190, 198, 199, 207, 210, 212, 215, 219, 222, 225, 233, 234, 237, 266, 267, 272, 287, 289, 290, 309, 317, 320, back cover
Stirling family archive: 130, 322
Sueddeutsche Zeitung Photo/Alamy: 263
Varian Fry Institute: 135
White's archive: 276

INDEX

Page numbers in bold refer to pictures or maps. 'n' indicates a footnote.